1 Introduction

2 Built-In Collections

3 Collection Protocols

4 Optionals

5 Structs and Classes

Introduction

Advanced Swift is quite a bold title for a book, so perhaps we should start with what we mean by it.

When we began writing the first edition of this book, Swift was barely a year old. We did so before the beta of 2.0 was released — albeit tentatively, because we suspected the language would continue to evolve as it entered its second year. Few languages — perhaps no other language — have been adopted so rapidly by so many developers.

But that left people with unanswered questions. How do you write "idiomatic" Swift? Is there a correct way to do certain things? The standard library provided some clues, but even that has changed over time, dropping some conventions and adopting others. Over the past two years, Swift has evolved at a high pace, and it has become clearer what idiomatic Swift is.

To someone coming from another language, Swift can resemble everything you like about your language of choice. Low-level bit twiddling can look very similar to (and can be as performant as) C, but without many of the undefined behavior gotchas. The lightweight trailing closure syntax of map or filter will be familiar to Rubyists. Swift generics are similar to C++ templates, but with type constraints to ensure generic functions are correct at the time of definition rather than at the time of use. The flexibility of higher-order functions and operator overloading means you can write code that's similar in style to Haskell or F#. And the @objc keyword allows you to use selectors and runtime dynamism in ways you would in Objective-C.

Given these resemblances, it's tempting to adopt the idioms of other languages. Case in point: Objective-C example projects can almost be mechanically ported to Swift. The same is true for Java or C# design patterns. And monad tutorials appeared to be everyone's favorite blog post topic in the first few months after Swift's introduction.

But then comes the frustration. Why can't we use protocol extensions with associated types like interfaces in Java? Why are arrays not covariant in the way we expect? Why can't we write "functor?" Sometimes the answer is because the part of Swift in question isn't yet implemented. But more often, it's either because there's a different Swift-like way to do what you want to do, or because the Swift feature you thought was like the equivalent in some other language is not quite what you think.

Swift is a complex language — most programming languages are. But it hides that complexity well. You can get up and running developing apps in Swift without needing to know about generics or overloading or the difference between static and dynamic dispatch. You may never need to call into a C library or write your own collection type, but after a while, we think you'll find it necessary to know about these things — either to improve your code's performance, to make it more elegant or expressive, or just to get certain things done.

Learning more about these features is what this book is about. We intend to answer many of the "How do I do this?" or "Why does Swift behave like that?" questions we've seen come up on various forums. Hopefully, once you've read our book, you'll have gone from being aware of the basics of the language to knowing about many advanced features and having a much better understanding of how Swift works. Being familiar with the material presented is probably necessary, if not sufficient, for calling yourself an advanced Swift programmer.

Who Is This Book For?

This book targets experienced (though not necessarily expert) programmers — such as existing Apple-platform developers, or those coming from other languages such as Java or C++ — who want to bring their knowledge of Swift to the same level as that of Objective-C or some other language. It's also suitable for new programmers who started on Swift, have grown familiar with the basics, and are looking to take things to the next level.

It's not meant as an introduction to Swift; it assumes you're familiar with the syntax and structure of the language. If you want some good, compact coverage of the basics of Swift, the best source is the official Apple Swift book (available on iBooks or on Apple's website). If you're already a confident programmer, you could try reading both our book and the Apple Swift book in parallel.

This is also not a book about programming for OS X or iOS devices. Of course, since Swift is currently mainly used on Apple platforms, we've tried to include examples of practical use, but we hope this book will be useful for non-Apple-platform programmers as well.

Themes

We've organized the book under the heading of basic concepts. There are in-depth chapters on some fundamental basic concepts like optionals or strings, and some deeper dives into topics like C interoperability. But throughout the book, hopefully a few themes regarding Swift emerge:

Swift is both a high- and low-level language. Swift allows you to write code similarly to Ruby and Python, with map and reduce, and to write your own higher-order functions easily. Swift also allows you to write fast code that compiles directly to native binaries with performance similar to code written in C.

What's exciting to us, and what's possibly the aspect of Swift we most admire, is that you're able to do both these things *at the same time*. Mapping a closure expression over an array compiles to the same assembly code as looping over a contiguous block of memory does.

However, there are some things you need to know about to make the most of this feature. For example, it will benefit you to have a strong grasp on how structs and classes differ, or an understanding of the difference between dynamic and static method dispatch. We'll cover topics such as these in more depth later on.

Swift is a multi-paradigm language. You can use it to write object-oriented code or pure functional code using immutable values, or you can write imperative C-like code using pointer arithmetic.

This is both a blessing and a curse. It's great, in that you have a lot of tools available to you, and you aren't forced into writing code one way. But it also exposes you to the risk of writing Java or C or Objective-C in Swift.

Swift still has access to most of the capabilities of Objective-C, including message sending, runtime type identification, and KVO. But Swift introduces many capabilities not available in Objective-C.

Erik Meijer, a well-known programming language expert, tweeted the following in October 2015:

> At this point, @SwiftLang is probably a better, and more valuable, vehicle for learning functional programming than Haskell.

Swift is a good introduction to a more functional style through its use of generics, protocols, value types, and closures. It's even possible to write operators that compose functions together. The early months of Swift brought many functional programming blog posts into the world. But since the release of Swift 2.0 and the introduction of protocol extensions, this trend has shifted.

Swift is very flexible. In the introduction to the book *On Lisp*, Paul Graham writes that:

> Experienced Lisp programmers divide up their programs differently. As well as top-down design, they follow a principle which could be called bottom-up design– changing the language to suit the problem. In Lisp, you don't just write your program down toward the language, you also build the language up toward your program. As you're writing a program you may think "I wish Lisp had such-and-such an operator." So you go and write it. Afterward you realize that using the new operator would simplify the design of another part of the program, and so on. Language and program evolve together.

Swift is a long way from Lisp. But still, we feel like Swift shares this characteristic of encouraging "bottom-up" programming — of making it easy to write very general reusable building blocks that you then combine into larger features, which you then use to solve your actual problem. Swift is particularly good at making these building blocks feel like primitives — like part of the language. A good demonstration of this is that the many features you might think of as fundamental building blocks, like optionals or basic operators, are actually defined in a library — the Swift standard library — rather than directly in the language. Trailing closures enable you to extend the language with features that feel like they're built in.

Swift code can be compact and concise while still being clear. Swift lends itself to relatively terse code. There's an underlying goal here, and it isn't to save on typing. The idea is to get to the point quicker and to make code readable by dropping a lot of the "ceremonial" boilerplate you often see in other languages that obscure rather than clarify the meaning of the code.

For example, type inference removes the clutter of type declarations that are obvious from the context. Semicolons and parentheses that add little or no value are gone. Generics and protocol extensions encourage you to avoid repeating yourself by packaging common operations into reusable functions. The goal is to write code that's readable at a glance.

At first, this can be off-putting. If you've never used functions like map, filter, and reduce before, they might look harder to read than a simple for loop. But our hope is that this is a short learning curve and that the reward is code that is more "obviously correct" at first glance.

Swift tries to be as safe as is practical, until you tell it not to be. This is unlike languages such as C and C++ (where you can be unsafe easily just by forgetting to do something), or like Haskell or Java (which are sometimes safe whether or not you like it).

Eric Lippert, one of the principal designers of C#, wrote about his 10 regrets of C#, including the lesson that:

> sometimes you need to implement features that are only for experts who are building infrastructure; those features should be clearly marked as dangerous—not invitingly similar to features from other languages.

Eric was specifically referring to C#'s finalizers, which are similar to C++ destructors. But unlike destructors, they run at a nondeterministic time (perhaps never) at the behest of the garbage collector (and on the garbage collector's thread). However, Swift, being reference counted, *does* execute a class's deinit deterministically.

Swift embodies this sentiment in other ways. Undefined and unsafe behavior is avoided by default. For example, a variable can't be used until it's been initialized, and using out-of-bounds subscripts on an array will trap, as opposed to continuing with possibly garbage values.

There are a number of "unsafe" options available (such as the unsafeBitcast function, or the UnsafeMutablePointer type) for when you really need them. But with great power comes great undefined behavior. You can write the following:

```
var someArray = [1,2,3]
```

```
let uhOh = someArray.withUnsafeBufferPointer { ptr in
    // ptr is only valid within this block, but
    // there is nothing stopping you letting it
    // escape into the wild:
    return ptr
}
// Later...
print(uhOh[10])
```

It'll compile, but who knows what it'll do. However, you can't say nobody warned you.

Swift is an opinionated language. We as authors have strong opinions about the "right" way to write Swift. You'll see many of them in this book, sometimes expressed as if they're facts. But they're just, like, our opinions, man. Feel free to disagree! Swift is still a young language, and many things aren't settled. What's more is that many blog posts are flat-out wrong or outdated (including several ones we wrote, especially in the early days). Whatever you're reading, the most important thing is to try things out for yourself, check how they behave, and decide how you feel about them. Think critically, and beware of out-of-date information.

Terminology

> 'When I use a word,' Humpty Dumpty said, in rather a scornful tone, 'it means just what I choose it to mean — neither more nor less.'
>
> — *Through the Looking Glass*, by Lewis Carroll

Programmers throw around terms of art a lot. To avoid confusion, what follows are some definitions of terms we use throughout this book. Where possible, we're trying to adhere to the same usage as the official documentation, or sometimes a definition that's been widely adopted by the Swift community. Many of these definitions are covered in more detail in later chapters, so don't worry if not everything makes sense on first reading. If you're already familiar with all of these terms, it's still best to skim through to make sure your accepted meanings don't differ from ours.

In Swift, we make the distinctions between values, variables, references, and constants.

A **value** is immutable and forever — it never changes. For example, 1, true, and [1,2,3] are all values. These are examples of **literals**, but values can also be generated at runtime. The number you get when you square the number five is a value.

When we assign a value to a name using var x = [1,2], we're creating a **variable** named x that holds the value [1,2]. By changing x, e.g. by performing x.append(3), we didn't change the original value. Rather, we replaced the value that x holds with the new value, [1,2,3] — at least *logically*, if not in the actual implementation (which might actually just tack a new entry on the back of some existing memory). We refer to this as **mutating** the variable.

We can declare **constant** variables (constants, for short) with let instead of var. Once a constant has been assigned a value, it can never be assigned a new value.

We also don't need to give a variable a value immediately. We can declare the variable first (let x: Int) and then later assign a value to it (x = 1). Swift, with its emphasis on safety, will check that all possible code paths lead to a variable being assigned a value before its value can be read. There's no concept of a variable having an as-yet-undefined value. Of course, if the variable was declared with let, it can only be assigned to once.

Structs and enums are **value types**. When you assign one struct variable to another, the two variables will then contain the same value. You can think of the contents as being copied, but it's more accurate to say that one variable was changed to contain the same value as the other.

A **reference** is a special kind of value: a value that "points to" another value. Because two references can refer to the same value, this introduces the possibility of that value getting mutated by two different parts of the program at once.

Classes are **reference types**. You can't hold an instance of a class (which we might occasionally call an **object** — a term fraught with troublesome overloading!) directly in a variable. Instead, you must hold a reference to it in a variable and access it via that reference.

Reference types have **identity** — you can check if two variables are referring to the exact same object by using ===. You can also check if they're equal, assuming == is implemented for the relevant type. Two objects with different identity can still be equal.

Value types don't have identity. You can't check if a particular variable holds the "same" number 2 as another. You can only check if they both contain the value 2. === is really asking: "Do both these variables hold the same reference as their value?" In programming language literature, == is sometimes called *structural equality*, and === is called *pointer equality* or *reference equality*.

Class references aren't the only kind of reference in Swift. For example, there are also pointers, accessed through withUnsafeMutablePointer functions and the like. But classes are the simplest reference type to use, in part because their reference-like nature is partially hidden from you by syntactic sugar. You don't need to do any explicit "dereferencing" like you do with pointers in some other languages. (We'll cover the other kind of references in more detail in the chapter on interoperability.)

A variable that holds a reference can be declared with let — that is, the reference is constant. This means that the variable can never be changed to refer to something else. But — and this is important — it *doesn't* mean that the object it *refers to* can't be changed. So when referring to a variable as a constant, be careful — it's only constant in what it points to. It doesn't mean what it points to is constant. (Note: if those last few sentences sound like doublespeak, don't worry, as we cover this again in the chapter on structs and classes). Unfortunately, this means that when looking at a declaration of a variable with let, you can't tell at a glance whether or not what's being declared is completely immutable. Instead, you have to *know* whether it's holding a value type or a reference type.

We refer to types as having **value semantics** to distinguish a value type that performs a *deep copy*. This copy can occur eagerly (whenever a new variable is introduced) or lazily (whenever a variable gets mutated).

Here we hit another complication. If our struct contains reference types, the reference types won't automatically get copied upon assigning the struct to a new variable. Instead, the references themselves get copied. This is called a *shallow copy*.

For example, the Data struct in Foundation is a wrapper around the NSData reference type. However, the authors of the Data struct took extra steps to also perform a deep copy of the NSData object whenever the Data struct is mutated. They do this efficiently using a technique called copy-on-write, which we'll explain in the chapter on structs and classes. For now, it's important to know that this behavior doesn't come for free.

The collections in Swift are also wrapping reference types and use copy-on-write to efficiently provide value semantics. However, if the elements in a collection are references (for example, an array containing objects), the objects won't get copied. Instead, only the references get copied. This means that a Swift array only has value semantics if the elements have value semantics too. In the next chapter, we'll look at how Swift's collections differ from Foundation collections such as NSArray and NSDictionary.

Some classes are completely immutable — that is, they provide no methods for changing their internal state after they're created. This means that even though they're classes, they also have value semantics (because even if they're shared, they can never change). Be careful though — only final classes can be guaranteed not to be subclassed with added mutable state.

In Swift, functions are also values. You can assign a function to a variable, have an array of functions, and call the function held in a variable. Functions that take other functions as arguments (such as map, which takes a function to transform every element of a sequence) or return functions are referred to as **higher-order functions**.

Functions don't have to be declared at the top level — you can declare a function within another function or in a do or other scope. Functions defined within an outer scope, but passed out from it (say, as the returned value of a function), can "capture" local variables, in which case those local variables aren't destroyed when the local scope ends, and the function can hold state through them. This behavior is called "closing over" variables, and functions that do this are called **closures**.

Functions can be declared either with the func keyword or by using a shorthand { } syntax called a **closure expression**. Sometimes this gets shortened to "closures," but don't let it give you the impression that only closure expressions can be closures. Functions declared with the func keyword are closures too.

Functions are held by reference. This means assigning a function that has state via closed-over variables to another variable doesn't copy that state; it shares it, similar to object references. What's more is that when two closures close over the same local variable, they both share that variable, so they share state. This can be quite surprising, and we'll discuss this more in the chapter on functions.

Functions defined inside a class or protocol are **methods**, and they have an implicit self parameter. A function that, instead of taking multiple arguments, takes some arguments and returns another function representing the partial application of the arguments to that function, is a **curried function**. Sometimes we call functions that aren't methods **free functions**. This is to distinguish them from methods.

Free functions, and methods called on structs, are **statically dispatched**. This means the function that'll be called is known at compile time. This also means the compiler might be able to **inline** the function, i.e. not call the function at all, but instead replace it with the code the function would execute. It can also discard or simplify code that it can prove at compile time won't actually run.

Methods on classes or protocols might be **dynamically dispatched**. This means the compiler doesn't necessarily know at compile time which function will run. This dynamic behavior is done either by using vtables (similar to how Java or C++ dynamic dispatch works), or in the case of @objc classes and protocols, by using selectors and objc_msgSend.

Subtyping and method **overriding** is one way of getting **polymorphic** behavior, i.e. behavior that varies depending on the types involved. A second way is function **overloading**, where a function is written multiple times for different types. (It's important not to mix up overriding and overloading, as they behave very differently.) A third way is via generics, where a function or method is written once to take any type that provides certain functions or methods, but the implementations of those functions can vary. Unlike method overriding, the results of function overloading and generics are known statically at compile time. We'll cover this more in the generics chapter.

Swift Style Guide

When writing this book, and when writing Swift code for our own projects, we try to stick to the following rules:

→ For naming, clarity *at the point of use* is the most important consideration. Since APIs are used many more times than they're declared, their names should be optimized for how well they work at the call site. Familiarize yourself with the Swift API Design Guidelines[1] and try to adhere to them in your own code.

→ Clarity is often helped by conciseness, but brevity should never be a goal in and of itself.

→ Always add documentation comments to functions — *especially* generic ones.

→ Types start with UpperCaseLetters. Functions, variables, and enum cases start with lowerCaseLetters.

→ Use type inference. Explicit but obvious types get in the way of readability.

→ Don't use type inference in cases of ambiguity or when defining contracts (which is why, for example, funcs have an explicit return type).

→ Default to structs unless you actually need a class-only feature or reference semantics.

→ Mark classes as final unless you've explicitly designed them to be inheritable. If you want to use inheritance internally but not allow subclassing for external clients, mark a class public but not open.

→ Use the trailing closure syntax, except when that closure is immediately followed by another opening brace.

→ Use guard to exit functions early.

→ Eschew force-unwraps and implicitly unwrapped optionals. They're occasionally useful, but needing them constantly is usually a sign something is wrong.

→ Don't repeat yourself. If you find you've written a very similar piece of code more than a couple of times, extract it into a function. Consider making that function a protocol extension.

→ Favor map and filter. But don't force it: use a for loop when it makes sense. The purpose of higher-order functions is to make code more readable. An obfuscated use of reduce when a simple for loop would be clearer defeats this purpose.

→ Favor immutable variables: default to let unless you know you need mutation. But use mutation when it makes the code clearer or more

---

1 https://swift.org/documentation/api-design-guidelines/

efficient. Again, don't force it: a mutating method on structs is often more idiomatic and efficient than returning a brand new struct.

→ Swift generics tend to lead to very long function signatures. Unfortunately, we have yet to settle on a good way of breaking up long function declarations into multiple lines. We'll try to be consistent in how we do this in sample code.

→ Leave off self. when you don't need it. In closure expressions, it's a clear signal that self is being captured by the closure.

→ Write extensions on existing types and protocols, instead of free functions, whenever you can. This helps readability and discoverability.

Built-In Collections

Collections of elements are among the most important data types in any programming language. Good language support for different kinds of containers has a big impact on programmer productivity and happiness. Swift places special emphasis on sequences and collections — so much of the standard library is dedicated to this topic that we sometimes have the feeling it deals with little else. The resulting model is way more extensible than what you may be used to from other languages, but it's also quite complex.

In this chapter, we're going to take a look at the major collection types Swift ships with, with a focus on how to work with them effectively and idiomatically. In the next chapter, we'll climb up the abstraction ladder and see how the collection protocols in the standard library work.

Arrays

Arrays and Mutability

Arrays are the most common collections in Swift. An array is an ordered container of elements that all have the same type, with random access to each element. As an example, to create an array of numbers, we can write the following:

```
// The Fibonacci numbers
let fibs = [0, 1, 1, 2, 3, 5]
```

If we try to modify the array defined above (by using append(_:), for example), we get a compile error. This is because the array is defined as a constant, using let. In many cases, this is exactly the right thing to do; it prevents us from accidentally changing the array. If we want the array to be a variable, we have to define it using var:

```
var mutableFibs = [0, 1, 1, 2, 3, 5]
```

Now we can easily append a single element or a sequence of elements:

```
mutableFibs.append(8)
mutableFibs.append(contentsOf: [13, 21])
mutableFibs // [0, 1, 1, 2, 3, 5, 8, 13, 21]
```

There are a couple of benefits that come with making the distinction between var and let. Constants defined with let are easier to reason about because

they're immutable. When you read a declaration like let fibs = ..., you know
that the value of fibs will never change — it's enforced by the compiler. This
helps greatly when reading through code. However, note that this is only true
for types that have value semantics. A let variable to a class instance (i.e. a
reference type) guarantees that the *reference* will never change, i.e. you can't
assign another object to that variable. However, the object the reference points
to *can* change. We'll go into more detail on these differences in the chapter on
structs and classes.

Arrays, like all collection types in the standard library, have value semantics.
When you assign an existing array to another variable, the array contents are
copied over. For example, in the following code snippet, x is never modified:

```
var x = [1,2,3]
var y = x
y.append(4)
y // [1, 2, 3, 4]
x // [1, 2, 3]
```

The statement var y = x makes a copy of x, so appending 4 to y won't change x
— the value of x will still be [1, 2, 3]. The same thing happens when you pass an
array into a function; the function gets a local copy, and any changes it makes
don't affect the caller.

Contrast this with the approach to mutability taken by NSArray in Foundation.
NSArray has no mutating methods — to mutate an array, you need an
NSMutableArray. But just because you have a non-mutating NSArray reference
does *not* mean the array can't be mutated underneath you:

```
let a = NSMutableArray(array: [1,2,3])

// I don't want to be able to mutate b
let b: NSArray = a

// But it can still be mutated - via a
a.insert(4, at: 3)
b // ( 1, 2, 3, 4 )
```

The correct way to write this is to manually create a copy upon assignment:

```
let c = NSMutableArray(array: [1,2,3])

// I don't want to be able to mutate d
let d = c.copy() as! NSArray
```

```
c.insert(4, at: 3)
d // ( 1, 2, 3 )
```

In the example above, it's very clear that we need to make a copy — a is mutable, after all. However, when passing around arrays between methods and functions, this isn't always so easy to see.

In Swift, instead of needing two types, there's just one, and mutability is defined by declaring with var instead of let. But there's no reference sharing — when you declare a second array with let, you're guaranteed it'll never change.

Making so many copies could be a performance problem, but in practice, all collection types in the Swift standard library are implemented using a technique called copy-on-write, which makes sure the data is only copied when necessary. So in our example, x and y shared internal storage up the point where y.append was called. In the chapter on structs and classes, we'll take a deeper look at value semantics, including how to implement copy-on-write for your own types.

Arrays and Optionals

Swift arrays provide all the usual operations you'd expect, like isEmpty and count. Arrays also allow for direct access of elements at a specific index through subscripting, like fibs[3]. Keep in mind that you need to make sure the index is within bounds before getting an element via subscript. Fetch the element at index 3, and you'd better be sure the array has at least four elements in it. Otherwise, your program will trap, i.e. abort with a fatal error.

The reason for this is mainly driven by how array indices are used. It's pretty rare in Swift to actually need to calculate an index:

→ Want to iterate over the array?
   for x in array

→ Want to iterate over all but the first element of an array?
   for x in array.dropFirst()

→ Want to iterate over all but the last 5 elements? for x in array.dropLast(5)

→ Want to number all the elements in an array?
   for (num, element) in collection.enumerated()

→ Want to find the location of a specific element?
if let idx = array.index { someMatchingLogic($0) }

→ Want to transform all the elements in an array?
array.map { someTransformation($0) }

→ Want to fetch only the elements matching a specific criterion?
array.filter { someCriteria($0) }

Another sign that Swift wants to discourage you from doing index math is the removal of traditional C-style for loops from the language in Swift 3. Manually fiddling with indices is a rich seam of bugs to mine, so it's often best avoided. And if it can't be, well, we'll see in the generics chapter that it's easy enough to write a new reusable general function that does what you need and in which you can wrap your carefully tested index calculations.

But sometimes you do have to use an index. And with array indices, the expectation is that when you do, you'll have thought very carefully about the logic behind the index calculation. So to have to unwrap the value of a subscript operation is probably overkill — it means you don't trust your code. But chances are you do trust your code, so you'll probably resort to force-unwrapping the result, because you *know* that the index must be valid. This is (a) annoying, and (b) a bad habit to get into. When force-unwrapping becomes routine, eventually you're going to slip up and force-unwrap something you don't mean to. So to avoid this habit becoming routine, arrays don't give you the option.

> While a subscripting operation that responds to a invalid index with a controlled crash could arguably be called *unsafe*, that's only one aspect of safety. Subscripting is totally safe in regard to *memory safety* — the standard library collections always perform bounds checks to prevent unauthorized memory access with an out-of-bounds index.

Other operations behave differently. The first and last properties return an optional; they return nil if the array is empty. first is equivalent to isEmpty ? nil : self[0]. Similarly, the removeLast method will trap if you call it on an empty array, whereas popLast will only delete and return the last element if the array isn't empty and otherwise do nothing and return nil. Which one you'd want to use depends on your use case. When you're using the array as a stack, you'll probably always want to combine checking for empty and removing the last entry. On the other hand, if you already know through invariants whether or not the array is empty, dealing with the optional is fiddly.

We'll encounter these tradeoffs again later in this chapter when we talk about dictionaries. Additionally, there's an entire chapter dedicated to optionals.

Transforming Arrays

Map

It's common to need to perform a transformation on every value in an array. Every programmer has written similar code hundreds of times: create a new array, loop over all elements in an existing array, perform an operation on an element, and append the result of that operation to the new array. For example, the following code squares an array of integers:

```
var squared: [Int] = []
for fib in fibs {
    squared.append(fib * fib)
}
squared // [0, 1, 1, 4, 9, 25]
```

Swift arrays have a map method, adopted from the world of functional programming. Here's the exact same operation, using map:

```
let squares = fibs.map { fib in fib * fib }
squares // [0, 1, 1, 4, 9, 25]
```

This version has three main advantages. It's shorter, of course. There's also less room for error. But more importantly, it's clearer. All the clutter has been removed. Once you're used to seeing and using map everywhere, it acts as a signal — you see map, and you know immediately what's happening: a function is going to be applied to every element, returning a new array of the transformed elements.

The declaration of squared no longer needs to be made with var, because we aren't mutating it any longer — it'll be delivered out of the map fully formed, so we can declare squares with let, if appropriate. And because the type of the contents can be inferred from the function passed to map, squares no longer needs to be explicitly typed.

map isn't hard to write — it's just a question of wrapping up the boilerplate parts of the for loop into a generic function. Here's one possible implementation (though in Swift, it's actually an extension of Sequence, something we'll cover in the chapter on writing generic algorithms):

```
extension Array {
  func map<T>(_ transform: (Element) -> T) -> [T] {
    var result: [T] = []
    result.reserveCapacity(count)
    for x in self {
      result.append(transform(x))
    }
    return result
  }
}
```

Element is the generic placeholder for whatever type the array contains. And T is a new placeholder that can represent the result of the element transformation. The map function itself doesn't care what Element and T are; they can be anything at all. The concrete type T of the transformed elements is defined by the return type of the transform function the caller passes to map.

> Really, the signature of this method should be
> func map<T>(_ transform: (Element) throws -> T) rethrows -> [T],
> indicating that map will forward any error the transformation
> function might throw to the caller. We'll cover this in detail in the
> errors chapter. We've left the error handling annotations out here
> for simplicity. If you'd like, you can check out the source code for
> Sequence.map in the Swift repository on GitHub.

Parameterizing Behavior with Functions

Even if you're already familiar with map, take a moment and consider the map code. What makes it so general yet so useful?

map manages to separate out the boilerplate — which doesn't vary from call to call — from the functionality that always varies: the logic of how exactly to transform each element. It does this through a parameter the caller supplies: the transformation function.

This pattern of parameterizing behavior is found throughout the standard library. There are more than a dozen separate functions that take a closure that allows the caller to customize the key step:

→ **map** and **flatMap** — how to transform an element

→ **filter** — should an element be included?

→ **reduce** — how to fold an element into an aggregate value

→ **sequence** — what should the next element of the sequence be?

→ **forEach** — what side effect to perform with an element

→ **sort, lexicographicallyPrecedes**, and **partition** — in what order should two elements come?

→ **index, first**, and **contains** — does this element match?

→ **min** and **max** — which is the min/max of two elements?

→ **elementsEqual** and **starts** — are two elements equivalent?

→ **split** — is this element a separator?

The goal of all these functions is to get rid of the clutter of the uninteresting parts of the code, such as the creation of a new array, the for loop over the source data, and the like. Instead, the clutter is replaced with a single word that describes what's being done. This brings the important code – the logic the programmer wants to express – to the forefront.

Several of these functions have a default behavior. sort sorts elements in ascending order when they're comparable, unless you specify otherwise. contains can take a value to check for, so long as the elements are equatable. These help make the code even more readable. Ascending order sort is natural, so the meaning of array.sort() is intuitive. array.index(of: "foo") is clearer than array.index { $0 == "foo" }.

But in every instance, these are just shorthand for the common cases. Elements don't have to be comparable or equatable, and you don't have to compare the whole element — you can sort an array of people by their ages (people.sort { $0.age < $1.age }) or check if the array contains anyone underage (people.contains { $0.age < 18 }). You can also compare some transformation of the element. For example, an admittedly inefficient case-insensitive sort could be performed via
people.sort { $0.name.uppercased() < $1.name.uppercased() }.

There are other functions of similar usefulness that would also take a closure to specify their behaviors but aren't in the standard library. You could easily define them yourself (and might like to try):

→ **accumulate** — combine elements into an array of running values (like reduce, but returning an array of each interim combination)

→ **all(matching:)** and **none(matching:)** — test if all or no elements in a sequence match a criterion (can be built with contains, with some carefully placed negation)

→ **count(where:)** — count the number of elements that match (similar to filter, but without constructing an array)

→ **indices(where:)** — return a list of indices matching a criteria (similar to index(where:), but doesn't stop on the first one)

→ **prefix(while:)** — filter elements while a predicate returns true, then drop the rest (similar to filter, but with an early exit, and useful for infinite or lazily computed sequences)

→ **drop(while:)** — drop elements until the predicate ceases to be true, and then return the rest (similar to prefix(while:), but this returns the inverse)

Many of these we define elsewhere in the book. (prefix(while:) and drop(while:) are actually planned additions to the standard library, but they didn't make the cut for Swift 3.0. They'll be added in a future release.)

You might find yourself writing something that fits a pattern more than a couple of times — something like this, where you search an array in reverse order for the first element that matches a certain condition:

```
let names = ["Paula", "Elena", "Zoe"]

var lastNameEndingInA: String?
for name in names.reversed() where name.hasSuffix("a") {
  lastNameEndingInA = name
  break
}
lastNameEndingInA // Optional("Elena")
```

If that's the case, consider writing a short extension to Sequence. The method last(where:) wraps this logic — we use a closure to abstract over the part of our for loop that varies:

```
extension Sequence {
```

```
func last(where predicate: (Iterator.Element) -> Bool) -> Iterator.Element? {
    for element in reversed() where predicate(element) {
        return element
    }
    return nil
  }
}
```

This then allows you to replace your for loop with the following:

```
let match = names.last { $0.hasSuffix("a") }
match // Optional("Elena")
```

This has all the same benefits we described for map. The example with last(where:) is more readable than the example with the for loop; even though the for loop is simple, you still have to run the loop through in your head, which is a small mental tax. Using last(where:) introduces less chance of error (such as accidentally forgetting to reverse the array), and it allows you to declare the result variable with let instead of var.

It also works nicely with guard — in all likelihood, you're going to terminate a flow early if the element isn't found:

```
guard let match = someSequence.last(where: { $0.passesTest() })
    else { return }
// Do something with match
```

We'll say more about extending collections and using functions later in the book.

Mutation and Stateful Closures

When iterating over an array, you could use map to perform side effects (e.g. inserting the elements into some lookup table). We don't recommend doing this. Take a look at the following:

```
array.map { item in
    table.insert(item)
}
```

This hides the side effect (the mutation of the lookup table) in a construct that looks like a transformation of the array. If you ever see something like the above, then it's a clear case for using a plain for loop instead of a function like map. The forEach method would also be more appropriate than map in this case, but it has its own issues. We'll look at forEach in a bit.

Performing side effects is different than deliberately giving the closure *local* state, which is a particularly useful technique, and it's what makes closures — functions that can capture and mutate variables outside their scope — so powerful a tool when combined with higher-order functions. For example, the accumulate function described above could be implemented with map and a stateful closure, like this:

```
extension Array {
  func accumulate<Result>(_ initialResult: Result,
    _ nextPartialResult: (Result, Element) -> Result) -> [Result]
  {
    var running = initialResult
    return map { next in
      running = nextPartialResult(running, next)
      return running
    }
  }
}
```

This creates a temporary variable to store the running value and then uses map to create an array of the running value as it progresses:

```
[1,2,3,4].accumulate(0, +) // [1, 3, 6, 10]
```

Note that this code assumes that map performs its transformation in order over the sequence. In the case of our map above, it does. But there are possible implementations that could transform the sequence out of order — for example, one that performs the transformation of the elements concurrently. The official standard library version of map doesn't specify whether or not it transforms the sequence in order, though it seems like a safe bet.

Filter

Another very common operation is to take an array and create a new array that only includes those elements that match a certain condition. The pattern of looping over an array and selecting the elements that match the given predicate is captured in the filter method:

```
nums.filter { num in num % 2 == 0 } // [2, 4, 6, 8, 10]
```

We can use Swift's shorthand notation for arguments of a closure expression to make this even shorter. Instead of naming the num argument, we can write the above code like this:

```
nums.filter { $0 % 2 == 0 } // [2, 4, 6, 8, 10]
```

For very short closures, this can be more readable. If the closure is more complicated, it's almost always a better idea to name the arguments explicitly, as we've done before. It's really a matter of personal taste — choose whichever is more readable at a glance. A good rule of thumb is this: if the closure fits neatly on one line, shorthand argument names are a good fit.

By combining map and filter, we can easily write a lot of operations on arrays without having to introduce a single intermediate array, and the resulting code will become shorter and easier to read. For example, to find all squares under 100 that are even, we could map the range 0..<10 in order to square it, and then filter out all odd numbers:

```
(1..<10).map { $0 * $0 }.filter { $0 % 2 == 0 } // [4, 16, 36, 64]
```

The implementation of filter looks much the same as map:

```
extension Array {
    func filter(_ isIncluded: (Element) -> Bool) -> [Element] {
        var result: [Element] = []
        for x in self where isIncluded(x) {
            result.append(x)
        }
        return result
    }
}
```

For more on the where clause we use in the for loop, see the optionals chapter.

One quick performance tip: if you ever find yourself writing something like the following, stop!

```
bigArray.filter { someCondition }.count > 0
```

filter creates a brand new array and processes every element in the array. But this is unnecessary. This code only needs to check if one element matches — in which case, contains(where:) will do the job:

```
bigArray.contains { someCondition }
```

This is much faster for two reasons: it doesn't create a whole new array of the filtered elements just to count them, and it exits early, as soon as it matches the first element. Generally, only ever use filter if you want all the results.

Often you want to do something that can be done by contains, but it looks pretty ugly. For example, you can check if every element of a sequence matches a predicate using !sequence.contains { !condition }, but it's much more readable to wrap this in a new function that has a more descriptive name:

```
extension Sequence {
    public func all(matching predicate: (Iterator.Element) -> Bool) -> Bool {
        // Every element matches a predicate if no element doesn't match it:
        return !contains { !predicate($0) }
    }
}
```

```
let evenNums = nums.filter { $0 % 2 == 0 } // [2, 4, 6, 8, 10]
evenNums.all { $0 % 2 == 0 } // true
```

Reduce

Both map and filter take an array and produce a new, modified array. Sometimes, however, you want to combine all elements into a new value. For example, to sum up all the elements, we could write the following code:

```
var total = 0
for num in fibs {
    total = total + num
}
total // 12
```

The reduce method takes this pattern and abstracts two parts: the initial value (in this case, zero), and the function for combining the intermediate value (total) and the element (num). Using reduce, we can write the same example like this:

```
let sum = fibs.reduce(0) { total, num in total + num } // 12
```

Operators are functions too, so we could've also written the same example like this:

```
fibs.reduce(0, +) // 12
```

The output type of reduce doesn't have to be the same as the element type. For example, if we want to convert a list of integers into a string, with each number followed by a space, we can do the following:

```
fibs.reduce("") { str, num in str + "\(num) " } // 0 1 1 2 3 5
```

Here's the implementation for reduce:

```
extension Array {
  func reduce<Result>(_ initialResult: Result,
    _ nextPartialResult: (Result, Element) -> Result) -> Result
  {
    var result = initialResult
    for x in self {
      result = nextPartialResult(result, x)
    }
    return result
  }
}
```

Another performance tip: reduce is very flexible, and it's common to see it used to build arrays and perform other operations. For example, you can implement map and filter using only reduce:

```
extension Array {
  func map2<T>(_ transform: (Element) -> T) -> [T] {
    return reduce([]) {
      $0 + [transform($1)]
    }
  }

  func filter2(_ isIncluded: (Element) -> Bool) -> [Element] {
    return reduce([]) {
      isIncluded($1) ? $0 + [$1] : $0
    }
  }
}
```

This is kind of beautiful and has the benefit of not needing those icky imperative for loops. But Swift isn't Haskell, and Swift arrays aren't lists. What's happening here is that every time, through the combine function, a brand new array is being created by appending the transformed or included element to the previous one. This means that both these implementations are

$O(n^2)$, not $O(n)$ — as the length of the array increases, the time these functions take increases quadratically.

A Flattening Map

Sometimes, you want to map an array where the transformation function returns another array and not a single element.

For example, let's say we have a function, links, which reads a Markdown file and returns an array containing the URLs of all the links in the file. The function type looks like this:

```
func extractLinks(markdownFile: String) -> [URL]
```

If we have a bunch of Markdown files and want to extract the links from all files into a single array, we could try to write something like markdownFiles.map(extractLinks). But this returns an array of arrays containing the URLs: one array per file. Now you could just perform the map, get back an array of arrays, and then call joined to flatten the results into a single array:

```
let markdownFiles: [String] = // ...
let nestedLinks = markdownFiles.map(extractLinks)
let links = nestedLinks.joined()
```

The flatMap method combines these two operations into a single step. So markdownFiles.flatMap(extractLinks) returns all the URLs in an array of Markdown files as a single array.

The implementation for flatMap is almost identical to map, except it takes a function argument that returns an array. It uses append(contentsOf:) instead of append(_:) to flatten the results when appending:

```
extension Array {
  func flatMap<T>(_ transform: (Element) -> [T]) -> [T] {
    var result: [T] = []
    for x in self {
      result.append(contentsOf: transform(x))
    }
    return result
  }
}
```

Another great use case for flatMap is combining elements from different arrays. To get all possible pairs of two arrays, flatMap over one array and then map over the other:

```
let suits = ["♠", "♥", "♣", "♦"]

let ranks = ["J","Q","K","A"]

let result = suits.flatMap { suit in
  ranks.map { rank in
    (suit, rank)
  }
}
```

Iteration using forEach

The final operation we'd like to discuss is forEach. It works almost like a for loop: the passed-in function is executed once for each element in the sequence. And unlike map, forEach doesn't return anything. Let's start by mechanically replacing a loop with forEach:

```
for element in [1,2,3] {
  print(element)
}

[1,2,3].forEach { element in
  print(element)
}
```

This isn't a big win, but it can be handy if the action you want to perform is a single function call on each element in a collection. Passing a function name to forEach instead of a closure expression can lead to clear and concise code. For example, if you're inside a view controller and want to add an array of subviews to the main view, you can just do theViews.forEach(view.addSubview).

However, there are some subtle differences between for loops and forEach. For instance, if a for loop has a return statement in it, rewriting it with forEach can significantly change the code's behavior. Consider the following example, which is written using a for loop with a where condition:

```
extension Array where Element: Equatable {
  func index(of element: Element) -> Int? {
```

```
    for idx in self.indices where self[idx] == element {
      return idx
    }
    return nil
  }
}
```

We can't directly replicate the where clause in the forEach construct, so we might (incorrectly) rewrite this using filter:

```
extension Array where Element: Equatable {
  func index_foreach(of element: Element) -> Int? {
    self.indices.filter { idx in
      self[idx] == element
    }.forEach { idx in
      return idx
    }
    return nil
  }
}
```

The return inside the forEach closure doesn't return out of the outer function; it only returns from the closure itself. In this particular case, we'd probably have found the bug because the compiler generates a warning that the argument to the return statement is unused, but you shouldn't rely on it finding every such issue.

Also, consider the following simple example:

```
(1..<10).forEach { number in
  print(number)
  if number > 2 { return }
}
```

It's not immediately obvious that this prints out all the numbers in the input range. The return statement isn't breaking the loop, rather it's returning from the closure.

In some situations, such as the addSubview example above, forEach can be nicer than a for loop. And it really shines as part of a sequence of chained operations. For instance, imagine you've chained several calls to map and filter in a single statement, and during debugging you want to log the intermediate values somewhere in the middle of the chain. Inserting a forEach step at the desired position is probably the quickest way to do this.

However, because of the non-obvious behavior with return, we recommend against most other uses of forEach. Just use a regular for loop instead.

Array Types

Slices

In addition to accessing a single element of an array by subscript (e.g. fibs[0]), we can also access a range of elements by subscript. For example, to get all but the first element of an array, we can do the following:

```
let slice = fibs[1..<fibs.endIndex]
slice // [1, 1, 2, 3, 5]
type(of: slice) // ArraySlice<Int>
```

This gets us a slice of the array starting at the second element, including the last element. The type of the result is ArraySlice, not Array. ArraySlice is a *view* on arrays. It's backed by the original array, yet it provides a view on just the slice. This makes certain the array doesn't need to get copied. The ArraySlice type has the same methods defined as Array does, so you can use them as if they were arrays. If you do need to convert them into an array, you can just construct a new array out of the slice:

```
Array(fibs[1..<fibs.endIndex]) // [1, 1, 2, 3, 5]
```

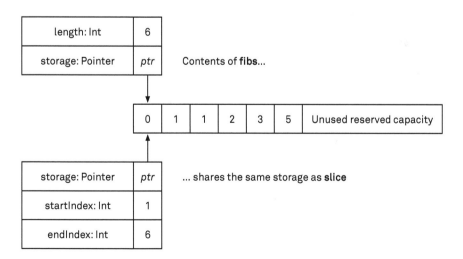

Figure 2.1: Array Slices

Bridging

Swift arrays can bridge to Objective-C. They can also be used with C, but we'll cover that in a later chapter. Because NSArray can only hold objects, there used to be a requirement that the elements of a Swift array had to be convertible to AnyObject in order for it to be bridgeable. This constrained the bridging to class instances and a small number of value types (such as Int, Bool, and String) that supported automatic bridging to their Objective-C counterparts.

This limitation no longer exists in Swift 3. The Objective-C id type is now imported into Swift as Any instead of AnyObject, which means that any Swift array is now bridgeable to NSArray. NSArray still always expects objects, of course, so the compiler and runtime will automatically wrap incompatible values in an opaque box class behind the scenes. Unwrapping in the reverse direction also happens automatically.

> A universal bridging mechanism for all Swift types to Objective-C doesn't just make working with arrays more pleasant. It also applies to other collections, like dictionaries and sets, and it opens up a lot of potential for future enhancements to the interoperability between Swift and Objective-C. For example, now that Swift values can be bridged to Objective-C objects, a future Swift version could conceivably allow Swift value types to conform to @objc protocols.

Dictionaries

Another key data structure in Swift is Dictionary. A dictionary contains keys with corresponding values; duplicate keys aren't supported. Retrieving a value by its key takes constant time on average, whereas searching an array for a particular element grows linearly with the array's size. Unlike arrays, dictionaries aren't ordered. The order in which pairs are enumerated in a for loop is undefined.

In the following example, we use a dictionary as the model data for a fictional settings screen in a smartphone app. The screen consists of a list of settings, and each individual setting has a name (the keys in our dictionary) and a value. A value can be one of several data types, such as text, numbers, or booleans. We use an enum with associated values to model this:

```
enum Setting {
  case text(String)
  case int(Int)
  case bool(Bool)
}

let defaultSettings: [String:Setting] = [
  "Airplane Mode": .bool(true),
  "Name": .text("My iPhone"),
]

defaultSettings["Name"] // Optional(Setting.text("My iPhone"))
```

We use subscripting to get the value of a setting (for example, defaultSettings["Name"]). Dictionary lookup always returns an *optional value*. When the specified key doesn't exist, it returns nil. Contrast this with arrays, which respond to an out-of-bounds access by crashing the program.

The rationale for this difference is that array indices and dictionary keys are used very differently. We've already seen that it's quite rare that you actually need to work with array indices directly. And if you do, an array index is usually directly derived from the array in some way (e.g. from a range like 0..<array.count); thus, using an invalid index is a programmer error. On the other hand, it's very common for dictionary keys to come from some source other than the dictionary itself.

Unlike arrays, dictionaries are also sparse. The existence of the value under the key "name" doesn't tell you anything about whether or not the key "address" also exists.

Mutation

Just like with arrays, dictionaries defined using let are immutable: no entries can be added, removed, or changed. And just like with arrays, we can define a mutable variant using var. To remove a value from a dictionary, we can either set it to nil using subscripting or call removeValue(forKey:). The latter additionally returns the deleted value, or nil if the key didn't exist. If we want to take an immutable dictionary and make changes to it, we have to make a copy:

```
var localizedSettings = defaultSettings
localizedSettings["Name"] = .text("Mein iPhone")
```

localizedSettings["Do Not Disturb"] = .bool(**true**)

Note that, again, the value of defaultSettings didn't change. As with key removal, an alternative to updating via subscript is the updateValue(_:forKey:) method, which returns the previous value (if any):

let oldName = localizedSettings
  .updateValue(.text("Il mio iPhone"), forKey: "Name")
localizedSettings["Name"] // *Optional(Setting.text("Il mio iPhone"))*
oldName // *Optional(Setting.text("Mein iPhone"))*

Some Useful Dictionary Extensions

What if we wanted to combine the default settings dictionary with any custom settings the user has changed? Custom settings should override defaults, but the resulting dictionary should still include default values for any keys that haven't been customized. Essentially, we want to merge two dictionaries, where the dictionary that's being merged in overwrites duplicate keys. The standard library doesn't include a function for this, so let's write one.

We can extend Dictionary with a merge method that takes the key-value pairs to be merged in as its only argument. We could make this argument another Dictionary, but this is a good opportunity for a more generic solution. Our requirements for the argument are that it must be a sequence we can loop over, and the sequence's elements must be key-value pairs of the same type as the receiving dictionary. Any Sequence whose Iterator.Element is a (Key, Value) pair meets these requirements, so that's what the method's generic constraints should express (Key and Value here are the generic type parameters of the Dictionary type we're extending):

```
extension Dictionary {
  mutating func merge<S>(_ other: S)
    where S: Sequence, S.Iterator.Element == (key: Key, value: Value) {
    for (k, v) in other {
      self[k] = v
    }
  }
}
```

We can use this to merge one dictionary into another, as shown in the following example, but the method argument could just as well be an array of key-value pairs or any other sequence:

```
var settings = defaultSettings
let overriddenSettings: [String:Setting] = ["Name": .text("Jane's iPhone")]
settings.merge(overriddenSettings)
settings
// ["Name": Setting.text("Jane\'s iPhone"), "Airplane Mode": Setting.bool(true)]
```

Another interesting extension is creating a dictionary from a sequence of
(Key, Value) pairs. The standard library provides a similar initializer for arrays
that comes up very frequently; you use it every time you create an array from a
range (Array(1...10)) or convert an ArraySlice back into a proper array
(Array(someSlice)). However, there's no such initializer for Dictionary. (There is
a Swift-Evolution proposal to add one, though, so we may see it in the future.)

We can start with an empty dictionary and then just merge in the sequence.
This makes use of the merge method defined above to do the heavy lifting:

```
extension Dictionary {
    init<S: Sequence>(_ sequence: S)
        where S.Iterator.Element == (key: Key, value: Value) {
        self = [:]
        self.merge(sequence)
    }
}
```

```
// All alarms are turned off by default
let defaultAlarms = (1..<5).map { (key: "Alarm \($0)", value: false) }
let alarmsDictionary = Dictionary(defaultAlarms)
```

A third useful extension is a map over the dictionary's values. Because
Dictionary is a Sequence, it already has a map method that produces an array.
However, sometimes we want to keep the dictionary structure intact and only
transform its values. Our mapValues method first calls the standard map to
create an array of *(key, transformed value)* pairs and then uses the new
initializer we defined above to turn it back into a dictionary:

```
extension Dictionary {
    func mapValues<NewValue>(transform: (Value) -> NewValue)
        -> [Key:NewValue] {
        return Dictionary<Key, NewValue>(map { (key, value) in
            return (key, transform(value))
        })
    }
}
```

```
let settingsAsStrings = settings.mapValues { setting -> String in
  switch setting {
  case .text(let text): return text
  case .int(let number): return String(number)
  case .bool(let value): return String(value)
  }
}
settingsAsStrings // ["Name": "Jane\'s iPhone", "Airplane Mode": "true"]
```

Hashable Requirement

Dictionaries are hash tables. The dictionary assigns each key a position in its underlying storage array based on the key's hashValue. This is why Dictionary requires its Key type to conform to the Hashable protocol. All the basic data types in the standard library already do, including strings, integers, floating-point, and Boolean values. Enumerations without associated values also get automatic Hashable conformance for free.

If you want to use your own custom types as dictionary keys, you must add Hashable conformance manually. This requires an implementation of the hashValue property and, because Hashable extends Equatable, an overload of the == operator function for your type. Your implementation must hold an important invariant: two instances that are equal (as defined by your == implementation) *must* have the same hash value. The reverse isn't true: two instances with the same hash value don't necessarily compare equally. This makes sense, considering that there's only a finite number of distinct hash values, while many hashable types (like strings) have essentially infinite cardinality.

The potential for duplicate hash values means that Dictionary must be able to handle collisions. Nevertheless, a good hash function should strive for a minimal number of collisions in order to preserve the collection's performance characteristics, i.e. the hash function should produce a uniform distribution over the full integer range. In the extreme case where your implementation returns the same hash value (e.g. zero) for every instance, a dictionary's lookup performance degrades to $O(n)$.

The second characteristic of a good hash function is that it's fast. Keep in mind that the hash value is computed every time a key is inserted, removed, or looked up. If your hashValue implementation takes too much time, it might eat up any gains you got from the $O(1)$ complexity.

Writing a good hash function that meets these requirements isn't easy. For types that are composed of basic data types that are Hashable themselves, XOR'ing the members' hash values can be a good starting point:

```
struct Person {
    var name: String
    var zipCode: Int
    var birthday: Date
}
```

```
extension Person: Equatable {
    static func ==(lhs: Person, rhs: Person) -> Bool {
        return lhs.name == rhs.name
            && lhs.zipCode == rhs.zipCode
            && lhs.birthday == rhs.birthday
    }
}
```

```
extension Person: Hashable {
    var hashValue: Int {
        return name.hashValue ^ zipCode.hashValue ^ birthday.hashValue
    }
}
```

One limitation of this technique is that XOR is symmetric (i.e. a ^ b == b ^ a), which, depending on the characteristics of the data being hashed, could make collisions more likely than necessary. You can add a bitwise rotation[1] to the mix to avoid this.

Finally, be extra careful when you use types that don't have value semantics (e.g. mutable objects) as dictionary keys. If you mutate an object after using it as a dictionary key in a way that changes its hash value and/or equality, you'll not be able to find it again in the dictionary. The dictionary now stores the object in the wrong slot, effectively corrupting its internal storage. This isn't a problem with value types because the key in the dictionary doesn't share your copy's storage and therefore can't be mutated from the outside.

---

1 https://www.mikeash.com/pyblog/friday-qa-2010-06-18-implementing-equality-and-hashing.html

Sets

The third major collection type in the standard library is Set. A set is an unordered collection of elements, with each element appearing only once. You can essentially think of a set as a dictionary that only stores keys and no values. Like Dictionary, Set is implemented with a hash table and has similar performance characteristics and requirements. Testing a value for membership in the set is a constant-time operation, and set elements must be Hashable, just like dictionary keys.

Use a set instead of an array when you need to test efficiently for membership (an $O(n)$ operation for arrays) and the order of the elements is not important, or when you need to ensure that a collection contains no duplicates.

Set conforms to the ExpressibleByArrayLiteral protocol, which means that we can initialize it with an array literal like this:

```
let naturals: Set = [1, 2, 3, 2]
naturals // [2, 3, 1]
naturals.contains(3) // true
naturals.contains(0) // false
```

Note that the number 2 appears only once in the set; the duplicate never even gets inserted.

Like all collections, sets support the common operations we've already seen: you can iterate over the elements in a for loop, map or filter them, and do all other sorts of things.

Set Algebra

As the name implies, Set is closely related to the mathematical concept of a set; it supports all common set operations you learned in math class. For example, we can *subtract* one set from another:

```
let iPods: Set = ["iPod touch", "iPod nano", "iPod mini",
    "iPod shuffle", "iPod Classic"]
let discontinuedIPods: Set = ["iPod mini", "iPod Classic"]
let currentIPods = iPods.subtracting(discontinuedIPods)
// ["iPod shuffle", "iPod nano", "iPod touch"]
```

We can also form the *intersection* of two sets, i.e. find all elements that are in both:

```
let touchscreen: Set = ["iPhone", "iPad", "iPod touch", "iPod nano"]
let iPodsWithTouch = iPods.intersection(touchscreen)
// ["iPod touch", "iPod nano"]
```

Or, we can form the *union* of two sets, i.e. combine them into one (removing duplicates, of course):

```
var discontinued: Set = ["iBook", "Powerbook", "Power Mac"]
discontinued.formUnion(discontinuedIPods) // ()
```

Here, we used the mutating variant formUnion to mutate the original set (which, as a result, must be declared with var). Almost all set operations have both non-mutating and mutating forms, the latter beginning with form.... For even more set operations, check out the SetAlgebra protocol.

Index Sets and Character Sets

Set is the only type in the standard library that conforms to SetAlgebra, but the protocol is also adopted by two interesting types in Foundation: IndexSet and CharacterSet. Both of these date back to a time long before Swift was a thing. The way these and other Objective-C classes are now bridged into Swift as fully featured value types — adopting common standard library protocols in the process — is great because they'll instantly feel familiar to Swift developers.

IndexSet represents a set of positive integer values. You can, of course, do this with a Set<Int>, but IndexSet is way more storage efficient because it uses a list of ranges internally. Say you have a table view with 1,000 elements and you want to use a set to manage the indices of the rows the user has selected. A Set<Int> needs to store up to 1,000 elements, depending on how many rows are selected. An IndexSet, on the other hand, stores continuous ranges, so a selection of the first 500 rows in the table only takes two integers to store (the selection's lower and upper bounds).

However, as a user of an IndexSet, you don't have to worry about the internal structure, as it's completely hidden behind the familiar SetAlgebra and Collection interfaces. (Unless you want to work on the ranges directly, that is. IndexSet exposes a view to them via its rangeView property, which itself is a collection.) For example, you can add a few ranges to an index set and then map over the indices as if they were individual members:

```
var indices = IndexSet()
indices.insert(integersIn: 1..<5)
indices.insert(integersIn: 11..<15)
let evenIndices = indices.filter { $0 % 2 == 0 } // [2, 4, 12, 14]
```

CharacterSet is an equally efficient way to store a set of Unicode characters. It's often used to check if a particular string only contains characters from a specific character subset, such as alphanumerics or decimalDigits. Unlike IndexSet, CharacterSet isn't a collection, though. We'll talk a bit more about CharacterSet in the chapter on strings.

Using Sets Inside Closures

Dictionaries and sets can be very handy data structures to use inside your functions, even when you're not exposing them to the caller. For example, if we want to write an extension on Sequence to retrieve all unique elements in the sequence, we could easily put the elements in a set and return its contents. However, that won't be *stable*: because a set has no defined order, the input elements might get reordered in the result. To fix this, we can write an extension that maintains the order by using an internal Set for bookkeeping:

```
extension Sequence where Iterator.Element: Hashable {
  func unique() -> [Iterator.Element] {
    var seen: Set<Iterator.Element> = []
    return filter {
      if seen.contains($0) {
        return false
      } else {
        seen.insert($0)
        return true
      }
    }
  }
}
```

```
[1,2,3,12,1,3,4,5,6,4,6].unique() // [1, 2, 3, 12, 4, 5, 6]
```

The method above allows us to find all unique elements in a sequence while still maintaining the original order (with the constraint that the elements must be Hashable). Inside the closure we pass to filter, we refer to the variable seen that we defined outside the closure, thus maintaining state over multiple iterations of the closure. In the chapter on functions, we'll look at this technique in more detail.

Ranges

A range is an interval of values, defined by its lower and upper bounds. You create ranges with the two range operators: ..< for half-open ranges that don't include their upper bound, and ... for closed ranges that include both bounds:

```
// 0 to 9, 10 is not included
let singleDigitNumbers = 0..<10

// "z" is included
let lowercaseLetters = Character("a")...Character("z")
```

Ranges seem like a natural fit to be sequences or collections, so it may surprise you to learn that they're *neither* — at least not all of them are.

There are now four range types in the standard library. They can be classified in a two-by-two matrix, as follows:

	Half-open range	Closed range
Elements are Comparable	Range	ClosedRange
Elements are Strideable (with integer steps)	CountableRange	CountableClosedRange

The columns of the matrix correspond to the two range operators we saw above, which create a [Countable]Range (half-open) or a [Countable]ClosedRange (closed), respectively. Half-open and closed ranges both have their place:

→ Only a **half-open range** can represent an **empty interval** (when the lower and upper bounds are equal, as in 5..<5).

→ Only a **closed range** can contain the **maximum value** its element type can represent (e.g. 0...Int.max). A half-open range always requires at least one representable value that's greater than the highest value in the range.

(In Swift 2, all ranges were technically half-open ranges, even if they were created with the ... operator; no range could contain the maximum expressible value. The standard library used to have additional types, HalfOpenInterval and ClosedInterval, to remedy this. They've been removed in Swift 3.)

The rows in the table distinguish between "normal" ranges whose element type only conforms to the Comparable protocol (which is the minimum requirement), and ranges over types that are Strideable *and* use integer steps between elements. Only the latter ranges are collections, inheriting all the powerful functionality we've seen in this chapter.

Swift calls these more capable ranges *countable* because only they can be iterated over. Valid bounds for countable ranges include integer and pointer types, but not floating-point types, because of the integer constraint on the type's Stride. If you need to iterate over consecutive floating-point values, you can use the stride(from:to:by) and stride(from:through:by) functions to create such a sequence.

This means that you can iterate over some ranges but not over others. For example, the range of Character values we defined above isn't a sequence, so this won't work:

```
for char in lowercaseLetters {
    // ...
}
// Error: Type 'ClosedRange<Character>' does not conform to protocol 'Sequence'
```

(The answer why iterating over characters isn't as straightforward as it would seem has to do with Unicode, and we'll cover it at length in the chapter on strings.)

Meanwhile, the following is no problem because an integer range is a countable range and thus a collection:

```
singleDigitNumbers.map { $0 * $0 } // [0, 1, 4, 9, 16, 25, 36, 49, 64, 81]
```

The standard library currently has to have separate types for countable ranges, CountableRange and CountableClosedRange. Ideally, these wouldn't be distinct types, but rather extensions on Range and ClosedRange that add collection conformance on the condition that the generic parameters meet the required constraints. We'll talk a lot more about this in the next chapter, but the code would look like this:

```
// Invalid in Swift 3
extension Range: RandomAccessCollection
  where Bound: Strideable, Bound.Stride: SignedInteger
{
  // Implement RandomAccessCollection
}
```

Alas, Swift 3's type system can't express this idea, so separate types are needed. Support for conditional conformance is expected for Swift 4, and CountableRange and CountableClosedRange will be folded into Range and ClosedRange when it lands.

The distinction between the half-open Range and the closed ClosedRange will likely remain, and it can sometimes make working with ranges harder than it used to be. Say you have a function that takes a Range<Character> and you want to pass it the closed character range we created above. You may be surprised to find out that it's not possible! Inexplicably, there appears to be no way to convert a ClosedRange into a Range. But why? Well, to turn a closed range into an equivalent half-open range, you'd have to find the element that comes after the original range's upper bound. And that's simply not possible unless the element is Strideable, which is only guaranteed for countable ranges.

This means the caller of such a function will have to provide the correct type. If the function expects a Range, you can't use the ... operator to create it. We're not certain how big of a limitation this is in practice, since most ranges are likely integer based, but it's definitely unintuitive.

Collection
Protocols

We saw in the previous chapter that Array, Dictionary, and Set don't exist in a vacuum. They're all implemented on top of a rich set of abstractions for processing series of elements, provided by the Swift standard library. This chapter is all about the Sequence and Collection protocols, which form the cornerstones of this model. We'll cover how these protocols work, why they work they way they do, and how you can write your own sequences and collections.

Sequences

The Sequence protocol stands at the base of the hierarchy. A sequence is a series of values of the same type that lets you iterate over the values. The most common way to traverse a sequence is a for loop:

```
for element in someSequence {
    doSomething(with: element)
}
```

This seemingly simple capability of stepping over elements forms the foundation for a large number of useful operations Sequence provides to adopters of the protocol. We already mentioned many of them in the previous chapter. Whenever you come up with a common operation that depends on sequential access to a series of values, you should consider implementing it on top of Sequence, too. We'll see many examples of how to do this throughout this chapter and the rest of the book.

The requirements for a type to conform to Sequence are fairly small. All it must do is provide a makeIterator() method that returns an *iterator*:

```
protocol Sequence {
    associatedtype Iterator: IteratorProtocol
    func makeIterator() -> Iterator
}
```

The only thing we learn about iterators from the definition of Sequence is that they're types that conform to IteratorProtocol. So let's first take a closer look at them.

Iterators

Sequences provide access to their elements by creating an iterator. The iterator produces the values of the sequence one at a time and keeps track of its iteration state as it traverses through the sequence. The only method defined in the IteratorProtocol protocol is next(), which must return the next element in the sequence on each subsequent call, or nil when the sequence is exhausted:

```
protocol IteratorProtocol {
    associatedtype Element
    mutating func next() -> Element?
}
```

The associated Element type specifies the type of the values the iterator produces. For example, the element type of the iterator for String.CharacterView is Character. By extension, the iterator also defines its sequence's element type; the fact that Element is an associated type of IteratorProtocol is why you often see references to Iterator.Element in method signatures or generic constraints for Sequence. We'll talk a lot more about protocols with associated types later in this chapter and in the chapter on protocols.

You normally only have to care about iterators when you implement one for your own custom sequence type. Other than that, you rarely need to use iterators directly, because a for loop is the idiomatic way to traverse a sequence. In fact, this is what a for loop does under the hood: the compiler creates a fresh iterator for the sequence and calls next on that iterator repeatedly, until nil is returned. The for loop example we showed above is essentially shorthand for the following:

```
var iterator = someSequence.makeIterator()
while let element = iterator.next() {
    doSomething(with: element)
}
```

Iterators are single-pass constructs; they can only be advanced, and never reversed or reset. While most iterators will produce a finite number of elements and eventually return nil from next(), nothing stops you from vending an infinite series that never ends. As a matter of fact, the simplest iterator imaginable — short of one that immediately returns nil — is one that just returns the same value over and over again:

```swift
struct ConstantIterator: IteratorProtocol {
  typealias Element = Int
  mutating func next() -> Int? {
    return 1
  }
}
```

The explicit typealias for Element is optional (but often useful for documentation purposes, especially in larger protocols). If we omit it, the compiler infers the concrete type of Element from the return type of next():

```swift
struct ConstantIterator: IteratorProtocol {
  mutating func next() -> Int? {
    return 1
  }
}
```

Notice that the next() method is declared as mutating. This isn't strictly necessary in this simplistic example because our iterator has no mutable state. In practice, though, iterators are inherently stateful. Almost any useful iterator requires mutable state to keep track of its position in the sequence.

We can create a new instance of ConstantIterator and loop over the sequence it produces in a while loop, printing an endless stream of ones:

```swift
var iterator = ConstantIterator()
while let x = iterator.next() {
  print(x)
}
```

Let's look at a more elaborate example. FibsIterator produces the Fibonacci sequence. It keeps track of the current position in the sequence by storing the upcoming two numbers. The next method then returns the first number and updates the state for the following call. Like the previous example, this iterator also produces an "infinite" stream; it keeps generating numbers until it reaches integer overflow, and then the program crashes:

```swift
struct FibsIterator: IteratorProtocol {
  var state = (0, 1)
  mutating func next() -> Int? {
    let upcomingNumber = state.0
    state = (state.1, state.0 + state.1)
    return upcomingNumber
  }
}
```

```
}
```

Conforming to Sequence

An example of an iterator that produces a finite sequence is the following PrefixIterator, which generates all prefixes of a string (including the string itself). It starts at the beginning of the string, and with each call of next, increments the slice of the string it returns by one character until it reaches the end:

```
struct PrefixIterator: IteratorProtocol {
    let string: String
    var offset: String.Index

    init(string: String) {
        self.string = string
        offset = string.startIndex
    }

    mutating func next() -> String? {
        guard offset < string.endIndex else { return nil }
        offset = string.index(after: offset)
        return string[string.startIndex..<offset]
    }
}
```

(string[string.startIndex..<offset] is a slicing operation that returns the substring between the start and the offset — we'll talk more about slicing later.)

With PrefixIterator in place, defining the accompanying PrefixSequence type is easy. Again, it isn't necessary to specify the associated Iterator type explicitly because the compiler can infer it from the return type of the makeIterator method:

```
struct PrefixSequence: Sequence {
    let string: String

    func makeIterator() -> PrefixIterator {
        return PrefixIterator(string: string)
    }
}
```

Now we can use a for loop to iterate over all the prefixes:

```
for prefix in PrefixSequence(string: "Hello") {
  print(prefix)
}
/*
H
He
Hel
Hell
Hello
*/
```

Or we can perform any other operation provided by Sequence:

```
PrefixSequence(string: "Hello").map { $0.uppercased() }
// ["H", "HE", "HEL", "HELL", "HELLO"]
```

We can create sequences for ConstantIterator and FibsIterator in the same way. We're not showing them here, but you may want to try this yourself. Just keep in mind that these iterators create infinite sequences. Use a construct like for i in fibsSequence.prefix(10) to slice off a finite piece.

Iterators and Value Semantics

The iterators we've seen thus far all have value semantics. If you make a copy of one, the iterator's entire state will be copied, and the two instances will behave independently of one other, as you'd expect. Most iterators in the standard library also have value semantics, but there are exceptions.

To illustrate the difference between value and reference semantics, we first take a look at StrideToIterator. It's the underlying iterator for the sequence that's returned from the stride(from:to:by:) function. Let's create a StrideToIterator and call next a couple of times:

```
// A sequence from 0 to 9
let seq = stride(from: 0, to: 10, by: 1)
var i1 = seq.makeIterator()
i1.next() // Optional(0)
i1.next() // Optional(1)
```

i1 is now ready to return 2. Now, say you make a copy of it:

var i2 = i1

Both the original and the copy are now separate and independent, and both
return 2 when you call next:

```
i1.next() // Optional(2)
i1.next() // Optional(3)
i2.next() // Optional(2)
i2.next() // Optional(3)
```

This is because StrideToIterator, a pretty simple struct whose implementation
is not too dissimilar from our Fibonacci iterator above, has value semantics.

Now let's look at an iterator that doesn't have value semantics. AnyIterator is
an iterator that wraps another iterator, thus "erasing" the base iterator's
concrete type. An example where this might be useful is if you want to hide
the concrete type of a complex iterator that would expose implementation
details in your public API. The way AnyIterator does this is by wrapping the
base iterator in an internal box object, which is a reference type. (If you want
to learn exactly how this works, check out the section on type erasure in the
protocols chapter.)

To see why this is relevant, we create an AnyIterator that wraps i1, and then we
make a copy:

```
var i3 = AnyIterator(i1)
var i4 = i3
```

In this situation, original and copy aren't independent because, despite being
a struct, AnyIterator doesn't have value semantics. The box object AnyIterator
uses to store its base iterator is a class instance, and when we assigned i3 to i4,
only the reference to the box got copied. The storage of the box is shared
between the two iterators. Any calls to next on either i3 or i4 now increment
the same underlying iterator:

```
i3.next() // Optional(4)
i4.next() // Optional(5)
i3.next() // Optional(6)
i3.next() // Optional(7)
```

Obviously, this could lead to bugs, although in all likelihood, you'll rarely
encounter this particular problem in practice. Iterators are usually not
something you pass around in your code. You're much more likely to create

one locally — sometimes explicitly, but mostly implicitly through a for loop — use it once to loop over the elements, and then throw it away. If you find yourself sharing iterators with other objects, consider wrapping the iterator in a sequence instead.

Function-Based Iterators and Sequences

AnyIterator has a second initializer that takes the next function directly as its argument. Together with the corresponding AnySequence type, this allows us to create iterators and sequences without defining any new types. For example, we could've defined the Fibonacci iterator alternatively as a function that returns an AnyIterator:

```
func fibsIterator() -> AnyIterator<Int> {
    var state = (0, 1)
    return AnyIterator {
        let upcomingNumber = state.0
        state = (state.1, state.0 + state.1)
        return upcomingNumber
    }
}
```

By keeping the state variable outside of the iterator's next closure and capturing it inside the closure, the closure can mutate the state every time it's invoked. There's only one functional difference between the two Fibonacci iterators: the definition using a custom struct has value semantics, and the definition using AnyIterator doesn't.

Creating a sequence out of this is even easier now because AnySequence provides an initializer that takes a function, which in turn produces an iterator:

```
let fibsSequence = AnySequence(fibsIterator)
Array(fibsSequence.prefix(10)) // [0, 1, 1, 2, 3, 5, 8, 13, 21, 34]
```

Another alternative is to use the sequence function that was introduced in Swift 3. The function has two variants. The first, sequence(first:next:), returns a sequence whose first element is the first argument you passed in; subsequent elements are produced by the closure passed in the next argument. In this example, we generate a sequence of random numbers, each smaller than the previous one, stopping when we reach zero:

```
let randomNumbers = sequence(first: 100) { (previous: UInt32) in
  let newValue = arc4random_uniform(previous)
  guard newValue > 0 else {
    return nil
  }
  return newValue
}
Array(randomNumbers) // [100, 1]
```

The other variant, sequence(state:next:), is even more powerful because it can keep some arbitrary mutable state around between invocations of the next closure. We can use this to build the Fibonacci sequence with a single function call:

```
let fibsSequence2 = sequence(state: (0, 1)) {
  // The compiler needs a little type inference help here
  (state: inout (Int, Int)) -> Int? in
  let upcomingNumber = state.0
  state = (state.1, state.0 + state.1)
  return upcomingNumber
}

Array(fibsSequence2.prefix(10)) // [0, 1, 1, 2, 3, 5, 8, 13, 21, 34]
```

> The return type of sequence(first:next:) and sequence(state:next:) is UnfoldSequence. This term comes from functional programming, where the same operation is often called *unfold*. sequence is the natural counterpart to reduce (which is often called *fold* in functional languages). Where reduce reduces (or *folds*) a sequence into a single return value, sequence *unfolds* a single value to generate a sequence.

The two sequence functions are extremely versatile. They're often a good fit for replacing a traditional C-style for loop that uses non-linear math.

Infinite Sequences

Like all iterators we've seen so far, the sequence functions apply their next closures lazily, i.e. the next value isn't computed until it's requested by the caller. This makes constructs like fibsSequence2.prefix(10) work. prefix(10) only asks the sequence for its first (up to) 10 elements and then stops. If the sequence had tried to compute all its values eagerly, the program would've crashed with an integer overflow before the next step had a chance to run.

The possibility of creating infinite sequences is one thing that sets sequences apart from collections, which can't be infinite.

Unstable Sequences

Sequences aren't limited to classic collection data structures, such as arrays or lists. Network streams, files on disk, streams of UI events, and many other kinds of data can all be modeled as sequences. But not all of these behave like an array when you iterate over the elements more than once.

While the Fibonacci sequence isn't affected by a traversal of its elements (and a subsequent traversal starts again at zero), a sequence that represents a stream of network packets is consumed by the traversal; it won't produce the same values again if you do another iteration. Both are valid sequences, though, so the documentation is very clear that Sequence makes no guarantee about multiple traversals:

> The Sequence protocol makes no requirement on conforming types regarding whether they will be destructively consumed by iteration. As a consequence, don't assume that multiple for-in loops on a sequence will either resume iteration or restart from the beginning:
>
> ```
> for element in sequence {
>   if ... some condition { break }
> }
>
> for element in sequence {
>   // No defined behavior
> }
> ```

> A conforming sequence that is not a collection is allowed to produce an arbitrary sequence of elements in the second for-in loop.

This also explains why the seemingly trivial first property is only available on collections, and not on sequences. Invoking a property getter ought to be non-destructive.

As an example of a destructively consumed sequence, consider this wrapper on the readLine function, which reads lines from the standard input:

```
let standardIn = AnySequence {
  return AnyIterator {
    readLine()
  }
}
```

Now you can use this sequence with the various extensions of Sequence. For example, you could write a line-numbering version of the Unix cat utility:

```
let numberedStdIn = standardIn.enumerated()

for (i, line) in numberedStdIn {
  print("\(i+1): \(line)")
}
```

The enumerated method wraps a sequence in a new sequence that produces pairs of the original sequence's elements and an incrementing number. Just like our wrapper of readLine, elements are lazily generated. The consumption of the base sequence only happens when you move through the enumerated sequence using its iterator, and not when it's created. So if you run the above code from the command line, you'll see it waiting inside the for loop. It prints the lines you type in as you hit return; it does *not* wait until the input is terminated with control-D. But nonetheless, each time enumerated serves up a line from standardIn, it's consuming the standard input. You can't iterate over it twice to get the same results.

As an author of a Sequence extension, you don't need to take into account whether or not the sequence is destructively consumed by iteration. But as a *caller* of a method on a sequence type, you should keep it in mind.

A certain sign that a sequence is stable is if it also conforms to Collection because this protocol makes that guarantee. The reverse isn't true. Even the standard library has some sequences that can be traversed safely multiple times although they aren't collections. Examples include the StrideTo and StrideThrough types, as returned by stride(from:to:by:) and stride(from:through:by:). The fact that you can stride over floating-point numbers would make it tricky (though probably not impossible) to render them as a collection, so they're just sequences.

The Relationship Between Sequences and Iterators

Sequences and iterators are so similar that you may wonder why these need to be separate types at all. Can't we just fold the IteratorProtocol functionality into Sequence? This would indeed work fine for destructively consumed sequences, like our standard input example. Sequences of this kind carry their own iteration state and are mutated as they're traversed.

Stable sequences, like arrays or our Fibonacci sequence, must not be mutated by a for loop; they require separate traversal state, and that's what the iterator provides (along with the traversal logic, but that might as well live in the sequence). The purpose of the makeIterator method is to create this traversal state.

Every iterator can also be seen as an *unstable* sequence over the elements it has yet to return. As a matter of fact, you can turn every iterator into a sequence simply by declaring conformance; Sequence comes with a default implementation for makeIterator that returns self if the conforming type is an iterator. The Swift team has expressed on the swift-evolution mailing list[1] that IteratorProtocol would actually inherit from Sequence if it weren't for language limitations (namely, lack of support for circular associated type constraints).

Though it may not currently be possible to enforce this relationship, most iterators in the standard library do conform to Sequence.

Subsequences

Sequence has another associated type, named SubSequence:

```
protocol Sequence {
  associatedtype Iterator: IteratorProtocol
  associatedtype SubSequence
  // ...
}
```

SubSequence is used as the return type for operations that return slices of the original sequence:

1 https://lists.swift.org/pipermail/swift-evolution/Week-of-Mon-20160104/005525.html

→ **prefix** and **suffix** — take the first or last *n* elements

→ **dropFirst** and **dropLast** — return subsequences where the first or last *n* elements have been removed

→ **split** — break up the sequence at the specified separator elements and return an array of subsequences

If you don't specify a type for SubSequence, the compiler will infer it to be AnySequence<Iterator.Element> because Sequence provides default implementations for the above methods with that return type. If you want to use your own subsequence type, you must provide custom implementations for these methods.

It can sometimes be convenient if SubSequence == Self, i.e. if subsequences have the same type as the base sequence. A standard library type for which this is the case is String.CharacterView. In the chapter on strings, we show some examples where this feature makes working with character views more pleasant.

In an ideal world, the associated type declaration would include constraints to ensure that SubSequence (a) is also a sequence, and (b) has the same element and subsequence types as its base sequence. It should look something like this:

```
// Invalid in Swift 3.0
associatedtype SubSequence: Sequence
  where Iterator.Element == SubSequence.Iterator.Element,
    SubSequence.SubSequence == SubSequence
```

This isn't possible in Swift 3.0 because the compiler lacks support for two required features: recursive protocol constraints (Sequence would reference itself) and where clauses on associated types. We expect both of these in a future Swift release. Until then, you may find yourself having to add some or all of these constraints to your own Sequence extensions to help the compiler understand the types.

The following example checks if a sequence starts with the same *n* elements from the head and the tail. It does this by comparing the sequence's prefix element with the reversed suffix. The comparison using elementsEqual only works if we tell the compiler that the subsequence is also a sequence, and that its elements have the same type as the base sequence's elements (which we constrained to Equatable):

```
extension Sequence
  where Iterator.Element: Equatable,
    SubSequence: Sequence,
    SubSequence.Iterator.Element == Iterator.Element
{
  func headMirrorsTail(_ n: Int) -> Bool {
    let head = prefix(n)
    let tail = suffix(n).reversed()
    return head.elementsEqual(tail)
  }
}
```

```
[1,2,3,4,2,1].headMirrorsTail(2) // true
```

We show another example of this in the chapter on generics.

Collections

A collection is a stable sequence that can be traversed nondestructively multiple times. In addition to linear traversal, a collection's elements can also be accessed via subscript with an index. Subscript indices are often integers, as they are in arrays. But as we'll see, indices can also be opaque values (as in dictionaries or strings), which sometimes makes working with them non-intuitive. A collection's indices invariably form a finite range, with a defined start and end. This means that unlike sequences, collections can't be infinite.

The Collection protocol builds on top of Sequence. In addition to all the methods inherited from Sequence, collections gain new capabilities that either depend on accessing elements at specific positions or rely on the guarantee of stable iteration, like the count property (if counting the elements of an unstable sequence consumed the sequence, it would kind of defeat the purpose).

Even if you don't need the special features of a collection, you can use Collection conformance to signal to users that your own sequence type is finite and supports multi-pass iteration. It's somewhat strange that you have to come up with an index if all you want is to document that your sequence is multi-pass. Picking a suitable index type to represent positions in the collection is often the hardest part of implementing the Collection protocol. One reason for this design is that the Swift team wanted to avoid the potential confusion of having a distinct protocol for multi-pass sequences[2] that had requirements identical to Sequence but different semantics.

Collections are used extensively throughout the standard library. In addition to Array, Dictionary, and Set, the four String views are all collections, as are CountableRange and UnsafeBufferPointer. Increasingly, we're also seeing types outside the standard library adopt the Collection protocol. Two examples of types that gained a ton of new capabilities in this way are Data and IndexSet, both from Foundation.

To demonstrate how collections in Swift work, we'll implement one of our own. Probably the most useful container type not present in the Swift standard library is a queue. Swift arrays are able to easily be used as stacks, with append to push and popLast to pop. However, they're not ideal to use as queues. You could use push combined with remove(at: 0), but removing anything other than the last element of an array is an $O(n)$ operation — because arrays are held in contiguous memory, every element has to shuffle down to fill the gap (unlike popping the last element, which can be done in constant time).

Designing a Protocol for Queues

Before we implement a queue, maybe we should define what we mean by it. A good way to do this is to define a protocol that describes what a queue is. Let's try the following definition:

```
/// A type that can `enqueue` and `dequeue` elements.
protocol Queue {
    /// The type of elements held in `self`.
    associatedtype Element
    /// Enqueue `element` to `self`.
    mutating func enqueue(_ newElement: Element)
    /// Dequeue an element from `self`.
    mutating func dequeue() -> Element?
}
```

As simple as this is, it says a lot about what our definition of queue is: it's defined generically. It can contain any type, represented by the associated type Element. It imposes no restrictions on what Element is.

---

2 https://lists.swift.org/pipermail/swift-evolution/Week-of-Mon-20151228/004989.html

It's important to note that the comments above the methods are as much a part of a protocol as the actual method names and types. Here, what we don't say tells us as much as what we do: there's no guarantee of the complexity of enqueue or dequeue. We could've said, for example, that both should operate in constant ($O(1)$) time. This would give users adopting this protocol a good idea of the performance characteristics of *any* kind of queue implementing this protocol. But it would rule out data structures, such as priority queues, that might have an $O(log_n)$ enqueueing operation.

It also doesn't offer a peek operation to check without dequeuing, which means it could be used to represent a queue that doesn't have such a feature (such as, say, a queue interface over an operating system or networking call that could only pop, not peek). It doesn't specify whether the two operations are thread-safe. It doesn't specify that the queue is a Collection (though the implementation we're about to write will be).

It doesn't even specify that it's a FIFO queue — it could be a LIFO queue, and we could conform Array to it, with append for enqueue and dequeue implemented via isEmpty/popLast.

Speaking of which, here *is* something the protocol specifies: like Array's popLast, dequeue returns an optional. If the queue is empty, it returns nil. Otherwise, it removes and returns the last element. We don't provide an equivalent for Array.removeLast, which traps if you call it on an empty array.

By making dequeue an optional, the most common operation of repeatedly dequeuing an element until the queue is empty becomes a one-liner, along with the safety of not being able to get it wrong:

```
while let x = queue.dequeue() {
    // Process queue element
}
```

The downside is the inconvenience of always having to unwrap, even when you already know the queue *can't* be empty. The right tradeoff for your particular data type depends on how you envision it to be used. (Conforming your custom collection to the Collection protocol gives you both variants for free, anyway, since Collection provides both a popFirst and a removeFirst method.)

A Queue Implementation

Now that we've defined what a queue is, let's implement it. Below is a very simple FIFO queue, with just enqueue and dequeue methods implemented on top of a couple of arrays.

Since we've named our queue's generic placeholder Element, the same name as the required associated type, there's no need to define it. It's not necessary to name it Element though — the placeholder is just an arbitrary name of your choosing. If it were named Foo, you could either define typealias Element = Foo, or leave Swift to infer it implicitly from the return types of the enqueue and dequeue implementations:

```swift
/// An efficient variable-size FIFO queue of elements of type `Element`
struct FIFOQueue<Element>: Queue {
    fileprivate var left: [Element] = []
    fileprivate var right: [Element] = []

    /// Add an element to the back of the queue.
    /// - Complexity: O(1).
    mutating func enqueue(_ newElement: Element) {
        right.append(newElement)
    }

    /// Removes front of the queue.
    /// Returns `nil` in case of an empty queue.
    /// - Complexity: Amortized O(1).
    mutating func dequeue() -> Element? {
        if left.isEmpty {
            left = right.reversed()
            right.removeAll()
        }
        return left.popLast()
    }
}
```

This implementation uses a technique of simulating a queue through the use of two stacks (two regular Swift arrays). As elements are enqueued, they're pushed onto the "right" stack. Then, when elements are dequeued, they're popped off the "left" stack, where they're held in reverse order. When the left stack is empty, the right stack is reversed onto the left stack.

You might find the claim that the dequeue operation is $O(1)$ slightly surprising. Surely it contains a reverse call that is $O(n)$? But while this is true, the overall *amortized* time to pop an item is constant — over a large number of pushes and pops, the time taken for them all is constant, even though the time for individual pushes or pops might not be.

The key to why this is lies in understanding how often the reverse happens and on how many elements. One technique to analyze this is the "banker's methodology." Imagine that each time you put an element on the queue, you pay a token into the bank. Single enqueue, single token, so constant cost. Then when it comes time to reverse the right-hand stack onto the left-hand one, you have a token in the bank for every element enqueued, and you use those tokens to pay for the reversal. The account never goes into debit, so you never spend more than you paid.

This kind of reasoning is good for explaining why the "amortized" cost of an operation over time is constant, even though individual calls might not be. The same kind of justification can be used to explain why appending an element to an array in Swift is a constant time operation. When the array runs out of storage, it needs to allocate bigger storage and copy all its existing elements into it. But since the storage size doubles with each reallocation, you can use the same "append an element, pay a token, double the array size, spend all the tokens but no more" argument.

Conforming to Collection

We now have a container that can enqueue and dequeue elements. The next step is to add Collection conformance to FIFOQueue. Unfortunately, figuring out the minimum set of implementations you must provide to conform to a protocol can sometimes be a frustrating experience in Swift.

At the time of writing, the Collection protocol has a whopping four associated types, four properties, seven instance methods, and two subscripts:

```swift
protocol Collection: Indexable, Sequence {
    associatedtype Iterator: IteratorProtocol = IndexingIterator<Self>
    associatedtype SubSequence: IndexableBase, Sequence = Slice<Self>
    associatedtype IndexDistance: SignedInteger = Int
    associatedtype Indices: IndexableBase, Sequence = DefaultIndices<Self>

    var first: Iterator.Element? { get }
    var indices: Indices { get }
    var isEmpty: Bool { get }
    var count: IndexDistance { get }
```

```
func makeIterator() -> Iterator
func prefix(through position: Index) -> SubSequence
func prefix(upTo end: Index) -> SubSequence
func suffix(from start: Index) -> SubSequence
func distance(from start: Index, to end: Index) -> IndexDistance
func index(_ i: Index, offsetBy n: IndexDistance) -> Index
func index(_ i: Index, offsetBy n: IndexDistance, limitedBy limit: Index) -> Index?

subscript(position: Index) -> Iterator.Element { get }
subscript(bounds: Range<Index>) -> SubSequence { get }
}
```

It also inherits from Sequence and Indexable, so we need to add those protocols' requirements to the "to-do list" of things we have to provide for our custom type. Quite a daunting task, isn't it?

Well, it turns out it's actually not that bad. Notice that all associated types have default values, so you don't need to care about those unless your type has special requirements. The same is true for most of the functions, properties, and subscripts: protocol extensions on Collection provide the default implementations. Some of these extensions have associated type constraints that match the protocol's default associated types; for example, Collection only provides a default implementation of the makeIterator method if its Iterator is an IndexingIterator<Self>:

```
extension Collection where Iterator == IndexingIterator<Self> {
    /// Returns an iterator over the elements of the collection.
    func makeIterator() -> IndexingIterator<Self>
}
```

If you decide that your type should have a different iterator type, you'd have to implement this method.

Working out what's required and what's provided through defaults isn't exactly hard, but it's a lot of manual work, and unless you're very careful not to overlook anything, it's easy to end up in an annoying guessing game with the compiler. The most frustrating part of the process may be that the compiler *has* all the information to guide you; the diagnostics just aren't helpful enough yet.

For the time being, your best hope is to find the minimal conformance requirements spelled out in the documentation, as is in fact the case for Collection.

Conforming to the Collection Protocol

... To add Collection conformance to your type, declare startIndex and endIndex properties, a subscript that provides at least read-only access to your type's elements, and the index(after:) method for advancing your collection's indices.

So in the end, we end up with these requirements:

```
protocol Collection: Indexable, Sequence {
    /// A type that represents a position in the collection.
    associatedtype Index: Comparable
    /// The position of the first element in a nonempty collection.
    var startIndex: Index { get }
    /// The collection's "past the end" position---that is, the position one
    /// greater than the last valid subscript argument.
    var endIndex: Index { get }
    /// Returns the position immediately after the given index.
    func index(after i: Index) -> Index
    /// Accesses the element at the specified position.
    subscript(position: Index) -> Element { get }
}
```

From the original requirements of the Collection protocol, only the subscript remains. The other requirements are inherited from IndexableBase by way of Indexable. Both of these protocols should be considered implementation details that only exist because of compiler limitations in Swift 3 (namely, the lack of support for circular protocol constraints). We expect them to be removed in Swift 4, with their functionality folded into Collection. You shouldn't need to use these protocols directly.

We can conform FIFOQueue to Collection like so:

```
extension FIFOQueue: Collection {
    public var startIndex: Int { return 0 }
    public var endIndex: Int { return left.count + right.count }

    public func index(after i: Int) -> Int {
        precondition(i < endIndex)
```

```
    return i + 1
  }

  public subscript(position: Int) -> Element {
    precondition((0..<endIndex).contains(position), "Index out of bounds")
    if position < left.endIndex {
      return left[left.count - position - 1]
    } else {
      return right[position - left.count]
    }
  }
}
```

We use Int as our queue's Index type. We don't specify an explicit typealias for the associated type; just like with Element, Swift can infer it from the method and property definitions. Note that since the indexing returns elements from the front first, Queue.first returns the next item that will be dequeued (so it serves as a kind of peek).

With just a handful of lines, queues now have more than 40 methods and properties at their disposal. We can iterate over queues:

```
var q = FIFOQueue<String>()
for x in ["1", "2", "foo", "3"] {
  q.enqueue(x)
}

for s in q {
  print(s, terminator: " ")
} // 1 2 foo 3
```

We can pass queues to methods that take sequences:

```
var a = Array(q) // ["1", "2", "foo", "3"]
a.append(contentsOf: q[2...3]) // ()
```

We can call methods and properties that extend Sequence:

```
q.map { $0.uppercased() } // ["1", "2", "FOO", "3"]
q.flatMap { Int($0) } // [1, 2, 3]
q.filter { $0.characters.count > 1 } // ["foo"]
q.sorted() // ["1", "2", "3", "foo"]
q.joined(separator: " ") // 1 2 foo 3
```

And we can call methods and properties that extend Collection:

```
q.isEmpty // false
q.count // 4
q.first // Optional("1")
```

Conforming to ExpressibleByArrayLiteral

When implementing a collection like this, it's nice to implement ExpressibleByArrayLiteral too. This will allow users to create a queue using the familiar [value1, value2, etc] syntax. This can be done easily, like so:

```
extension FIFOQueue: ExpressibleByArrayLiteral {
  public init(arrayLiteral elements: Element...) {
    self.init(left: elements.reversed(), right: [])
  }
}
```

For our queue logic, we want to reverse the elements to have them ready for use on the left-hand buffer. Of course, we could just copy the elements to the right-hand buffer, but since we're going to be copying elements anyway, it's more efficient to copy them in reverse order so that they don't need reversing later when they're dequeued.

Now queues can easily be created from literals:

```
let queue: FIFOQueue = [1,2,3] // FIFOQueue<Int>(left: [3, 2, 1], right: [])
```

It's important here to underline the difference between literals and types in Swift. [1,2,3] here is *not* an array. Rather, it's an "array literal" — something that can be used to create any type that conforms to ExpressibleByArrayLiteral. This particular literal contains other literals — integer literals — which can create any type that conforms to ExpressibleByIntegerLiteral.

These literals have "default" types — types that Swift will assume if you don't specify an explicit type when you use a literal. So array literals default to Array, integer literals default to Int, float literals default to Double, and string literals default to String. But this only occurs in the absence of you specifying otherwise. For example, the queue declared above is a queue of integers, but it could've been a queue of some other integer type:

```
let byteQueue: FIFOQueue<UInt8> = [1,2,3]
// FIFOQueue<UInt8>(left: [3, 2, 1], right: [])
```

Often, the type of the literal can be inferred from the context. For example, this is what it looks like if a function takes a type that can be created from literals:

```
func takesSetOfFloats(floats: Set<Float>) {
  //...
}

takesSetOfFloats(floats: [1,2,3])
```

This literal will be interpreted as Set<Float>, not as Array<Int>.

Associated Types

We've seen that Collection provides defaults for all but one of its associated types; types adopting the protocol only have to specify an Index type. While you don't *have* to care much about the other associated types, it's a good idea to take a brief look at each of them in order to better understand what they do. Let's go through them one by one.

Iterator. Inherited from Sequence. We already looked at iterators in detail in our discussion on sequences. The default iterator type for collections is IndexingIterator<Self>. This is a simple struct that wraps the collection and uses the collection's own indices to step over each element. The implementation is straightforward:

```
struct IndexingIterator<Elements: IndexableBase>: IteratorProtocol, Sequence {
  private let _elements: Elements
  private var _position: Elements.Index

  init(_elements: Elements) {
    self._elements = _elements
    self._position = _elements.startIndex
  }

  mutating func next() -> Elements._Element? {
    guard _position < _elements.endIndex else {
      return nil
    }
    let element = _elements[_position]
    _elements.formIndex(after: &_position)
    return element
  }
```

}

(The generic constraint <Elements: IndexableBase> should really be <Elements: Collection> once the compiler allows circular associated type constraints.)

Most collections in the standard library use IndexingIterator as their iterator. There should be little reason to write your own iterator type for a custom collection.

SubSequence. Also inherited from Sequence, but Collection restates this type with tighter constraints. A collection's SubSequence should itself also be a Collection. (We say "should" rather than "must" because this constraint is currently not fully expressible in the type system.) The default is Slice<Self>, which wraps the original collection and stores the slice's start and end index in terms of the base collection.

It can make sense for a collection to customize its SubSequence type, especially if it can be Self (i.e. a slice of the collection has the same type as the collection itself). We'll talk more about slicing later in this chapter.

IndexDistance. A signed integer type that represents the number of steps between two indices. There should be no reason to change this from the default Int.

Indices. The return type of the collection's indices property. It represents a collection containing all indices that are valid for subscripting the base collection, in ascending order. Note that the endIndex is not included because it signifies the "past the end" position and thus is not a valid subscript argument.

In Swift 2, the indices property returned a Range<Index> that could be used to iterate over all valid indices in the collection. In Swift 3, Range<Index> is no longer iterable because indices can no longer be advanced on their own; it's now up to the collection to advance an index. The Indices type replaces Range<Index> to keep index iterations working.

The default type is the imaginatively named DefaultIndices<Self>. Like Slice, it's a pretty simple wrapper for the base collection and a start and end index — it needs to keep a reference to the base collection to be able to advance the indices. This can lead to unexpected performance problems if users mutate the collection while iterating over its indices: if the collection is implemented using copy-on-write (as all collections in the standard library are), the extra reference to the collection can trigger unnecessary copies.

We cover copy-on-write in the chapter on structs and classes. For now, it's enough to know that if your custom collection can provide an alternative Indices type that doesn't need to keep a reference to the base collection, doing so is a worthwhile optimization. This is true for all collections whose index math doesn't rely on the collection itself, like arrays or our queue. If your index is an integer type, you can use CountableRange<Index>:

```
extension FIFOQueue: Collection {
    ...
    typealias Indices = CountableRange<Int>
    var indices: CountableRange<Int> {
        return startIndex..<endIndex
    }
}
```

Indices

An index represents a position in the collection. Every collection has two special indices, startIndex and endIndex. The startIndex designates the collection's first element, and endIndex is the index that comes *after* the last element in the collection. As a result, endIndex isn't a valid index for subscripting; you use it to form ranges of indices (someIndex..<endIndex) or to compare other indices against, e.g. as the break condition in a loop (while someIndex < endIndex).

Up to this point, we've been using integers as the index into our collections. Array does this, and (with a bit of manipulation) our FIFOQueue type does too. Integer indices are very intuitive, but they're not the only option. The only requirement for a collection's Index is that it must be Comparable, which is another way of saying that indices have a defined order.

Take Dictionary, for instance. It would seem that the natural candidates for a dictionary's indices would be its keys; after all, the keys are what we use to address the values in the dictionary. But the key can't be the index because you can't advance it — there's no way to tell what the next index after a given key would be. Also, subscripting on an index is expected to give direct element access, without detours for searching or hashing.

As a result, DictionaryIndex is an opaque value that points to a position in the dictionary's internal storage buffer. It really is just a wrapper for a single Int offset, but that's an implementation detail of no interest to users of the collection. (In fact, the reality is somewhat more complex because dictionaries that get passed to or returned from Objective-C APIs use an NSDictionary as their backing store for efficient bridging, and the index type for those dictionaries is different. But you get the idea.)

This also explains why subscripting a Dictionary with an index doesn't return an optional value, whereas subscripting with a key does. The subscript(_ key: Key) we're so used to is an additional overload of the subscript operator that's defined directly on Dictionary. It returns an optional Value:

```
struct Dictionary {
    ...
    subscript(key: Key) -> Value?
}
```

In contrast, subscripting on an index is part of the Collection protocol and *always* returns a non-optional value, because addressing a collection with an invalid index (like an out-of-bounds index on an array) is considered a programmer error and doing so will trap:

```
protocol Collection {
    subscript(position: Index) -> Element { get }
}
```

Notice the return type Element. A dictionary's Element type is the tuple type (key: Key, value: Value), so for Dictionary, this subscript returns a key-value pair and not just a Value.

In the section on array indexing in the built-in collections chapter, we discussed why it makes sense even for a "safe" language like Swift not to wrap every failable operation in an optional or error construct. "If every API can fail, then you can't write useful code.[3] You need to have some fundamental basis that you can rely on, and trust to operate correctly," otherwise your code gets bogged down in safety checks.

---

3 https://lists.swift.org/pipermail/swift-evolution/Week-of-Mon-20160411/014776.html

Index Invalidation

Indices may become invalid when the collection is mutated. Invalidation could mean that the index remains valid but now addresses a different element or that the index is no longer a valid index for the collection and using it to access the collection will trap. This should be intuitively clear when you consider arrays. When you append an element, all existing indices remain valid. When you remove the first element, an existing index to the last element becomes invalid. Meanwhile smaller indices remain valid, but the elements they point to have changed.

A dictionary index remains stable when new key-value pairs are added *until* the dictionary grows so much that it triggers a reallocation. This is because the element's location in the dictionary's storage buffer doesn't change, as elements are inserted until the buffer has to be resized, forcing all elements to be rehashed. Removing elements from a dictionary invalidates indices.

An index should be a dumb value that only stores the minimal amount of information required to describe an element's position. In particular, indices shouldn't keep a reference to their collection, if at all possible. Similarly, a collection usually can't distinguish one of its "own" indices from one that came from another collection of the same type. Again, this is trivially evident for arrays. Of course, you can use an integer index that was derived from one array to index another:

```
let numbers = [1,2,3,4]
let squares = numbers.map { $0 * $0 }
let numbersIndex = numbers.index(of: 4)! // 3
squares[numbersIndex] // 16
```

This also works with opaque index types, such as String.Index. In this example, we use one string's startIndex to access the first character of another string:

```
let hello = "Hello"
let world = "World"
let helloIdx = hello.startIndex
world[helloIdx] // W
```

However, the fact that you can do this doesn't mean it's generally a good idea. If we had used the index to subscript into an empty string, the program would've crashed because the index was out of bounds.

There are legitimate use cases for sharing indices between collections, though. The biggest one is working with slices. Subsequences usually share the underlying storage with their base collection, so an index of the base collection will address the same element in the slice.

Advancing Indices

Swift 3 introduced a major change to the way index traversal is handled for collections. The task of advancing an index forward or backward (i.e. deriving a new index from a given index) is now a responsibility of the collection, whereas up until Swift 2, indices were able to advance themselves. Where you used to write someIndex.successor() to step to the next index, you now write collection.index(after: someIndex).

Why did the Swift team decide to make this change? In short, performance. It turns out that deriving an index from another very often requires information about the collection's internals. It doesn't for arrays, where advancing an index is a simple addition operation. But a string index, for example, needs to inspect the actual character data because characters have variable sizes in Swift.

In the old model of self-advancing indices, this meant that the index had to store a reference to the collection's storage. That extra reference was enough to defeat the copy-on-write optimizations used by the standard library collections and would result in unnecessary copies when a collection was mutated during iteration.

By allowing indices to remain dumb values, the new model doesn't have this problem. It's also conceptually easier to understand and can make implementations of custom index types simpler. When you do implement your own index type, keep in mind that the index shouldn't keep a reference to the collection if at all possible. In most cases, an index can likely be represented with one or two integers that efficiently encode the position to the element in the collection's underlying storage.

The downside of the new indexing model is a slightly more verbose syntax in some cases.

A Linked List

As an example of a collection that doesn't have an integer index, let's implement one of the most basic collections of all: a singly linked list. To do this, we'll first demonstrate another way of implementing data structures using an indirect enum.

A linked list node is one of either two things: a node with a value and a reference to the next node, or a node indicating the end of the list. We can define it like this:

```
/// A simple linked list enum
enum List<Element> {
  case end
  indirect case node(Element, next: List<Element>)
}
```

The use of the indirect keyword here indicates that the compiler should represent this value as a reference. Swift enums are value types. This means they hold their values directly in the variable, rather than the variable holding a reference to the location of the value. This has many benefits, as we'll see in the structs and classes chapter, but it also means they can't contain a reference to themselves. The indirect keyword allows an enum case to be held as a reference and thus hold a reference to itself.

We prepend another element to the list by creating a new node, with the next: value set to the current node. To make this a little easier, we can create a method for it. We name this prepending method cons, because that's the name of the operation in LISP (it's short for "construct," and adding elements onto the front of the list is sometimes called "consing"):

```
extension List {
  /// Return a new list by prepending a node with value `x` to the
  /// front of a list.
  func cons(_ x: Element) -> List {
    return .node(x, next: self)
  }
}

// A 3-element list, of (3 2 1)
let list = List<Int>.end.cons(1).cons(2).cons(3)
// node(3, List<Swift.Int>.node(2, List<Swift.Int>.node(1, List<Swift.Int>.end)))
```

The chaining syntax makes it clear how a list is constructed, but it's also kind of ugly. As with our queue type, we can add conformance to ExpressibleByArrayLiteral to be able to initialize a list with an array literal. The implementation first reverses the input array (because lists are built from the end) and then uses reduce to prepend the elements to the list one by one, starting with the .end node:

```
extension List: ExpressibleByArrayLiteral {
  init(arrayLiteral elements: Element...) {
    self = elements.reversed().reduce(.end) { partialList, element in
      partialList.cons(element)
    }
  }
}
```

```
let list2: List = [3,2,1]
// node(3, List<Swift.Int>.node(2, List<Swift.Int>.node(1, List<Swift.Int>.end)))
```

This list type has an interesting property: it's "persistent[4]." The nodes are immutable — once created, you can't change them. Consing another element onto the list doesn't copy the list; it just gives you a new node that links onto the front of the existing list.

This means two lists can share a tail:

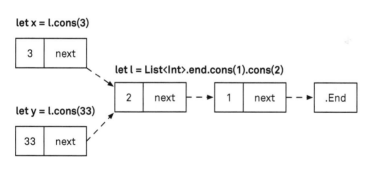

let x = l.cons(3)

| 3 | next |

let l = List<Int>.end.cons(1).cons(2)

| 2 | next | ---▶ | 1 | next | ---▶ | .End |

let y = l.cons(33)

| 33 | next |

Figure 3.1: List Sharing

4 https://en.wikipedia.org/wiki/Persistent_data_structure

The immutability of the list is key here. If you could change the list (say, remove the last entry, or update the element held in a node), then this sharing would be a problem — x might change the list, and the change would affect y.

Stacks

This list is a stack, with consing as push, and unwrapping the next element as pop. As we've mentioned before, arrays are also stacks. Let's define a common protocol for stacks, as we did with queues:

```
/// A LIFO stack type with constant-time push and pop operations
protocol Stack {
    /// The type of element held stored in the stack
    associatedtype Element

    /// Pushes `x` onto the top of `self`
    /// - Complexity: Amortized O(1).
    mutating func push(_: Element)

    /// Removes the topmost element of `self` and returns it,
    /// or `nil` if `self` is empty.
    /// - Complexity: O(1)
    mutating func pop() -> Element?
}
```

We've been a bit more proscriptive in the documentation comments about what it means to conform to Stack, including giving some minimum performance guarantees.

Array can be made to conform to Stack, like this:

```
extension Array: Stack {
    mutating func push(_ x: Element) { append(x) }
    mutating func pop() -> Element? { return popLast() }
}
```

So can List:

```
extension List: Stack {
    mutating func push(_ x: Element) {
        self = self.cons(x)
    }

    mutating func pop() -> Element? {
```

```
    switch self {
    case .end: return nil
    case let .node(x, next: xs):
      self = xs
      return x
    }
  }
}
```

But didn't we just say that the list had to be immutable for the persistence to work? How can it have mutating methods?

These mutating methods don't change the list. Instead, they just change the part of the list the variables refer to:

```
var stack: List<Int> = [3,2,1]
var a = stack
var b = stack

a.pop() // Optional(3)
a.pop() // Optional(2)
a.pop() // Optional(1)

stack.pop() // Optional(3)
stack.push(4)

b.pop() // Optional(3)
b.pop() // Optional(2)
b.pop() // Optional(1)

stack.pop() // Optional(4)
stack.pop() // Optional(2)
stack.pop() // Optional(1)
```

This shows us the difference between values and variables. The nodes of the list are values; they can't change. A node of three and a reference to the next node can't become some other value; it'll be that value forever, just like the number three can't change. It just is. Just because these values in question are structures with references to each other doesn't make them less value-like.

A variable a, on the other hand, can change the value it holds. It can be set to hold a value of an indirect reference to any of the nodes, or to the value end. But changing a doesn't change these nodes; it just changes which node a refers to.

This is what these mutating methods on structs do — they take an implicit
inout argument of self, and they can change the value self holds. This doesn't
change the list, but rather which part of the list the variable currently
represents. In this sense, through indirect, the variables have become iterators
into the list:

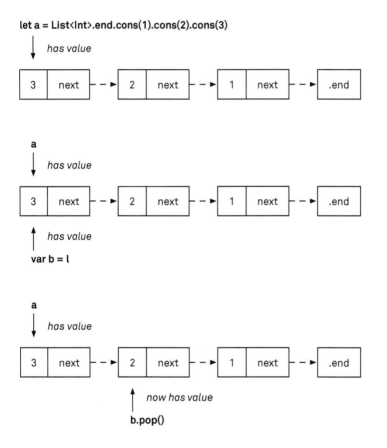

Figure 3.2: List Iteration

You can, of course, declare your variables with let instead of var, in which case
the variables will be constant (i.e. you can't change the value they hold once
they're set). But let is about the variables, not the values. Values are constant
by definition.

Now this is all just a logical model of how things work. In reality, the nodes are
actually places in memory that point to each other. And they take up space,

which we want back if it's no longer needed. Swift uses automated reference counting (ARC) to manage this and frees the memory for the nodes that are no longer used:

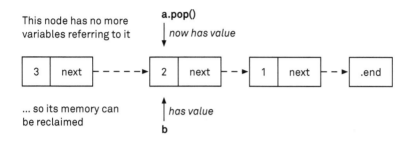

Figure 3.3: List Memory Management

We'll discuss inout in more detail in the chapter on functions, and we'll cover mutating methods as well as ARC in the structs and classes chapter.

Conforming List to Sequence

Since list variables are iterators into the list, this means you can use them to conform List to Sequence. As a matter of fact, List is an example of an unstable sequence that carries its own iteration state, like we saw when we talked about the relationship between sequences and iterators. We can add conformance to IteratorProtocol and Sequence in one go just by providing a next() method; the implementation of this is exactly the same as for pop:

```
extension List: IteratorProtocol, Sequence {
  mutating func next() -> Element? {
    return pop()
  }
}
```

Now you can use lists with for ... in:

```
let list: List = ["1", "2", "3"]
for x in list {
  print("\(x) ", terminator: "")
} // 1 2 3
```

This also means that, through the power of protocol extensions, we can use List with dozens of standard library functions:

```
list.joined(separator: ",") // 1,2,3
list.contains("2") // true
list.flatMap { Int($0) } // [1, 2, 3]
list.elementsEqual(["1", "2", "3"]) // true
```

Conforming List to Collection

Next, we make List conform to Collection. To do that, we need to decide on an index type for List. We said above that the best index is often a simple integer offset into the collection's storage, but that doesn't work in this case because a linked list has no contiguous storage. An integer-based index (e.g. the number of steps to the node from the beginning of the list) would have to traverse the list from the startIndex every time, making subscript access an $O(n)$ operation. However, the documentation for Collection requires this to be $O(1)$, "because many collection operations depend on $O(1)$ subscripting performance for their own performance guarantees."

As a result, our index must reference the list nodes directly. This isn't a problem for performance, because List, being immutable, doesn't use copy-on-write optimizations.

Since we already used List directly as an iterator, it's tempting to do the same here and use the enum itself as the index. But this will lead to problems. For example, index and collection need very different implementations of ==:

→ The index needs to know if two indices from the same list are at the same position. It shouldn't need the elements to conform to Equatable.

→ The collection, on the other hand, should be able to compare two different lists to see if they hold the same elements. It'll need the elements to conform to Equatable.

By creating separate types to represent the index and collection, we'll be able to implement different behavior for the two different == operators. And by having neither be the node enum, we'll be able to make that node implementation private, hiding the details from users of the collection. The new ListNode type looks just like our first variant of List:

/// Private implementation detail of the List collection

```
fileprivate enum ListNode<Element> {
  case end
  indirect case node(Element, next: ListNode<Element>)

  func cons(_ x: Element) -> ListNode<Element> {
    return .node(x, next: self)
  }
}
```

The index type wraps ListNode. In order to be a collection index, a type needs to conform to Comparable, which has only two requirements: it needs a less-than operator (<), and it needs an is-equal operator (==), which the protocol inherits from Equatable. The other operators, >, <=, and >=, have default implementations like the first two do.

We need some additional information to allow us to implement == and <. As we've discussed, nodes are values, and values don't have identity. So how can we tell if two variables are pointing to the same node? To do this, we tag each index with an incrementing number (the .end node has the tag zero). As we'll see in a bit, storing the tags with the nodes will allow for very efficient operations. The way the list works, two indices in the same list must be the same if they have the same tag:

```
public struct ListIndex<Element>: CustomStringConvertible {
  fileprivate let node: ListNode<Element>
  fileprivate let tag: Int

  public var description: String {
    return "ListIndex(\(tag))"
  }
}
```

Another thing to note is that ListIndex is a public struct but has private properties (node and tag). This means it's not publicly constructible — its default memberwise initializer of ListIndex(node:tag:) won't be accessible to users. So you can be handed a ListIndex from a List, but you can't create one yourself. This is a useful technique for hiding implementation details and providing safety.

We also need to adopt Comparable. As we discussed above, we do this by comparing the tag:

```
extension ListIndex: Comparable {
  public static func == <T>(lhs: ListIndex<T>, rhs: ListIndex<T>) -> Bool {
```

```
    return lhs.tag == rhs.tag
  }

  public static func < <T>(lhs: ListIndex<T>, rhs: ListIndex<T>) -> Bool {
    // startIndex has the highest tag, endIndex the lowest
    return lhs.tag > rhs.tag
  }
}
```

Now that we have a suitable index type, the next step is to create a List struct that conforms to Collection:

```
public struct List<Element>: Collection {
  // Index's type could be inferred, but it helps make the rest of
  // the code clearer:
  public typealias Index = ListIndex<Element>

  public let startIndex: Index
  public let endIndex: Index

  public subscript(position: Index) -> Element {
    switch position.node {
    case .end: fatalError("Subscript out of range")
    case let .node(x, _): return x
    }
  }

  public func index(after idx: Index) -> Index {
    switch idx.node {
    case .end: fatalError("Subscript out of range")
    case let .node(_, next): return Index(node: next, tag: idx.tag - 1)
    }
  }
}
```

Note that List requires no other storage besides the startIndex and endIndex. Since the index wraps the list node and the nodes link to each other, the entire list is accessible from startIndex. And endIndex will be the same ListIndex(node: .end, tag: 0) for all instances (at least until we get to slicing, below).

To make lists easier to construct, we again implement ArrayLiteralConvertible:

```
extension List: ExpressibleByArrayLiteral {
  public init(arrayLiteral elements: Element...) {
```

```
    startIndex = ListIndex(node: elements.reversed().reduce(.end) {
      partialList, element in
      partialList.cons(element)
    }, tag: elements.count)
    endIndex = ListIndex(node: .end, tag: 0)
  }
}
```

The capabilities inherited from Sequence also make it very easy to write a simple implementation of description for nicer debug output. We map over the list elements, convert them to their string representations, and join them into a single string:

```
extension List: CustomStringConvertible {
  public var description: String {
    let elements = self.map { String(describing: $0) }
      .joined(separator: ", ")
    return "List: (\(elements))"
  }
}
```

And now our list gains the extensions on Collection:

```
let list: List = ["one", "two", "three"] // List: (one, two, three)
list.first // Optional("one")
list.index(of: "two") // Optional(ListIndex(2))
```

As an added bonus, since the tag is the count of nodes prepended to .end, List gets a constant-time count property, even though this is normally an $O(n)$ operation for a linked list:

```
extension List {
  public var count: Int {
    return startIndex.tag - endIndex.tag
  }
}
list.count // 3
```

The subtraction of the end index (which, up until now, will always be a tag of zero) is to support slicing, which we'll come to shortly.

Finally, since List and ListIndex are two different types, we can give List a different implementation of == — this time, comparing the elements:

```swift
public func == <T: Equatable>(lhs: List<T>, rhs: List<T>) -> Bool {
  return lhs.elementsEqual(rhs)
}
```

In a perfect type system, we wouldn't just implement the overload for ==, but also add Equatable conformance to List itself, with a constraint that the Element type must be Equatable, like so:

```swift
extension List: Equatable where Element: Equatable { }
// Error: Extension of type 'List' with constraints cannot have an inheritance clause
```

This would allow us to compare a list of lists, for example, or use List in any other place that requires Equatable conformance. Sadly, the language currently can't express this kind of constraint. However, *conditional protocol conformance* is a highly anticipated feature, and it's very likely to come with Swift 4.

Slices

All collections get a default implementation of the slicing operation and have an overload for subscript that takes a Range<Index>. This is the equivalent of list.dropFirst():

```swift
let list: List = [1,2,3,4,5]
let onePastStart = list.index(after: list.startIndex)
let firstDropped = list[onePastStart..<list.endIndex]
Array(firstDropped) // [2, 3, 4, 5]
```

Since operations like list[somewhere..<list.endIndex] (slice from a specific point to the end) and list[list.startIndex..<somewhere] (slice from the start to a specific point) are very common, there are default operations in the standard library that do this in a more readable way:

```swift
let firstDropped2 = list.suffix(from: onePastStart)
```

By default, the type of firstDropped won't be a list — it'll be a Slice<List<String>>. Slice is a lightweight wrapper on top of any collection. The implementation looks something like this:

```swift
struct Slice<Base: Collection>: Collection {
  typealias Index = Base.Index
  typealias IndexDistance = Base.IndexDistance
```

```
let collection: Base

var startIndex: Index
var endIndex: Index

init(base: Base, bounds: Range<Index>) {
  collection = base
  startIndex = bounds.lowerBound
  endIndex = bounds.upperBound
}

func index(after i: Index) -> Index {
  return collection.index(after: i)
}

subscript(position: Index) -> Base.Iterator.Element {
  return collection[position]
}

typealias SubSequence = Slice<Base>

subscript(bounds: Range<Base.Index>) -> Slice<Base> {
  return Slice(base: collection, bounds: bounds)
}
}
```

In addition to a reference to the original collection, Slice stores the start and end index of the slice's bounds. This makes it twice as big as it needs to be in List's case, because the storage of a list itself consists of two indices:

```
// Size of a list is size of two nodes, the start and end:
MemoryLayout.size(ofValue: list) // 32

// Size of a list slice is size of a list, plus size of the slice's
// start and end index, which in List's case are also list nodes.
MemoryLayout.size(ofValue: list.dropFirst()) // 64
```

Implementing Custom Slicing

We can do better, because lists could instead return themselves as subsequences by holding different start and end indices. We can give List a custom implementation that does this:

```
extension List {
  public subscript(bounds: Range<Index>) -> List<Element> {
    return List(startIndex: bounds.lowerBound, endIndex: bounds.upperBound)
  }
}
```

Using this implementation, list slices are themselves lists, so their size is only 32 bytes:

```
let list: List = [1,2,3,4,5]
MemoryLayout.size(ofValue: list.dropFirst()) // 32
```

Perhaps more important than the size optimization is that sequences and collections that are their own subsequence type are more pleasant to work with because you don't have to deal with another type. As one example, your carefully designed CustomStringConvertible implementation will also work on a subsequence without additional code.

Another thing to consider is that with many sliceable containers, including Swift's arrays and strings, a slice shares the storage buffer of the original collection. This has an unpleasant side effect: slices can keep the original collection's buffer alive in its entirety, even if the original collection falls out of scope. If you read a 1 GB file into an array or string, and then slice off a tiny part, the whole 1 GB buffer will stay in memory until both the collection and the slice are destroyed. This is why Apple explicitly warns in the documentation to "use slices only for transient computation."

With List, it isn't quite as bad. As we've seen, the nodes are managed by ARC: when the slices are the only remaining copy, any elements dropped from the front will be reclaimed as soon as no one is referencing them:

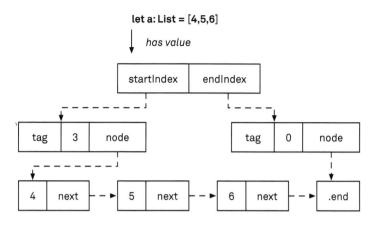

Figure 3.4: List Sharing and ARC

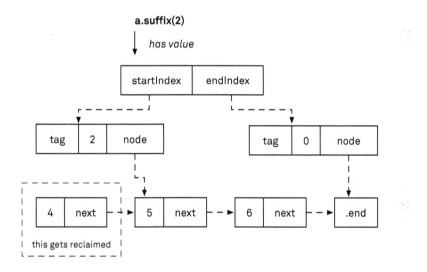

Figure 3.5: Memory Reclaiming

However, the back nodes won't be reclaimed, since the slice's last node still has a reference to what comes after it:

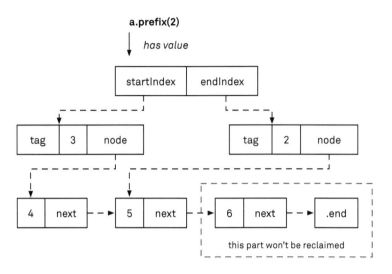

Figure 3.6: No Reclaiming of Memory

Slices Share Indices with the Base Collection

Indices of a slice can generally be used interchangeably with indices of the original collection. This isn't a formal requirement, but all slice types in the standard library behave in this way, so it's a good rule to follow in your own implementations.

An important implication of this model is that, even when using integer indices, a collection's index won't necessarily start at zero. Here's an example of the start and end indices of an array slice:

```
let cities = ["New York", "Rio", "London", "Berlin",
  "Rome", "Beijing", "Tokyo", "Sydney"]
let slice = cities[2...4]
cities.startIndex // 0
cities.endIndex // 8
slice.startIndex // 2
slice.endIndex // 5
```

Accidentally accessing slice[0] in this situation will crash your program. This is another reason to always prefer constructs like for x in collection or for index in collection.indices over manual index math if possible — with one exception: if you mutate a collection while iterating over its indices, any strong reference the indices object holds to the original collection will defeat the copy-on-write optimizations and may cause an unwanted copy to be made. Depending on the size of the collection, this can have a significant negative performance impact. (Not all collections use an Indices type that strongly references the base collection, but many do.)

To avoid this, you can replace the for loop with a while loop and advance the index manually in each iteration, thus avoiding the indices property. Just remember that if you do this, always start the loop at collection.startIndex and not at 0.

A Generic PrefixIterator

Now that we know any collection can be sliced, we could revisit our prefix iterator code from earlier in the chapter and write a version that works with any collection:

```
struct PrefixIterator<Base: Collection>: IteratorProtocol, Sequence {
  let base: Base
  var offset: Base.Index

  init(_ base: Base) {
    self.base = base
    self.offset = base.startIndex
  }

  mutating func next() -> Base.SubSequence? {
    guard offset != base.endIndex else { return nil }
    base.formIndex(after: &offset)
    return base.prefix(upTo: offset)
  }
}
```

By conforming the iterator directly to Sequence, we can use it with functions that work on sequences without having to define another type:

```
let numbers = [1,2,3]
Array(PrefixIterator(numbers))
// [ArraySlice([1]), ArraySlice([1, 2]), ArraySlice([1, 2, 3])]
```

Specialized Collections

Like all well-designed protocols, Collection strives to keep its requirements as small as possible. In order to allow a wide array of types to become collections, the protocol shouldn't require conforming types to provide more than is absolutely necessary to implement the desired functionality.

Two particularly interesting limitations are that a Collection can't move its indices backward, and that it doesn't provide any functionality for mutating the collection, such as inserting, removing, or replacing elements. That isn't to say that conforming types can't have these capabilities, of course, only that the protocol makes no assumptions about them.

Some operations have additional requirements, though, and it would be nice to have generic variants of them, even if only some collections can use them. For this purpose, the standard library includes four specialized collection protocols, each of which refines Collection in a particular way in order to enable new functionality (the quotes are from the standard library documentation):

→ **BidirectionalCollection** — "A collection that supports backward as well as forward traversal."

→ **RandomAccessCollection** — "A collection that supports efficient random-access index traversal."

→ **MutableCollection** — "A collection that supports subscript assignment."

→ **RangeReplaceableCollection** — "A collection that supports replacement of an arbitrary subrange of elements with the elements of another collection."

Let's discuss them one by one. But before we do that, we need to take a look at what it means to have forward-only index traversal.

Forward-Only Traversal

A singly linked list is famous for a particular trait: it can only be iterated forward. You can't leap into the middle of a linked list. You can't start at the end and work backward. You can only go forward.

For this reason, while our List collection has a first property, it doesn't have a last property. To get the last element of a list, you have to iterate all the way to the end, an $O(n)$ operation. It would be misleading to provide a cute little property for the last element — a list with a million elements takes a long time to fetch the last element.

A general rule of thumb for properties is probably that "they must be constant-time(-ish) operations only, unless it's incredibly obvious the operation couldn't be done in constant time." This is quite a wooly definition. "Must be constant-time operations" would be nicer, but the standard library does make some exceptions. For example, the default implementation of the count property is documented to be $O(n)$, though most collections will provide an overload that guarantees $O(1)$, like we did above for List.

Functions are a different matter. Our List type *does* have a reversed operation:

```
let list: List = ["red", "green", "blue"]
let reversed = list.reversed() // ["blue", "green", "red"]
```

In this case, what's being called is the reversed method provided by the standard library as an extension on Sequence, which returns the reversed elements in an array:

```
extension Sequence {
    /// Returns an array containing the elements of this sequence
    /// in reverse order. The sequence must be finite.
    func reversed() -> [Self.Iterator.Element]
}
```

But you might want to be able to stick with a list as the reverse of a list — in which case, we can overload the default implementation by extending List:

```
extension List {
    public func reversed() -> List<Element> {
        let reversedNodes: ListNode<Element> =
            self.reduce(.end) { $0.cons($1) }
        return List(
            startIndex: ListIndex(node: reversedNodes, tag: self.count),
            endIndex: ListIndex(node: .end, tag: 0))
    }
}
```

Now, when you call reversed on a list, you get another list. This will be chosen by default by Swift's overloading resolution mechanism, which always favors the most specialized implementation of a function or method on the basis that this almost always means it's a better choice. In this case, an implementation of reversed directly on List is more specific than the more general one that reverses any sequence:

```
let list: List = ["red", "green", "blue"]
let reversed = list.reversed() // List: (blue, green, red)
```

But it's possible you really want an array, in which case it'd be more efficient to use the sequence-reversing version rather than reversing the list and then converting it to an array in two steps. If you still wanted to choose the version that returns an array, you could force Swift to call it by specifying the type you're assigning to (rather than letting type inference default it for you):

```
let reversedArray: [String] = list.reversed() // ["blue", "green", "red"]
```

Or, you can use the as keyword if you pass the result into a function. For example, the following code tests that calling reversed on a list generates the same result as the version on an array:

```
list.reversed().elementsEqual(list.reversed() as [String]) // true
```

A quick testing tip: be sure to check that the overload is really in place and not accidentally missing. Otherwise, the above test will always pass, because you'll be comparing the two array versions.

You can test for this using is List, but assuming the overload is working, the compiler will warn you that your is is pointless (which would be true, so long as your overload has worked). To avoid that, you can cast via Any first:

```
list.reversed() as Any is List<String> // true
```

BidirectionalCollection

BidirectionalCollection adds a single but critical capability: the ability to move an index backward using the index(before:) method. This is sufficient to give your collection a default last property, matching first:

```
extension BidirectionalCollection {
    /// The last element of the collection.
    public var last: Iterator.Element? {
        return isEmpty ? nil : self[index(before: endIndex)]
    }
}
```

}

An example of a bidirectional collection in the standard library is
String.CharacterView. For Unicode-related reasons that we'll go into in the
chapter on strings, a character collection can't provide random access to its
characters, but you can move backward from the end, character by character.

BidirectionalCollection also adds more efficient implementations of some
operations that profit from traversing the collection backward, such as suffix,
removeLast, and reversed. The latter doesn't immediately reverse the
collection, but instead returns a lazy view:

```
extension BidirectionalCollection {
  /// Returns a view presenting the elements of the collection in reverse
  /// order.
  /// - Complexity: O(1)
  public func reversed() -> ReversedCollection<Self> {
    return ReversedCollection(_base: self)
  }
}
```

Just as with the enumerated wrapper on Sequence, no actual reversing takes
place. Instead, ReversedCollection holds the base collection and uses a
reversed index into the collection. The collection then reverses the logic of all
index traversal methods so that moving forward moves backward in the base
collection, and vice versa.

Value semantics play a big part in the validity of this approach. On
construction, the wrapper "copies" the base collection into its own storage so
that a subsequent mutation of the original collection won't change the copy
held by ReversedCollection. This means that it has the same observable
behavior as the version of reversed that returns an array. We'll see in the
chapter on structs and classes that, in the case of copy-on-write types such as
Array (or immutable persistent structures like List, or types composed of two
copy-on-write types like FIFOQueue), this is still an efficient operation.

RandomAccessCollection

A RandomAccessCollection provides the most efficient element access of all —
it can jump to any index in constant time. To do this, conforming types must
be able to (a) move an index any distance, and (b) measure the distance
between any two indices, both in $O(1)$ time. RandomAccessCollection

redeclares its associated Indices and SubSequence types with stricter constraints — both must be random-access themselves — but otherwise adds no new requirements over BidirectionalCollection. Adopters must ensure to meet the documented $O(1)$ complexity requirements, however. You can do this either by providing implementations of the index(_:offsetBy:) and distance(from:to:) methods, or by using an Index type that conforms to Strideable, such as Int.

At first, this might seem like it doesn't add much. Even a simple forward-traverse-only collection like our List can advance an index by an arbitrary distance. But there's a big difference. For Collection and BidirectionalCollection, index(_:offsetBy:) operates by incrementing the index successively until it reaches the destination. This clearly takes linear time — the longer the distance traveled, the longer it'll take to run. Random-access collections, on the other hand, can just move straight to the destination.

This ability is key in a number of algorithms, a couple of which we'll look at in the chapter on generics. There, we'll implement a generic binary search, but it's crucial this algorithm be constrained to random-access collections only — otherwise it'd be far less efficient than just searching through the collection from start to end.

Earlier, when we implemented our linked list, we wrote a custom version of count because we could get it from the tags. A random-access collection can compute the distance between its startIndex and endIndex in constant time, which means the collection can also compute count in constant time out of the box.

> Under the old Swift 2 indexing model, the capability of forward-only, bidirectional, or random-access traversal was a property of the index and not the collection. Instead of BidirectionalCollection and RandomAccessCollection, there were ForwardIndexType, BidirectionalIndexType, and RandomAccessIndexType. Through protocol extensions that were constrained on the index type, the collection would then have implementations for operations that depended on the index's capabilities.
>
> The new model — where index traversal is defined in terms of a refinement of Collection — is clearer and matches the existing scheme of MutableCollection and RangeReplaceableCollection.

MutableCollection

A mutable collection supports in-place element mutation. The single new requirement it adds to Collection is that the subscript now must also have a setter. We can't make List mutable, but we can add conformance to our queue type:

```
extension FIFOQueue: MutableCollection {
  public var startIndex: Int { return 0 }
  public var endIndex: Int { return left.count + right.count }

  public func index(after i: Int) -> Int {
    return i + 1
  }

  public subscript(position: Int) -> Element {
    get {
      precondition((0..<endIndex).contains(position), "Index out of bounds")
      if position < left.endIndex {
        return left[left.count - position - 1]
      } else {
        return right[position - left.count]
      }
    }
    set {
      precondition((0..<endIndex).contains(position), "Index out of bounds")
      if position < left.endIndex {
        left[left.count - position - 1] = newValue
      } else {
        return right[position - left.count] = newValue
      }
    }
  }
}
```

Notice that the compiler won't let us add the subscript setter in an extension to an existing Collection; it's neither allowed to provide a setter without a getter, nor can we redefine the existing getter, so we have to replace the existing Collection-conforming extension. Now the queue is mutable via subscripts:

```
var playlist: FIFOQueue = ["Shake It Off", "Blank Space", "Style"]
playlist.first // Optional("Shake It Off")
swap(&playlist[0], &playlist[1])
playlist.first // Optional("Blank Space")
```

Relatively few types in the standard library adopt MutableCollection. Of the three major collection types, only Array does. MutableCollection allows changing the values of a collection's elements but not the length of the collection or the order of the elements. This last point explains why Dictionary and Set do *not* conform to MutableCollection, although they're certainly mutable data structures.

Dictionaries and sets are *unordered* collections — the order of the elements is undefined as far as the code using the collection is concerned. However, *internally* , even these collections have a stable element order that's defined by their implementation. When you mutate a MutableCollection via subscript assignment, the index of the mutated element must remain stable, i.e. the position of the index in the indices collection must not change. Dictionary and Set can't satisfy this requirement because their indices point to the bucket in their internal storage where the corresponding element is stored, and that bucket could change when the element is mutated.

RangeReplaceableCollection

For operations that require adding or removing elements, use the RangeReplaceableCollection protocol. This protocol requires two things:

→ An empty initializer — this is useful in generic functions, as it allows a function to create new empty collections of the same type.

→ A replaceSubrange(_:with:) method — this takes a range to replace and a collection to replace it with.

RangeReplaceableCollection is a great example of the power of protocol extensions. You implement one uber-flexible method, replaceSubrange, and from that comes a whole bunch of derived methods for free:

→ **append(_:)** and **append(contentsOf:)** — replace endIndex..<endIndex (i.e. replace the empty range at the end) with the new element/elements

→ **remove(at:)** and **removeSubrange(_:)** — replace i...i or subrange with an empty collection

→ **insert(at:)** and **insert(contentsOf:)** — replace atIndex..<atIndex (i.e. replace the empty range at that point in the array) with a new element/elements

→ **removeAll** — replace startIndex..<endIndex with an empty collection

If a specific collection type can use knowledge about its implementation to perform these functions more efficiently, it can provide custom versions that will take priority over the default protocol extension ones.

We chose to have a very simple inefficient implementation for our queue type. As we stated when defining the data type, the left stack holds the element in reverse order. In order to have a simple implementation, we need to reverse all the elements and combine them into the right array so that we can replace the entire range at once:

```
extension FIFOQueue: RangeReplaceableCollection {
  mutating func replaceSubrange<C: Collection>(_ subrange: Range<Int>,
    with newElements: C) where C.Iterator.Element == Element
  {
    right = left.reversed() + right
    left.removeAll()
    right.replaceSubrange(subrange, with: newElements)
  }
}
```

You might like to try implementing a more efficient version, which looks at whether or not the replaced range spans the divide between the left and right stacks. There's no need for us to implement the empty init in this example, since the FIFOQueue struct already has one by default.

Unlike BidirectionalCollection and RandomAccessCollection, where the latter extends the former, RangeReplaceableCollection doesn't inherit from MutableCollection; they form distinct hierarchies. An example of a standard library collection that does conform to RangeReplaceableCollection but isn't a MutableCollection is String.CharacterView. The reasons boil down to what we said above about indices having to remain stable during a single-element subscript mutation, which CharacterView can't guarantee. We'll talk more about this in the chapter on strings.

> The standard library knows twelve distinct kinds of collections that are the result of the combination of three traversal methods (forward-only, bidirectional, and random-access) with four mutability types (immutable, mutable, range-replaceable, and mutable-and-range-replaceable).

Because each of these needs a specialized default subsequence type, you may encounter types like MutableRangeReplaceableBidirectionalSlice. Don't let these monstrosities discourage you from working with them — they behave just like a normal Slice, with extra capabilities that match their base collection, and you rarely need to care about the specific type. And if and when Swift gets conditional protocol conformance, the types will be removed in favor of constrained extensions on Slice.

Composing Capabilities

The specialized collection protocols can be composed very elegantly into a set of constraints that exactly matches the requirements of each specific operation. As an example, take the sort method in the standard library for sorting a collection in place (unlike its non-mutating sibling, sorted, which returns the sorted elements in an array). Sorting in place requires the collection to be mutable. If you want the sort to be fast, you also need random access. Last but not least, you need to be able to compare the collection's elements to each other.

Combining these requirements, the sort method is defined in an extension to MutableCollection, with RandomAccessCollection and Element: Comparable as additional constraints:

```
extension MutableCollection
   where Self: RandomAccessCollection, Iterator.Element: Comparable {
   /// Sorts the collection in place.
   public mutating func sort() { ... }
}
```

Conclusion

The Sequence and Collection protocols form the foundation of Swift's collection types. They provide dozens of common operations to conforming types and act as constraints for your own generic functions. The specialized collection types, such as MutableCollection or RandomAccessCollection, give you very fine-grained control over the functionality and performance requirements of your algorithms.

The high level of abstraction necessarily makes the model complex, so don't feel discouraged if not everything makes sense immediately. It takes practice to become comfortable with the strict type system, especially since, more often than not, discerning what the compiler wants to tell you is an art form that forces you to carefully read between the lines. The reward is an extremely flexible system that can handle everything from a pointer to a memory buffer to a destructively consumed stream of network packets.

This flexibility means that once you've internalized the model, chances are that a lot of code you'll come across in the future will instantly feel familiar because it's built on the same abstractions and supports the same operations. And whenever you create a custom type that fits in the Sequence or Collection framework, consider adding the conformance. It'll make life easier both for you and for other developers who work with your code.

The next chapter is all about another fundamental concept in Swift: optionals.

Optionals

4

Sentinel Values

An extremely common pattern in programming is to have an operation that may or may not return a value.

Perhaps not returning a value is an expected outcome when you've reached the end of a file you were reading, as in the following C snippet:

```
int ch;
while ((ch = getchar()) != EOF) {
   printf("Read character %c\n", ch);
}
printf("Reached end-of-file\n");
```

EOF is just a #define for -1. As long as there are more characters in the file, getchar returns them. But if the end of the file is reached, getchar returns -1.

Or perhaps returning no value means "not found," as in this bit of C++:

```
auto vec = {1, 2, 3};
auto iterator = std::find(vec.begin(), vec.end(), someValue);
if (iterator != vec.end()) {
   std::cout << "vec contains " << *iterator << std::endl;
}
```

Here, vec.end() is the iterator "one past the end" of the container; it's a special iterator you can check against the container's end, but that you mustn't ever actually use to access a value — similar to a collection's endIndex in Swift. find uses it to indicate that no such value is present in the container.

Or maybe the value can't be returned because something went wrong during the function's processing. Probably the most notorious example is that of the null pointer. This innocuous-looking piece of Java code will likely throw a NullPointerException:

```
int i = Integer.getInteger("123")
```

It happens that Integer.getInteger doesn't parse strings into integers, but rather gets the integer value of a system property named "123." This property probably doesn't exist, in which case getInteger returns null. When the null then gets auto unboxed into an int, Java throws an exception.

Or take this example in Objective-C:

```
[[NSString alloc] initWithContentsOfURL:url
  encoding:NSUTF8StringEncoding error:&e];
```

Here, the NSString might be nil, in which case — and only then — the error
pointer should be checked. There's no guarantee the error pointer is valid if
the result is non-nil.

In all of the above examples, the function returns a special "magic" value to
indicate that it hasn't returned a real value. Magic values like these are called
"sentinel values."

But this approach is problematic. The result returned looks and feels like a real
value. An int of -1 is still a valid integer, but you don't ever want to print it out.
v.end() is an iterator, but the results are undefined if you try to use it. And
everyone loves seeing a stack dump when your Java program throws a
NullPointerException.

So sentinel values are error prone — you can forget to check the sentinel value
and accidentally use it instead. They also require prior knowledge. Sometimes
there's an idiom, as with the C++ end iterator, but not always. Often, you need
to check the documentation. And there's no way for the function to indicate it
can't fail. If a call returns a pointer, that pointer might never be nil. But there's
no way to tell except by reading the documentation, and even then, perhaps
the documentation is wrong.

In Objective-C, it's possible to safely send messages to nil. If the message
signature returns an object, it'll return nil instead, and if the message should
return a struct, all its values will be zeroed. However, consider the following
snippet:

```
NSString *someString = ...;
if ([someString rangeOfString:@"swift"].location != NSNotFound) {
  NSLog(@"Someone mentioned swift!");
}
```

If someString is nil, the rangeOfString: message will return a zeroed NSRange.
Hence, the .location will be zero, and NSNotFound is defined as NSIntegerMax.
Therefore, the body of the if-statement will be executed if someString is nil.

Null references cause so much heartache that Tony Hoare, credited with their
creation in 1965, calls them his "billion-dollar mistake":

> At that time, I was designing the first comprehensive type system for references in an object oriented language (ALGOL W). My goal was to ensure that all use of references should be absolutely safe, with checking performed automatically by the compiler. But I couldn't resist the temptation to put in a null reference, simply because it was so easy to implement. This has led to innumerable errors, vulnerabilities, and system crashes, which have probably caused a billion dollars of pain and damage in the last forty years.

Solving the Magic Value Problem with Enumerations

Of course, every good programmer knows magic numbers are bad. Most languages support some kind of enumeration type, which is a safer way of representing a set of discrete possible values for a type.

Swift takes enumerations further with the concept of "associated values." These are enumeration values that can also have another value associated with them:

```
enum Optional<Wrapped> {
  case none
  case some(wrapped)
}
```

In some languages, these are called "tagged unions" (or "discriminated unions") — a union being multiple different possible types all held in the same space in memory, with a tag to tell which type is actually held. In Swift enums, this tag is the enum case.

The only way to retrieve an associated value is via a switch or an if case let. Unlike with a sentinel value, you can't accidentally use the value embedded in an Optional without explicitly checking and unpacking it.

So instead of returning an index, the Swift equivalent of find — called index(of:) — returns an Optional<Index> with a protocol extension implementation somewhat similar to this:

```
extension Collection where Iterator.Element: Equatable {
```

```
  func index(of element: Iterator.Element) -> Optional<Index> {
    var idx = startIndex
    while idx != endIndex {
      if self[idx] == element {
        return .some(idx)
      }
      formIndex(after: &idx)
    }
    // Not found, return .none
    return .none
  }
}
```

Since optionals are so fundamental in Swift, there's lots of syntax support to neaten this up: Optional<Index> can be written Index?; optionals conform to ExpressibleByNilLiteral so that you can write nil instead of .none; and non-optional values (like idx) are automatically "upgraded" to optionals where needed so that you can write return idx instead of return .some(idx).

Now there's no way a user could mistakenly use the invalid value:

```
var array = ["one", "two", "three"]
let idx = array.index(of: "four")
// Compile-time error: removeIndex takes an Int, not an Optional<Int>
array.remove(at: idx)
```

Instead, you're forced to "unwrap" the optional in order to get at the index within, assuming you didn't get none back:

```
var array = ["one","two","three"]
switch array.index(of: "four") {
case .some(let idx):
  array.remove(at: idx)
case .none:
  break // do nothing
}
```

This switch statement writes the enumeration syntax for optionals out longhand, including unpacking the "associated type" when the value is the some case. This is great for safety, but it's not very pleasant to read or write. Swift 2.0 introduced the ? pattern suffix syntax to match a some optional inside a switch, and you can use the nil literal to match none:

```
switch array.index(of: "four") {
```

```
case let idx?:
  array.remove(at: idx)
case nil:
  break // Do nothing
}
```

But this is still clunky. Let's take a look at all the other ways you can make your optional processing short and clear, depending on your use case.

A Tour of Optional Techniques

Optionals have a lot of extra support built into the language. Some of the examples below might look very simple if you've been writing Swift, but it's important to make sure you know all of these concepts well, as we'll be using them again and again throughout the book.

if let

Optional binding with if let is just a short step away from the switch statement above:

```
var array = ["one", "two", "three", "four"]
if let idx = array.index(of: "four") {
  array.remove(at: idx)
}
```

An optional binding with if can have boolean clauses as well. So suppose you didn't want to remove the element if it happened to be the first one in the array:

```
if let idx = array.index(of: "four"), idx != array.startIndex {
  array.remove(at: idx)
}
```

You can also bind multiple entries in the same if statement. What's more is that later entries can rely on the earlier ones being successfully unwrapped. This is very useful when you want to make multiple calls to functions that return optionals themselves. For example, these URL and UIImage initializers are all "failable" — that is, they can return nil — if your URL is malformed, or if the data isn't an image. The Data initializer can throw an error, and by using

try?, we can convert it into an optional as well. All three can be chained
together, like this:

```
let urlString = "http://www.objc.io/logo.png"
if let url = URL(string: urlString),
   let data = try? Data(contentsOf: url),
   let image = UIImage(data: data)
{
   let view = UIImageView(image: image)
   PlaygroundPage.current.liveView = view
}
```

Separate parts of a multi-variable let can have a boolean clause as well:

```
if let url = URL(string: urlString), url.pathExtension == "png",
   let data = try? Data(contentsOf: url),
   let image = UIImage(data: data)
{
   let view = UIImageView(image: image)
}
```

If you need to perform a check *before* performing various if let bindings, you
can supply a leading boolean condition. Suppose you're using a storyboard
and want to check the segue identifier before casting to a specific kind of view
controller:

```
if segue.identifier == "showUserDetailsSegue",
   let userDetailVC = segue.destination
   as? UserDetailViewController
{
   userDetailVC.screenName = "Hello"
}
```

You can also mix and match optional bindings, boolean clauses, and case let
bindings within the same if statement.

if let binding can also help with Foundation's Scanner type, which returns a
boolean value to indicate whether or not it successfully scanned something,
after which you can unwrap the result:

```
let scanner = Scanner(string: "myUserName123")
var username: NSString?
let alphas = CharacterSet.alphanumerics
```

```
if scanner.scanCharacters(from: alphas, into: &username),
   let name = username {
   print(name)
}
```

while let

Very similar to the if let statement is while let — a loop that only terminates when a nil is returned.

The standard library's readLine function returns an optional string from the standard input. Once the end of input is reached, it returns nil. So to implement a very basic equivalent of the Unix cat command, you use while let:

```
while let line = readLine() {
   print(line)
}
```

Similar to if let, you can always add a boolean clause to your optional binding. So if you want to terminate this loop on either EOF or a blank line, add a clause to detect an empty string. Note that once the condition is false, the loop is terminated (you might mistakenly think the boolean condition functions like a filter):

```
while let line = readLine(), !line.isEmpty {
   print(line)
}
```

As we saw in the chapter on collection protocols, the for x in sequence loop requires sequence to conform to Sequence. This provides a makeIterator method that returns an iterator, which in turn has a next method. next returns values until the sequence is exhausted, and then it returns nil. while let is ideal for this:

```
let array = [1, 2, 3]
var iterator = array.makeIterator()
while let i = iterator.next() {
   print(i, terminator: " ")
} // 1 2 3
```

So given that for loops are really just while loops, it's not surprising that they also support boolean clauses, albeit with a where keyword:

```
for i in 0..<10 where i % 2 == 0 {
  print(i, terminator: " ")
} // 0 2 4 6 8
```

> Note that the where clause above doesn't work like the boolean clause
> in a while loop. In a while loop, iteration stops once the value is false,
> whereas in a for loop, it functions like filter. If we rewrite the above for
> loop using while, it looks like this:
>
> ```
> var iterator = (0..<10).makeIterator()
> while let i = iterator.next() {
>   if i % 2 == 0 {
>     print(i)
>   }
> }
> ```

This feature of for loops avoids a particularly strange bug with variable capture
that can occur in other languages. Consider the following code, written in
Ruby:

```
a = []
for i in 1..3
  a.push(lambda { i })
end
for f in a
  print "#{f.call()} "
end
```

Ruby lambdas are like Swift's closure expressions, and as with Swift, they
capture local variables. So the above code loops from 1 to 3 — adding a closure
to the array that captures i — and will print out the value of i when called.
Then it loops over that array, calling each of the closures. What do you think
will be printed out? If you're on a Mac, you can try it out by pasting the above
into a file and running ruby on it from the command line.

If you run it, you'll see it prints out three 3s in a row. Even though i held a
different value when each closure was created, they all captured the *same* i
variable. And when you call them, i now has the value 3 — its value at the end
of the loop.

Now for a similar Swift snippet:

```
var a: [() -> Int] = []
for i in 1...3 {
  a.append { i }
}
for f in a {
  print("\(f())", terminator: " ")
}
// 1 2 3
```

The output: 1, 2, and 3. This makes sense when you realize for...in is really
while let. To make the correspondence even clearer, imagine there *wasn't* a
while let, and that you had to use an iterator without it:

```
var g = (1...3).makeIterator()
var o: Int? = g.next()
while o != nil {
  let i = o!
  a.append { i }
  o = g.next()
}
```

This makes it easy to see that i is a fresh local variable in every iteration, so the
closure captures the correct value even when a *new* local i is declared on
subsequent iterations.

By contrast, the Ruby and Python code is more along the lines of the following:

```
var a: [() -> Int] = []

do {
  var g = (1...3).makeIterator()
  var i: Int
  var o: Int? = g.next()
  while o != nil {
    i = o!
    a.append { i }
    o = g.next()
  }
}
```

Here, i is declared *outside* the loop — and reused — so every closure captures
the same i. If you run each of them, they'll all return 3. The do is there because,
despite i being declared outside the loop, it's still scoped in such a way that it
isn't *accessible* outside that loop — it's sandwiched in a narrow outer shell.

C# had the same behavior as Ruby until C# 5, when it was decided that this behavior was dangerous enough to justify a breaking change in order to work like Swift.

Doubly Nested Optionals

This is a good time to point out that the type an optional wraps can itself be optional, which leads to optionals nested inside optionals. To see why this isn't just a strange edge case or something the compiler should automatically coalesce, suppose you have an array of strings of numbers, which you want to convert into integers. You might run them through a map to convert them:

```
let stringNumbers = ["1", "2", "three"]
let maybeInts = stringNumbers.map { Int($0) }
```

You now have an array of Optional<Int> — i.e. Int? — because Int.init(String) is failable, since the string might not contain a valid integer. Here, the last entry will be a nil, since "foo" isn't an integer.

When looping over the array with for, you'd rightly expect that each element would be an optional integer, because that's what maybeInts contains:

```
for maybeInt in maybeInts {
  // maybeInt is an Int?
  // Two numbers and a `nil`
}
```

Now consider that the implementation of for...in is shorthand for the while loop technique above. What's returned from next would be an Optional<Optional<Int>> — or Int?? — because next wraps each element in the sequence inside an optional. The while let unwraps it to check it isn't nil, and while it's non-nil, binds the unwrapped value and runs the body:

```
var iterator = maybeInts.makeIterator()
while let maybeInt = iterator.next() {
  print(maybeInt)
}
/*
Optional(1)
Optional(2)
nil
*/
```

When the loop gets to the final element — the nil from "foo" — what's returned from next is a non-nil value: .some(nil). It unwraps this and binds what's inside (a nil) to maybeInt. Without doubly wrapped optionals, this wouldn't be possible.

By the way, if you ever want to loop over only the non-nil values with for, you can use if case pattern matching:

```
for case let i? in maybeInts {
  // i will be an Int, not an Int?
  print(i, terminator: " ")
}
// 1 2

// Or only the nil values:
for case nil in maybeInts {
  // Will run once for each nil
  print("No value")
}
// No value
```

This uses a "pattern" of x?, which only matches non-nil values. This is shorthand for .some(x), so the loop could be written like this:

```
for case let .some(i) in maybeInts {
  print(i)
}
```

This case-based pattern matching is a way to apply the same rules that work in switch statements to if, for, and while. It's most useful with optionals, but it also has other applications — for example:

```
let j = 5
if case 0..<10 = j {
  print("\(j) within range")
} // 5 within range
```

Since case matching is extensible via implementations of the ~= operator, this means you can extend if case and for case in various interesting ways:

```
struct Substring {
  let s: String
  init(_ s: String) { self.s = s }
}
```

```
func ~=(pattern: Substring, value: String) -> Bool {
  return value.range(of: pattern.s) != nil
}

let s = "Taylor Swift"
if case Substring("Swift") = s {
  print("has substring \"Swift\"")
}
// has substring "Swift"
```

This has incredible potential, but you need to be careful, as it's very easy to accidentally write ~= operators that match a little too much. On that note, inserting the following into a common bit of library code would probably be a good April Fools' joke:

```
func ~=<T, U>(_: T, _: U) -> Bool { return true }
```

The code above will make every case match (unless a more specific version of ~= is already defined).

if var and while var

Instead of let, you can use var with if, while, and for:

```
let number = "1"
if var i = Int(number) {
  i += 1
  print(i)
} // 2
```

But note that i will be a local copy; any changes to i won't affect the value inside the original optional. Optionals are value types, and unwrapping them unwraps the value inside.

Scoping of Unwrapped Optionals

Sometimes it feels frustrating to only have access to an unwrapped variable within the if block it has defined. But really, this is no different than other techniques.

For example, take the first computed property on arrays — a property that returns an optional of the first element, or nil when the array is empty. This is convenient shorthand for the following common bit of code:

```
let array = [1,2,3]
if !array.isEmpty {
  print(array[0])
}
// Outside the block, no guarantee that array[0] is valid
```

Using the first property, you *have* to unwrap the optional in order to use it — you can't accidentally forget:

```
if let firstElement = array.first {
  print(firstElement)
}
// Outside the block, you can't use firstElement
```

The big exception to this is an early exit from a function. Sometimes you might write the following:

```
func doStuff(withArray a: [Int]) {
  guard !a.isEmpty else { return }
  // Now use a[0] safely
}
```

This early exit can help avoid annoying nesting or repeated guards later on in the function.

One option for using an unwrapped optional outside the scope it was bound in is to rely on Swift's deferred initialization capabilities. Consider the following example, which reimplements part of the pathExtension property from URL and NSString:

```
extension String {
  var fileExtension: String? {
    let period: String.Index
    if let idx = characters.index(of: ".") {
      period = idx
    } else {
      return nil
    }
    let extensionRange = characters.index(after: period)..<characters.endIndex
    return self[extensionRange]
```

```
  }
}
```

"hello.txt".fileExtension // *Optional("txt")*

Swift checks your code to confirm that there are only two possible paths: one in which the function returns early, and another where period is properly initialized. There's no way period could be nil (it isn't optional) or uninitialized (Swift won't let you use a variable that hasn't been initialized). So after the if statement, the code can be written without you having to worry about optionals at all.

However, this is pretty ugly. Really, what's needed is some kind of if not let — which is exactly what guard let does:

```
extension String {
  var fileExtension: String? {
    guard let period = characters.index(of: ".") else { return nil }
    let extensionRange = index(after: period)..<characters.endIndex
    return self[extensionRange]
  }
}
```

"hello.txt".fileExtension // *Optional("txt")*

Anything can go in the else clause here, including multiple statements just like an if ... else. The only requirement is that the end of the else must leave the current scope. That might mean return, or it might mean calling fatalError (or any other function that returns Never). If the guard were in a loop, it could be via break or continue.

A function that has the return type Never signals to the compiler that it'll never return. There are two common types of functions that do this: those that abort the program, such as fatalError; and those that run for the entire lifetime of the program, like dispatchMain. The compiler uses this information for its control flow diagnostics. For example, the else branch of a guard statement must either exit the current scope or call one of these never-returning functions.

Never is what's called an *uninhabited type*. It's a type that has no valid values and thus can't be constructed. Its only purpose is its signaling role for the compiler. A function declared to return an uninhabited type can never return normally. In Swift, an uninhabited type is implemented as an enum that has no cases.

You won't usually need to define your own never-returning functions unless you write a wrapper for fatalError or preconditionFailure. One interesting use case is while you're writing new code: say you're working on a complex switch statement, gradually filling in all the cases, and the compiler is bombarding you with error messages for empty case labels or missing return values, while all you'd like to do is concentrate on the one case you're working on. In this situation, a few carefully placed calls to fatalError() can do wonders to silence the compiler. Consider writing a function called unimplemented() in order to better communicate the temporary nature of these calls:

```
func unimplemented() -> Never {
    fatalError("This code path is not implemented yet.")
}
```

Of course, guard isn't limited to binding. Guard can take any condition you might find in a regular if statement, so the empty array example could be rewritten with it:

```
func doStuff(withArray a: [Int]) {
    guard !a.isEmpty else { return }
    // now, use a[0] safely
}
```

Unlike the optional binding case, this guard isn't a big win — in fact, it's slightly more verbose than the original return. But it's still worth considering doing this with any early exit situation. For one, sometimes (though not in this case) the inversion of the boolean condition can make things clearer. Additionally, guard is a clear signal when reading the code; it says: "We only continue if the following condition holds." Finally, the Swift compiler will check that you're definitely exiting the current scope and raise a compilation error if you don't. For this reason, we'd suggest using guard even when an if would do.

Optional Chaining

In Objective-C, sending a message to nil is a no-op. In Swift, the same effect can be achieved via "optional chaining":

```
delegate?.callback()
```

Unlike with Objective-C, though, the compiler will warn you when your value might be optional. If your value is non-optional, you're guaranteed that the method will actually be called. If not, the ? is a clear signal to the reader that it might not be called.

When the method you call via optional chaining returns a result, that result will also be optional. Consider the following code to see why this must be the case:

```
let str: String? = "Never say never"
// We want upper to be the uppercase string
let upper: String
if str != nil {
  upper = str!.uppercased()
} else {
  // No reasonable action to take at this point
  fatalError("No idea what to do now...")
}
```

If str is non-nil, upper will have the desired value. But if str is nil, then upper can't be set to a value. So in the optional chaining case, result *must* be optional, in order to account for the possibility that st could've been nil:

```
let result = str?.uppercased() // Optional("NEVER SAY NEVER")
```

As the name implies, you can chain calls on optional values:

```
let lower = str?.uppercased().lowercased() // Optional("never say never")
```

However, this might look a bit surprising. Didn't we just say that the result of optional chaining is an optional? So why don't you need a ?. after uppercased()? This is because optional chaining is a "flattening" operation. If str?.uppercased() returned an optional and you called ?.lowercased() on it, then logically you'd get an optional optional. But you just want a regular optional, so instead we write the second chained call without an optional to represent the fact that the optionality is already captured.

On the other hand, if the uppercased method itself returned an optional, then you'd need a ? after it to express that you were chaining *that* optional. For example, let's imagine adding a computed property, half, on the Int type. This property returns the result of dividing the integer by two, but only if the number is big enough to be divided. When the number is smaller than two, it returns nil:

```
extension Int {
  var half: Int? {
    guard self > 1 else { return nil }
    return self / 2
  }
}
```

Because calling half returns an optional result, we need to keep putting in ? when calling it repeatedly. After all, at every step, the function might return nil:

```
20.half?.half?.half // Optional(2)
```

Optional chaining also applies to subscript and function calls — for example:

```
let dictOfArrays = ["nine": [0, 1, 2, 3]]
dictOfArrays["nine"]?[3] // Optional(3)
```

Additionally, you can use optional chaining to call optional functions:

```
let dictOfFuncs: [String: (Int, Int) -> Int] = [
  "add": (+),
  "subtract": (-)
]
dictOfFuncs["add"]?(1, 1) // Optional(2)
```

You can even assign *through* an optional chain. Suppose you have an optional variable, and if it's non-nil, you wish to update one of its properties:

```
let splitViewController: UISplitViewController? = nil
let myDelegate: UISplitViewControllerDelegate? = nil
if let viewController = splitViewController {
  viewController.delegate = myDelegate
}
```

Instead, you can assign to the chained optional value, and if it isn't nil, the assignment will work:

```
splitViewController?.delegate = myDelegate
```

The nil-Coalescing Operator

Often you want to unwrap an optional, replacing nil with some default value. This is a job for the nil-coalescing operator:

```
let stringteger = "1"
let number = Int(stringteger) ?? 0
```

So if the string is of an integer, number will be that integer, unwrapped. If it isn't, and Int.init returns nil, the default value of 0 will be substituted. So lhs ?? rhs is analogous to the code lhs != nil ? lhs! : rhs.

"Big deal!" Objective-C developers might say. "We've had the ?: for ages." And ?? is very similar to Objective-C's ?:. But there are some differences, so it's worth stressing an important point when thinking about optionals in Swift: optionals are *not* pointers.

Yes, you'll often encounter optionals combined with references when dealing with Objective-C libraries. But optionals, as we've seen, can also wrap value types. So number in the above example is just an Int, not an NSNumber.

Through the use of optionals, you can guard against much more than just null pointers. Consider the case where you want to access the first value of an array — but in case the array is empty, you want to provide a default:

```
let array = [1,2,3]
!array.isEmpty ? array[0] : 0
```

Because Swift arrays provide a first property that's nil if the array is empty, you can use the nil-coalescing operator instead:

```
array.first ?? 0 // 1
```

This is cleaner and clearer — the intent (grab the first element in the array) is up front, with the default tacked on the end, joined with a ?? that signals "this is a default value." Compare this with the ternary version, which starts first with the check, then the value, then the default. And the check is awkwardly negated (the alternative being to put the default in the middle and the actual value on the end). And, as is the case with optionals, it's impossible to forget that first is optional and accidentally use it without the check, because the compiler will stop you if you try.

Whenever you find yourself guarding a statement with a check to make sure the statement is valid, it's a good sign optionals would be a better solution. Suppose that instead of an empty array, you're checking a value that's within the array bounds:

```
array.count > 5 ? array[5] : 0 // 0
```

Unlike first and last, getting an element out of an array by its index doesn't return an Optional. But it's easy to extend Array to add this functionality:

```
extension Array {
  subscript(safe idx: Int) -> Element? {
    return idx < endIndex ? self[idx] : nil
  }
}
```

This now allows you to write the following:

```
array[safe: 5] ?? 0 // 0
```

Coalescing can also be chained — so if you have multiple possible optionals and you want to choose the first non-optional one, you can write them in sequence:

```
let i: Int? = nil
let j: Int? = nil
let k: Int? = 42
i ?? j ?? k // Optional(42)
```

Sometimes, you might have multiple optional values and you want to choose between them in an order, but you don't have a reasonable default if they're all nil. You can still use ?? for this, but if the final value is also optional, the full result will be optional:

```
let m = i ?? j ?? k
type(of: m) // Optional<Int>
```

This is often useful in conjunction with if let. You can think of this like an "or" equivalent of if let:

```
if let n = i ?? j { // similar to if i != nil || j != nil
  print(n)
}
```

If you think of the ?? operator as similar to an "or" statement, you can think of an if let with multiple clauses as an "and" statement:

```
if let n = i, let m = j {}
// similar to if i != nil && j != nil
```

Because of this chaining, if you're ever presented with a doubly nested optional and want to use the ?? operator, you must take care to distinguish between a ?? b ?? c (chaining) and (a ?? b) ?? c (unwrapping the inner and then outer layers):

```
let s1: String?? = nil // nil
(s1 ?? "inner") ?? "outer" // inner
let s2: String?? = .some(nil) // Optional(nil)
(s2 ?? "inner") ?? "outer" // outer
```

Optional map

Let's say we have an array of characters, and we want to turn the first character into a string:

```
let characters: [Character] = ["a", "b", "c"]
String(characters[0]) // a
```

However, if characters could be empty, we can use an if let to create the string only if the array is non empty:

```
var firstCharAsString: String? = nil
if let char = characters.first {
  firstCharAsString = String(char)
}
```

So now, if the characters array contains at least one element, firstCharAsString will contain that element as a String. But if it doesn't, firstCharAsString will be nil.

This pattern — take an optional, and transform it if it isn't nil — is common enough that there's a method on optionals to do this. It's called map, and it takes a closure that represents how to transform the contents of the optional. Here's the above function, rewritten using map:

```
let firstChar = characters.first.map { String($0) } // Optional("a")
```

This map is, of course, very similar to the map on arrays or other sequences. But instead of operating on a sequence of values, it operates on just one: the possible one inside the optional. You can think of optionals as being a collection of either zero or one values, with map either doing nothing to zero values or transforming one.

Given the similarities, the implementation of optional map looks a lot like collection map:

```
extension Optional {
  func map<U>(transform: (Wrapped) -> U) -> U? {
    if let value = self {
      return transform(value)
    }
    return nil
  }
}
```

An optional map is especially nice when you already want an optional result. Suppose you wanted to write another variant of reduce for arrays. Instead of taking an initial value, it uses the first element in the array (in some languages, this might be called reduce1, but we'll call it reduce and rely on overloading):

Because of the possibility that the array might be empty, the result needs to be optional — without an initial value, what else could it be? You might write it like this:

```
extension Array {
  func reduce(_ nextPartialResult: (Element, Element) -> Element) -> Element? {
    // first will be nil if the array is empty
    guard let fst = first else { return nil }
    return dropFirst().reduce(fst, nextPartialResult)
  }
}
```

You can use it like this:

```
[1, 2, 3, 4].reduce(+) // Optional(10)
```

Since optional map returns nil if the optional is nil, reduce could be rewritten using a single return statement (and no guard):

```
extension Array {
  func reduce_alt(_ nextPartialResult: (Element, Element) -> Element)
```

```
    -> Element?
  {
    return first.map {
      dropFirst().reduce($0, nextPartialResult)
    }
  }
}
```

Optional flatMap

As we saw in the built-in collections chapter, it's common to want to map over a collection with a function that returns a collection, but collect the results as a single array rather than an array of arrays.

Similarly, if you want to perform a map on an optional value, but your transformation function also has an optional result, you'll end up with a doubly nested optional. An example of this is when you want to fetch the first element of an array of strings as a number, using first on the array and then map to convert it to a number:

```
let stringNumbers = ["1", "2", "3", "foo"]
let x = stringNumbers.first.map { Int($0) } // Optional(Optional(1))
```

The problem is that since map returns an optional (first might have been nil) and Int(someString) returns an optional (the string might not be an integer), the type of x will be Int??.

flatMap will instead flatten the result into a single optional:

```
let y = stringNumbers.first.flatMap { Int($0) } // Optional(1)
```

As a result, y will be of type Int?.

Instead, you could've written this with if let, because values that are bound later can be computed from earlier ones:

```
if let a = stringNumbers.first, let b = Int(a) {
  print(b)
} // 1
```

This shows that flatMap and if let are very similar. Earlier in this chapter, we saw an example that uses a multiple-if-let statement. We can rewrite it using map and flatMap instead:

```
let urlString = "http://www.objc.io/logo.png"
let view = URL(string: urlString)
    .flatMap { try? Data(contentsOf: $0) }
    .flatMap { UIImage(data: $0) }
    .map    { UIImageView(image: $0) }

if let view = view {
    PlaygroundPage.current.liveView = view
}
```

Optional chaining is also very similar to flatMap: i?.advance(by: 1) is essentially equivalent to i.flatMap { $0.advance(by: 1) }.

Since we've shown that a multiple-if-let statement is equivalent to flatMap, we could implement one in terms of the other:

```
extension Optional {
    func flatMap<U>(transform: (Wrapped) -> U?) -> U? {
        if let value = self, let transformed = transform(value) {
            return transformed
        }
        return nil
    }
}
```

Filtering Out nils with flatMap

If you have a sequence and it contains optionals, you might not care about the nil values. In fact, you might just want to ignore them.

Suppose you wanted to process only the numbers in an array of strings. This is easily done in a for loop using optional pattern matching:

```
let numbers = ["1", "2", "3", "foo"]

var sum = 0
for case let i? in numbers.map({ Int($0) }) {
    sum += i
}
sum // 6
```

You might also want to use ?? to replace the nils with zeros:

```
numbers.map { Int($0) }.reduce(0) { $0 + ($1 ?? 0) } // 6
```

But really, you just want a version of map that filters out nil and unwraps the non-nil values. Enter the standard library's overload of flatMap on sequences, which does exactly that:

```
numbers.flatMap { Int($0) }.reduce(0, +) // 6
```

We've already seen two flattening maps: flattening a sequence mapped to arrays, and flattening an optional mapped to an optional. This is a hybrid of the two: flattening a sequence mapped to an optional.

This makes sense if we return to our analogy of an optional being a collection of zero or one thing(s). If that collection were an array, flatMap would be exactly what we want.

To implement our own version of this operator, let's first define a flatten that filters out nil values and returns an array of non-optionals:

```
func flatten<S: Sequence, T>
  (source: S) -> [T] where S.Iterator.Element == T? {
  let filtered = source.lazy.filter { $0 != nil }
  return filtered.map { $0! }
}
```

Ewww, a free function? Why no protocol extension? Unfortunately, there's no way to constrain an extension on Sequence to only apply to sequences of optionals. You'd need a two-placeholder clause (one for S, and one for T, as given here), and protocol extensions currently don't support this.

Nonetheless, it does make flatMap simple to write:

```
extension Sequence {
  func flatMap<U>(transform: (Iterator.Element) -> U?) -> [U] {
    return flatten(source: self.lazy.map(transform))
  }
}
```

In both these functions, we used lazy to defer actual creation of the array until the last moment. This is possibly a micro-optimization, but it might be worthwhile for larger arrays. Using lazy saves the allocation of multiple buffers that would otherwise be needed to write the intermediary results into.

Equating Optionals

Often, you don't care whether a value is nil or not — just whether it contains (if non-nil) a certain value:

```
let regex = "^Hello$"
// ...
if regex.characters.first == "^" {
  // match only start of string
}
```

In this case, it doesn't matter if the value is nil or not — if the string is empty, the first character can't be a caret, so you don't want to run the block. But you still want the protection and simplicity of first. The alternative, if !regex.isEmpty && regex.characters[regex.startIndex] == "^", is horrible.

The code above relies on two things to work. First, there's a version of == that takes two optionals, with an implementation something like this:

```
func ==<T: Equatable>(lhs: T?, rhs: T?) -> Bool {
  switch (lhs, rhs) {
  case (nil, nil): return true
  case let (x?, y?): return x == y
  case (_?, nil), (nil, _?): return false
  }
}
```

This overload *only* works on optionals of equatable types. Given this, there are four possibilities: they're both nil, or they both have a value, or either one or the other is nil. The switch exhaustively tests all four possibilities (hence no need for a default clause). It defines two nils to be equal to each other, nil to never be equal to non-nil, and two non-nil values to be equal if their unwrapped values are equal.

But this is only half the story. Notice that we did *not* have to write the following:

```
if regex.characters.first == Optional("^") {
  // Match only start of string
}
```

This is because whenever you have a non-optional value, Swift will always be willing to upgrade it to an optional value in order to make the types match.

This implicit conversion is incredibly useful for writing clear, compact code. Suppose there was no such conversion, but to make things nice for the caller, you wanted a version of == that worked between both optional and non-optional types. You'd have to write three separate versions:

```
// Both optional
func == <T: Equatable>(lhs: T?, rhs: T?) -> Bool
// lhs non-optional
func == <T: Equatable>(lhs: T, rhs: T?) -> Bool
// rhs non-optional
func == <T: Equatable>(lhs: T?, rhs: T) -> Bool
```

But instead, only the first version is necessary, and the compiler will convert to optionals where necessary.

In fact, we've been relying on this throughout the book. For example, when we implemented optional map, we transformed the inner value and returned it. But the return value of map is optional. The compiler automatically converted the value for us — we didn't have to write return Optional(transform(value)).

Swift code constantly relies on this implicit conversion. For example, dictionary subscript lookup by key returns an optional (the key might not be present). But it also takes an optional on assignment — subscripts have to both take and receive the same type. Without implicit conversion, you'd have to write myDict["someKey"] = Optional(someValue).

Incidentally, if you're wondering what happens to dictionaries with key-based subscript assignment when you assign a nil value, the answer is that the key is removed. This can be useful, but it also means you need to be a little careful when dealing with a dictionary with an optional value type. Consider this dictionary:

```
var dictWithNils: [String: Int?] = [
  "one": 1,
  "two": 2,
  "none": nil
]
```

The dictionary has three keys, and one of them has a value of nil. Suppose we wanted to set the value of the "two" key to nil as well. This will *not* do that:

```
dictWithNils["two"] = nil
dictWithNils // ["none": nil, "one": Optional(1)]
```

Instead, it'll *remove* the "two" key.

To change the value for the key, you'd have to write one of the following (they all work, so choose whichever you feel is clearer):

```
dictWithNils["two"] = Optional(nil)
dictWithNils["two"] = .some(nil)
dictWithNils["two"]? = nil
dictWithNils // ["none": nil, "one": Optional(1), "two": nil]
```

Note that the third version above is slightly different than the other two. It works because the "two" key is already in the dictionary, so it uses optional chaining to set its value if successfully fetched. Now try this with a key that isn't present:

```
dictWithNils["three"]? = nil
dictWithNils.index(forKey: "three") // nil
```

You can see that nothing would be updated/inserted.

Equatable and ==

Even though optionals have an == operator, this doesn't mean they can conform to the Equatable protocol. This subtle but important distinction will hit you in the face if you try and do the following:

```
// Two arrays of optional integers
let a: [Int?] = [1, 2, nil]
let b: [Int?] = [1, 2, nil]

// Error: binary operator '==' cannot be applied to two [Int?] operands
a == b
```

The problem is that the == operator for arrays requires the elements of the array to be equatable:

```
func ==<Element : Equatable>(lhs: [Element], rhs: [Element]) -> Bool
```

Optionals don't conform to Equatable — that would require they implement == for any kind of type they contain, and they only can if that type is itself equatable. In the future, Swift will support conditional protocol conformance — maybe something like this:

```
extension Optional: Equatable where Wrapped: Equatable {
  // No need to implement anything; == is already implemented so long
  // as this condition is met.
}
```

In the meantime, you could implement a version of == for arrays of optionals, like so:

```
func ==<T: Equatable>(lhs: [T?], rhs: [T?]) -> Bool {
  return lhs.elementsEqual(rhs) { $0 == $1 }
}
```

switch-case Matching for Optionals:

Another consequence of optionals not being Equatable is that you can't check them in a case statement. case matching is controlled in Swift by the ~= operator, and the relevant definition looks a lot like the one that wasn't working for arrays:

```
func ~=<T: Equatable>(a: T, b: T) -> Bool
```

But it's simple to produce a matching version for optionals that just calls ==:

```
func ~=<T: Equatable>(pattern: T?, value: T?) -> Bool {
  return pattern == value
}
```

It's also nice to implement a range match at the same time:

```
func ~=<Bound>(pattern: Range<Bound>, value: Bound?) -> Bool {
  return value.map { pattern.contains($0) } ?? false
}
```

Here, we use map to check if a non-nil value is inside the interval. Because we want nil not to match any interval, we return false in case of nil.

Given this, we can now match optional values with switch:

```
for i in ["2", "foo", "42", "100"] {
  switch Int(i) {
  case 42:
    print("The meaning of life")
  case 0..<10:
```

```
    print("A single digit")
  case nil:
    print("Not a number")
  default:
    print("A mystery number")
  }
}
/*
A single digit
Not a number
The meaning of life
A mystery number
*/
```

Comparing Optionals

Similar to ==, there used to be implementations of <, >, >=, and >= for optionals. In SE-0121, these comparison operators were removed because they can easily yield unexpected results.

For example, nil < .some(_) would return true. In combination with higher-order functions or optional chaining, this can be very surprising. Consider the following example:

```
let temps = ["-459.67", "98.6", "0", "warm"]
let belowFreezing = temps.filter { Double($0) < 0 }
```

Because Double("warm") will return nil and nil is less than 0, it'll be included in the belowFreezing temperatures. This is unexpected indeed.

When to Force-Unwrap

Given all these techniques for cleanly unwrapping optionals, when should you use !, the force-unwrap operator? There are many opinions on this scattered throughout the Internet, such as "never," "whenever it makes the code clearer," and "when you can't avoid it." We propose the following rule, which encompasses most of them:

> Use ! when you're so certain that a value won't be nil that you *want* your program to crash if it ever is.

As an example, take the implementation of flatten:

Here, there's no possible way in the map that $0! will ever hit a nil, since the nil elements were all filtered out in the preceding filter step. This function could certainly be written to eliminate the force-unwrap operator by looping over the array and adding non-nil values into an array. But the filter/map version is cleaner and probably clearer, so the ! could be justified.

But these cases are pretty rare. If you have full mastery of all the unwrapping techniques described in this chapter, chances are that there's a better way. Whenever you do find yourself reaching for !, it's worth taking a step back and wondering if there really is no other way. For example, we could've also implemented flatten using a single method call: source.flatMap { $0 }.

As another example, consider the following code that fetches all the keys in a dictionary with values matching a certain condition:

```
let ages = [
  "Tim": 53, "Angela": 54, "Craig": 44,
  "Jony": 47, "Chris": 37, "Michael": 34,
]
ages.keys
  .filter { name in ages[name]! < 50 }
  .sorted()
// ["Chris", "Craig", "Jony", "Michael"]
```

Here, the ! is perfectly safe — since all the keys came from the dictionary, there's no possible way in which a key could be missing from the dictionary.

But you could also rewrite the statement to eliminate the need for a force-unwrap altogether. Using the fact that dictionaries present themselves as sequences of key/value pairs, you could just filter this sequence and then run it through a map to remove the value:

```
ages.filter { (_, age) in age < 50 }
  .map { (name, _) in name }
  .sorted()
// ["Chris", "Craig", "Jony", "Michael"]
```

This version even has a performance benefit: avoiding unnecessary key lookups.

Nonetheless, sometimes life hands you an optional, and you know *for certain* that it isn't nil. So certain are you of this that you'd *rather* your program crash than continue, because it'd mean a very nasty bug in your logic. Better to trap than to continue under those circumstances, so ! acts as a combined unwrap-or-error operator in one handy character. This approach is often a better move than just using the nil chaining or coalescing operators to sweep theoretically impossible situations under the carpet.

Improving Force-Unwrap Error Messages

That said, even when you're force-unwrapping an optional value, you have options other than using the ! operator. When your program does error, you don't get much by way of description as to why in the output log.

Chances are, you'll leave a comment as to why you're justified in force-unwrapping. So why not have that comment serve as the error message too? Here's an operator, !!; it combines unwrapping with supplying a more descriptive error message to be logged when the application exits:

```
infix operator !!
```

```
func !! <T>(wrapped: T?, failureText: @autoclosure () -> String) -> T {
  if let x = wrapped { return x }
  fatalError(failureText())
}
```

Now you can write a more descriptive error message, including the value you expected to be able to unwrap:

```
let s = "foo"
let i = Int(s) !! "Expecting integer, got \"\(s)\""
```

The @autoclosure annotation makes sure that we only evaluate the second operand when needed. In the chapter on functions, we'll go into this in more detail.

Asserting in Debug Builds

Still, choosing to crash even on release builds is quite a bold move. Often, you might prefer to assert during debug and test builds, but in production, you'd substitute a valid default value — perhaps zero or an empty array.

Enter the interrobang operator, !?. We define this operator to assert on failed unwraps and also to substitute a default value when the assertion doesn't trigger in release mode:

infix operator !?

```
func !?<T: ExpressibleByIntegerLiteral>
   (wrapped: T?, failureText: @autoclosure () -> String) -> T
{
   assert(wrapped != nil, failureText())
   return wrapped ?? 0
}
```

Now, the following will assert while debugging but print 0 in release:

```
let s = "20"
let i = Int(s) !? "Expecting integer, got \"\(s)\""
```

Overloading for other literal convertible protocols enables a broad coverage of types that can be defaulted:

```
func !?<T: ExpressibleByArrayLiteral>
   (wrapped: T?, failureText: @autoclosure () -> String) -> T
{
   assert(wrapped != nil, failureText())
   return wrapped ?? []
}

func !?<T: ExpressibleByStringLiteral>
   (wrapped: T?, failureText: @autoclosure () -> String) -> T
{
   assert(wrapped != nil, failureText)
   return wrapped ?? ""
}
```

And for when you want to provide a different explicit default, or for non-standard types, we can define a version that takes a pair — the default and the error text:

```
func !?<T>(wrapped: T?,
   nilDefault: @autoclosure () -> (value: T, text: String)) -> T
{
   assert(wrapped != nil, nilDefault().text)
   return wrapped ?? nilDefault().value
}
```

```
// Asserts in debug, returns 5 in release
Int(s) !? (5, "Expected integer")
```

Since optionally chained method calls on methods that return Void return
Void?, you can also write a non-generic version to detect when an optional
chain hits a nil, resulting in a no-op:

```
func !?(wrapped: ()?, failureText: @autoclosure () -> String) {
  assert(wrapped != nil, failureText)
}
```

```
var output: String? = nil
output?.write("something") !? "Wasn't expecting chained nil here"
```

There are three ways to halt execution. The first option, fatalError, takes a
message and stops execution unconditionally. The second option, assert,
checks a condition and a message and stops execution if the condition
evaluates to false. In release builds, the assert gets removed — the condition
isn't checked (and execution is never halted). The third option is precondition,
which has the same interface as assert, but doesn't get removed from release
builds, so if the condition evaluates to false, execution is stopped.

Living Dangerously: Implicit Optionals

Make no mistake: implicit optionals are still optionals — ones that are
automatically force-unwrapped whenever you use them. Now that we know
that force-unwraps will crash your application if they're ever nil, why on earth
would you use them? Well, two reasons really.

Reason 1: Temporarily, because you're calling code that hasn't been audited
for nullability into Objective-C.

Of course, on the first day you start writing Swift against your existing
Objective-C, any Objective-C method that returns a reference will translate
into an implicitly unwrapped optional. Since, for most of Objective-C's
lifetime, there was no way to indicate that a reference was nullable, there was
little option other than to assume any call returning a reference might return a
nil reference. But few Objective-C APIs *actually* return null references, so it'd
be incredibly annoying to automatically expose them as optionals. Since

everyone was used to dealing with the "maybe null" world of Objective-C objects, implicitly unwrapped optionals were a reasonable compromise.

So you see them in unaudited bridged Objective-C code. But you should *never* see a pure native Swift API returning an implicit optional (or passing one into a callback).

Reason 2: Because a value is nil *very* briefly, for a well-defined period of time, and is then never nil again.

For example, if you have a two-phase initialization, then by the time your class is ready to use, the implicitly wrapped optionals will all have a value. This is the reason Xcode/Interface Builder uses them.

Implicit Optional Behavior

While implicitly unwrapped optionals usually behave like non-optional values, you can still use most of the unwrap techniques to safely handle them like optionals — chaining, nil-coalescing, if let, and map all work the same:

```
var s: String! = "Hello"
s?.isEmpty // Optional(false)
if let s = s { print(s) }
s = nil
s ?? "Goodbye" // Goodbye
```

As much as implicit optionals try to hide their optional-ness from you, there are a few times when they behave slightly differently. For example, you can't pass an implicit optional into a function that takes the wrapped type as an inout:

```
func increment(_ x: inout Int) {
    x += 1
}

var i = 1    // Regular Int
increment(&i) // Increments i to 2

var j: Int! = 1 // Implicitly unwrapped Int
increment(&j)  // Error: Cannot pass immutable value of type 'Int' as inout argument
```

Conclusion

Optionals are very useful when dealing with values that might or might not be nil. Rather than using magic values such as NSNotFound, we can use nil to indicate a value is empty. Swift has many built-in features that work with optionals so that you can avoid forced unwrapping of optionals. Implicitly unwrapped optionals are useful when working with legacy code, but normal optionals should always be preferred (if possible). Finally, if you need more than just an optional (for example, you also need an error message if the result isn't present), you can use errors, which we cover in the errors chapter.

Structs and
Classes

In Swift, we can choose from multiple options to store structured data: structs, enums, classes, and capturing variables with closures. Most of the public types in Swift's standard library are defined as structs, with enums and classes making up a much smaller percentage. Part of this may be the nature of the types in the standard library, but it does give an indication as to the importance of structs in Swift. Likewise, in Swift, 3 many of the classes in Foundation now have struct counterparts specifically built for Swift. That said, we'll focus on the differences between structs and classes in this chapter. Meanwhile, enums behave in a way that's similar to structs.

Here are some of the major things that help distinguish between structs and classes:

→ Structs (and enums) are *value types*, whereas classes are *reference types*. When designing with structs, we can ask the compiler to enforce immutability. With classes, we have to enforce it ourselves.

→ How memory is managed differs. Structs can be held and accessed directly, whereas class instances are always accessed indirectly through their references. Structs aren't referenced but instead copied. Structs have a single owner, whereas classes can have many owners.

→ With classes, we can use inheritance to share code. With structs (and enums), inheritance isn't possible. Instead, to share code using structs and enums, we need to use different techniques, such as composition, generics, and protocol extensions.

In this chapter, we'll explore these differences in more detail. We'll start by looking at the differences between entities and values. Next, we'll continue by discussing issues with mutability. Then we'll take a look at structs and mutability. After that, we'll demonstrate how to wrap a reference type in a struct in order to use it as an efficient value type. Finally, we'll compare the differences in how memory is managed — particularly how memory is managed in combination with closures, and how to avoid reference cycles.

Value Types

We're often dealing with objects that need an explicit *lifecycle*: they're initialized, changed, and destroyed. For example, a file handle has a clear lifecycle: it's opened, actions are performed on it, and then we need to close it. If we open two file handles that otherwise have the same properties, we still want to keep them separate. In order to compare two file handles, we check whether they point to the same address in memory. Because we compare addresses, file handles are best implemented as reference types, using objects. This is what the FileHandle class in Foundation does.

Other types don't need to have a lifecycle. For example, a URL is created and then never changed. More importantly, it doesn't need to perform any action when it's destroyed (in contrast to the file handle, which needs to be closed). When we compare two URL variables, we don't care whether they point to the same address in memory, rather we check whether they point to the same URL. Because we compare URLs by their properties, we say that they're *values*. In Objective-C, they were implemented as immutable objects using the NSURL class. However, the Swift counterpart, URL, is a struct.

In all software, there are many objects that have a lifecycle — file handles, notification centers, networking interfaces, database connections, and view controllers are some examples. For all these types, we want to perform specific actions on initialization and when they're destroyed. When comparing these types, we don't compare their properties, but instead compare their memory addresses. All of these types are implemented using objects, and all of them are reference types.

There are also many values at play in most software. URLs, binary data, dates, errors, strings, notifications, and numbers are only defined by their properties. When we compare them, we're not interested in their memory addresses. All of these types can be implemented using structs.

Values never change; they're immutable. This is (mostly) a good thing, because code that works with immutable data is much easier to understand. The immutability automatically makes such code thread-safe too: anything that can't change can be safely shared across threads.

In Swift, structs are designed to build values. Structs can't be compared by reference; we can only compare their properties. And although we can declare mutable struct *variables* (using var), it's important to understand that the mutability only refers to the variable and not the underlying value. Mutating a property of a struct variable is conceptually the same as assigning a whole new struct (with a different value for the property) to the variable.

Structs have a single owner. For instance, if we pass a struct variable to a function, that function receives a copy of the struct, and it can only change its own copy. This is called *value semantics* (sometimes also called copy semantics). Contrast this with the way objects work: they get passed by reference and can have many owners. This is called *reference semantics*.

Because structs only have a single owner, it's not possible to create a reference cycle. But with classes and functions, we need to always be careful to not create reference cycles. We'll look at reference cycles in the section on memory.

The fact that values are copied all the time may sound inefficient; however, the compiler can optimize away many superfluous copy operations. It can do this because structs are very basic things. A struct copy is a shallow bitwise copy (except if it contains any classes — then it needs to increase the reference count for those). When structs are declared with let, the compiler knows for certain that none of those bits can be mutated later on. And there are no hooks for the developer to know *when* the struct is being copied, unlike with similar value types in C++. This simplicity gives the compiler many more possibilities for eliminating copy operations or optimizing a constant structure to be passed by reference rather than by value.

Copy optimizations of a value *type* that might be done by the compiler aren't the same as the copy-on-write behavior of a type with value *semantics*. Copy-on-write has to be implemented by the developer, and it works by detecting that the contained class has shared references.

Unlike the automatic elimination of value type copies, you don't get copy-on-write for free. But the two optimizations — the compiler potentially eliminating unnecessary "dumb" shallow copies, and the code inside types like arrays that perform "smart" copy-on-write — complement each other. We'll look at how to implement your own copy-on-write mechanism shortly.

If your struct is composed out of other structs, the compiler can enforce immutability. Also, when using structs, the compiler can generate really fast code. For example, the performance of operations on an array containing just structs is usually much better than the performance of operations on an array containing objects. This is because structs usually have less indirection: the values are stored directly inside the array's memory, whereas an array containing objects contains just the references to the objects. Finally, in many cases, the compiler can put structs on the stack, rather than on the heap.

When interfacing with Cocoa and Objective-C, we often need to use classes. For example, when implementing a delegate for a table view, there's no choice: we must use a class. Many of Apple's frameworks rely heavily on subclassing.

However, depending on the problem domain, we can still create a class where the objects are values. For example, in the Core Image framework, the CIImage objects are immutable: they represent an image that never changes.

It's not always easy to decide whether your new type should be a struct or a class. Both behave very differently, and knowing the differences will help you make a decision. In the examples in the rest of this chapter, we'll look in more detail at the implications of value types and provide some guidance for when to use structs.

Mutability

In recent years, mutability got a bad reputation. It's named as a major cause of bugs, and most experts recommend you work with immutable objects where possible, in order to write safe, maintainable code. Luckily, Swift allows us to write safe code while preserving an intuitive mutable coding style at the same time.

To see how this works, let's start by showing some of the problems with mutation. In Foundation, there are two classes for arrays: NSArray, and its subclass, NSMutableArray. We can write the following (crashing) program using NSMutableArray:

```
let mutableArray: NSMutableArray = [1,2,3]
for _ in mutableArray {
  mutableArray.removeLastObject()
}
```

You're not allowed to mutate an NSMutableArray while you're iterating through it, because the iterator works on the original array, and mutating it corrupts the iterator's internal state. Once you know this, the restriction makes sense, and you won't make that mistake again. However, consider that there could be a different method call in the place of mutableArray.removeLastObject(), and that method might mutate mutableArray. Now the violation becomes much harder to see, unless you know exactly what that method does.

Now let's consider the same example, but using Swift arrays:

```
var mutableArray = [1, 2, 3]
for _ in mutableArray {
```

```
    mutableArray.removeLast()
}
```

This example doesn't crash, because the iterator keeps a local, independent copy of the array. To see this even more clearly, you could write removeAll instead of removeLast, and if you open it up in a playground, you'll see that the statement gets executed three times because the iterator's copy of the array still contains three elements.

Classes are reference types. If you create an instance of a class and assign it to a new variable, both variables point to the same object:

```
let mutableArray: NSMutableArray = [1, 2, 3]
let otherArray = mutableArray
mutableArray.add(4)
otherArray // ( 1, 2, 3, 4 )
```

Because both variables refer to the same object, they now both refer to the array [1, 2, 3, 4], since changing the value of one variable also changes the value of the other variable. This is a very powerful thing, but it's also a great source of bugs. Calling a method might change something you didn't expect to change, and your invariant won't hold anymore.

Inside a class, we can control mutable and immutable properties with var and let. For example, we could create our own variant of Foundation's Scanner, but for binary data. The Scanner class allows you to scan values from a string, advancing through the string with each successful scanned value. A Scanner does this by storing a string and its current position in the string. Similarly, our class, BinaryScanner, contains the position (which is mutable), and the original data (which will never change). This is all we need to store in order to replicate the behavior of Scanner:

```
class BinaryScanner {
    var position: Int
    let data: Data
    init(data: Data) {
        self.position = 0
        self.data = data
    }
}
```

We can also add a method that scans a byte. Note that this method is mutating: it changes the position (unless we've reached the end of the data):

```
extension BinaryScanner {
  func scanByte() -> UInt8? {
    guard position < data.endIndex else {
      return nil
    }
    position += 1
    return data[position-1]
  }
}
```

To test it out, we can write a method that scans all the remaining bytes:

```
func scanRemainingBytes(scanner: BinaryScanner) {
  while let byte = scanner.scanByte() {
    print(byte)
  }
}
let scanner = BinaryScanner(data: "hi".data(using: .utf8)!)
scanRemainingBytes(scanner: scanner)
/*
104
105
*/
```

Everything works as expected. However, it's easy to construct an example with a race condition. If we use Grand Central Dispatch to call scanRemainingBytes from two different threads, it'll eventually run into a race condition. In the code below, the condition position < data.endIndex can be true on one thread, but then GCD switches to another thread and scans the last byte. Now, if it switches back, the position will be incremented and the subscript will access a value that's out of bounds:

```
for _ in 0..<Int.max {
  let newScanner = BinaryScanner(data: "hi".data(using: .utf8)!)
  DispatchQueue.global().async {
    scanRemainingBytes(scanner: newScanner)
  }
  scanRemainingBytes(scanner: newScanner)
}
```

The race condition doesn't occur too often (hence the Int.max), and is therefore difficult to find during testing. If we change BinaryScanner to a struct, this problem doesn't occur at all. In the next section, we'll look at why.

Structs

Value types imply that whenever a variable is copied, the value itself — and not just a reference to the value — is copied. For example, in almost all programming languages, scalar types are value types. This means that whenever a value is assigned to a new variable, it's copied rather than passed by reference:

```
var a = 42
var b = a
b += 1
b // 43
a // 42
```

After the above code executes, the value of b will be 43, but a will still be 42. This is so natural that it seems like stating the obvious. However, in Swift, all structs behave this way — not just scalar types.

Let's start with a simple struct that describes a Point. This is similar to CGPoint, except that it contains Ints, whereas CGPoint contains CGFloats:

```
struct Point {
    var x: Int
    var y: Int
}
```

For structs, Swift automatically adds a memberwise initializer. This means we can now initialize a new variable:

```
let origin = Point(x: 0, y: 0)
```

Because structs in Swift have value semantics, we can't change any of the properties of a struct variable that's defined using let. For example, the following code won't work:

```
origin.x = 10 // Error
```

Even though we defined x within the struct as a var property, we can't change it, because origin is defined using let. This has some major advantages. For example, if you read a line like let point = ..., and you know that point is a struct variable, then you also know that it'll never, ever, change. This is a great help when reading through code.

To create a mutable variable, we need to use var:

```
var otherPoint = Point(x: 0, y: 0)
otherPoint.x += 10
otherPoint // (x: 10, y: 0)
```

Unlike with objects, every struct variable is unique. For example, we can create a new variable, thirdPoint, and assign the value of origin to it. Now we can change thirdPoint, but origin (which we defined as an immutable variable using let) won't change:

```
var thirdPoint = origin
thirdPoint.x += 10
thirdPoint // (x: 10, y: 0)
origin // (x: 0, y: 0)
```

When you assign a struct to a new variable, Swift automatically makes a copy. Even though this sounds very expensive, many of the copies can be optimized away by the compiler, and Swift tries hard to make the copies very cheap. In fact, many structs in the standard library are implemented using a technique called copy-on-write, which we'll look at later.

If we have struct values that we plan to use more often, we can define them in an extension as a static property. For example, we can define an origin property on Point so that we can write Point.origin everywhere we need it:

```
extension Point {
    static let origin = Point(x: 0, y: 0)
}
Point.origin // (x: 0, y: 0)
```

Structs can also contain other structs. For example, if we define a Size struct, we can create a Rect struct, which is composed out of a point and a size:

```
struct Size {
    var width: Int
    var height: Int
}

struct Rectangle {
    var origin: Point
    var size: Size
}
```

Just like before, we get a memberwise initializer for Rectangle. The order of the parameters matches the order of the property definitions:

```
Rectangle(origin: Point.origin,
    size: Size(width: 320, height: 480))
```

If we want a custom initializer for our struct, we can add it directly inside the struct definition. However, if the struct definition contains a custom initializer, Swift doesn't generate a memberwise initializer. By defining our custom initializer in an extension, we also get to keep the memberwise initializer:

```
extension Rectangle {
    init(x: Int = 0, y: Int = 0, width: Int, height: Int) {
        origin = Point(x: x, y: y)
        size = Size(width: width, height: height)
    }
}
```

Instead of setting origin and size directly, we could've also called self.init(origin:size:).

If we define a mutable variable screen, we can add a didSet block that gets executed whenever screen changes. This didSet works for every definition of a struct, be it in a playground, in a class, or when defining a global variable:

```
var screen = Rectangle(width: 320, height: 480) {
    didSet {
        print("Screen changed: \(screen)")
    }
}
```

Maybe somewhat surprisingly, even if we change something deep inside the struct, the following will get triggered:

```
screen.origin.x = 10 // Screen changed: (10, 0, 320, 480)
```

Understanding why this works is key to understanding value types. Mutating a struct variable is semantically the same as assigning a new value to it. When we mutate something deep inside the struct, it still means we're mutating the struct, so didSet still needs to get triggered.

Although we semantically replace the entire struct with a new one, the compiler can still mutate the value in place; since the struct has no other owner, it doesn't actually need to make a copy. With copy-on-write structs (which we'll discuss later), this works differently.

Since arrays are structs, this naturally works with them, too. If we define an array containing other value types, we can modify one of the properties of an element in the array and still get a didSet trigger:

```
var screens = [Rectangle(width: 320, height: 480)] {
  didSet {
    print("Array changed")
  }
}
screens[0].origin.x += 100 // Array changed
```

The didSet trigger wouldn't fire if Rectangle were a class, because in that case, the reference the array stores doesn't change — only the object it's referring to does.

To add two Points together, we can write an overload for the + operator. Inside, we add both members and return a new Point:

```
func +(lhs: Point, rhs: Point) -> Point {
  return Point(x: lhs.x + rhs.x, y: lhs.y + rhs.y)
}
screen.origin + Point(x: 10, y: 10) // (x: 20, y: 10)
```

We can also make this operation work on rectangles and add a translate method, which moves the rectangle by a given offset. Our first attempt doesn't work:

```
extension Rectangle {
  func translate(by offset: Point) {
    // Error: Cannot assign to property: 'self' is immutable
    origin = origin + offset
  }
}
```

The compiler tells us that we can't assign to the origin property because self is immutable (writing origin = is shorthand for self.origin =). We can think of self as an extra, implicit parameter that gets passed to every method on Rectangle. You never have to pass the parameter, but it's always there inside the method body, and it's immutable so that value semantics can be guaranteed. If we want to mutate self, or any property of self, or even nested properties (e.g. self.origin.x), we need to mark our method as mutating:

```
extension Rectangle {
  mutating func translate(by offset: Point) {
    origin = origin + offset
  }
}
screen.translate(by: Point(x: 10, y: 10))
screen // (20, 10, 320, 480)
```

The compiler enforces the mutating keyword. Unless we use it, we're not allowed to mutate anything inside the method. By marking the method as mutating, we change the behavior of self. Instead of it being a let, it now works like a var: we can freely change any property. (To be precise, it's not even a var, but we'll get to that in a little bit).

If we define a Rectangle variable using let, we can't call translate on it, because the only Rectangles that are mutable are the ones defined using var:

```
let otherScreen = screen
// Error: Cannot use mutating member on immutable value
otherScreen.translate(by: Point(x: 10, y: 10))
```

Thinking back to the built-in collections chapter, we can now see how the difference between let and var applies to collections as well. The append method on arrays is defined as mutating, and therefore, we're not allowed to call it on an array declared with let.

Swift automatically marks property setters as mutating; you can't call a setter on a let variable. The same is true for subscript setters:

```
let point = Point.origin
// Error: Cannot assign to property: 'point' is a 'let' constant
point.x = 10
```

In many cases, it makes sense to have both a mutable and an immutable variant of the same method. For example, arrays have both a sort() method (which is mutating and sorts in place) and a sorted() method (which returns a new array). We can also add a non-mutating variant of our translate(by:_) method. Instead of mutating self, we create a copy, mutate that, and return a new Rectangle:

```
extension Rectangle {
  func translated(by offset: Point) -> Rectangle {
    var copy = self
    copy.translate(by: offset)
```

```
    return copy
  }
}
screen.translated(by: Point(x: 20, y: 20)) // (40, 30, 320, 480)
```

> The names sort and sorted aren't chosen at random; rather, they're
> names that conform to the Swift API Design Guidelines[a]. We applied
> the same guidelines to translate and translated. There's even specific
> documentation for methods that have a mutating and a non-mutating
> variant: because translate has a side effect, it should read as an
> imperative verb phrase. The non-mutating variant should have an -ed
> or -ing suffix.
>
> ───────────
> a https://swift.org/documentation/api-design-guidelines/

As we saw in the introduction of this chapter, when dealing with mutating
code, it's easy to introduce bugs: because the object you're just checking can
be modified from a different thread (or even a different method on the same
thread), your assumptions might be invalid.

Swift structs with mutating methods and properties don't have the same
problems. The mutation of the struct is a local side effect, and it only applies
to the current struct variable. Because every struct variable is unique (or in
other words: every struct value has exactly one owner), it's almost impossible
to introduce bugs this way. That is, unless you're referring to a global struct
variable across threads.

To understand how the mutating keyword works, we can look at the behavior
of inout. In Swift, we can mark function parameters as inout. Before we do that,
let's define a free function that moves a rectangle by 10 points on both axes.
We can't simply call translate directly on the rectangle parameter, because all
function parameters are immutable by default and get passed in as copies.
Instead, we need to use translated(by:). Then we need to re-assign the result of
the function to screen:

```
func translatedByTenTen(rectangle: Rectangle) -> Rectangle {
    return rectangle.translated(by: Point(x: 10, y: 10))
}
screen = translatedByTenTen(rectangle: screen)
screen // (30, 20, 320, 480)
```

How could we write a function that changes the rectangle in place? Looking back, the mutating keyword does exactly that. It makes the implicit self parameter mutable, and it changes the value of the variable.

In functions, we can mark parameters as inout. Just like with a regular parameter, a copy of the value gets passed in to the function. However, we can change the copy (it's as if it were defined as a var). And once the function returns, the original value gets overwritten. Now we can use translate(by:) instead of translated(by:):

```
func translateByTwentyTwenty(rectangle: inout Rectangle) {
    rectangle.translate(by: Point(x: 20, y: 20))
}
translateByTwentyTwenty(rectangle: &screen)
screen // (50, 40, 320, 480)
```

The translateByTwentyTwenty function takes the screen rectangle, changes it locally, and copies the new value back (overriding the previous value of screen). This behavior is exactly the same as that of a mutating method. In fact, mutating methods are just like regular methods on the struct, except the implicit self parameter is marked as inout.

We can't call translateByTwentyTwenty on a rectangle that's defined using let. We can only use it with mutable values:

```
let immutableScreen = screen
// Error: Cannot pass immutable value as inout argument
translateByTwentyTwenty(rectangle: &immutableScreen)
```

Now it also makes sense how we had to write a mutating operator like +=. Such operators modify the left-hand side, so that parameter must be inout:

```
func +=(lhs: inout Point, rhs: Point) {
    lhs = lhs + rhs
}
var myPoint = Point.origin
myPoint += Point(x: 10, y: 10)
myPoint // (x: 10, y: 10)
```

In the functions chapter, we'll go into more detail about inout. For now, it suffices to say that inout is in lots of places. For example, it's now easy to understand how mutating a value through a subscript works:

```
var array = [Point(x: 0, y: 0), Point(x: 10, y: 10)]
```

```
array[0] += Point(x: 100, y: 100)
array // [(x: 100, y: 100), (x: 10, y: 10)]
```

The expression array[0] is automatically passed in as an inout variable. In the functions chapter, we'll see why we can use expressions like array[0] as an inout parameter.

Let's revisit the BinaryScanner example from the introduction of this chapter. We had the following problematic code snippet:

```
for _ in 0..<Int.max {
  let newScanner = BinaryScanner(data: "hi".data(using: .utf8)!)
  DispatchQueue.global().async {
    scanRemainingBytes(scanner: newScanner)
  }
  scanRemainingBytes(scanner: newScanner)
}
```

If we make BinaryScanner a struct instead of a class, each call to scanRemainingBytes gets its own independent copy of newScanner. Therefore, the calls can safely keep iterating over the array without having to worry that the struct gets mutated from a different method or thread.

Structs don't magically make your code safe for multithreading. For example, if we keep BinaryScanner as a struct but inline the scanRemainingBytes method, we end up with the same race condition as we had before. Both the while loop inside the closure, as well as the while loop outside of the closure, refer to the same newScanner variable, and both will mutate it at the same time:

```
for _ in 0..<Int.max {
  let newScanner = BinaryScanner(data: "hi".data(using: .utf8)!)
  DispatchQueue.global().async {
    while let byte = newScanner.scanByte() {
     print(byte)
    }
  }
  while let byte = newScanner.scanByte() {
   print(byte)
  }
}
```

Copy-On-Write

In the Swift standard library, collections like Array, Dictionary, and Set are implemented using a technique called *copy-on-write*. Let's say we have an array of integers:

```
var x = [1,2,3]
var y = x
```

If we create a new variable, y, and assign the value of x to it, a copy gets made, and both x and y now contain independent structs. Internally, each of these Array structs contains a reference to some memory. This memory is where the elements of the array are stored, and it's located on the heap. At this point, the references of both arrays point to the same location in memory — the arrays are sharing this part of their storage. However, the moment we mutate x, the shared reference gets detected, and the memory is copied. This means we can mutate both variables independently, yet the (expensive) copy of the elements only happens when it has to — once we mutate one of the variables:

```
x.append(5)
y.removeLast()
x // [1, 2, 3, 5]
y // [1, 2]
```

If the reference inside the Array struct had been unique at the instant the array was mutated (for example, by not declaring y), then no copy would've been made; the memory would've been mutated in place. This behavior is called *copy-on-write*, and as the author of a struct, it's not something you get for free; you have to implement it yourself. Implementing copy-on-write behavior for your own types makes sense whenever you define a struct that contains one or more mutable references internally but should still retain value semantics, and at the same time, avoid unnecessary copying.

To see how this works, we'll reimplement the Data struct from Foundation and use the NSMutableData class as our internal reference type. Data is a value type, and it behaves just like you'd expect:

```
var input: [UInt8] = [0x0b,0xad,0xf0,0x0d]
var other: [UInt8] = [0x0d]
var d = Data(bytes: input)
var e = d
d.append(contentsOf: other)
```

```
d // 5 bytes
e // 4 bytes
```

As we can see above, d and e are independent: adding a byte to d doesn't change the value of e.

Writing the same example using NSMutableData, we can see that objects are shared:

```
var f = NSMutableData(bytes: &input, length: input.count)
var g = f
f.append(&other, length: other.count)
f // <0badf00d 0d>
g // <0badf00d 0d>
```

Both f and g refer to the same object (in other words: they point to the same piece of memory), so changing one also changes the other. We can even verify that they refer to the same object by using the === operator:

```
f===g // true
```

If we naively wrap NSMutableData in a struct, we don't get value semantics automatically. For example, we could try the following:

```
struct MyData {
  var _data: NSMutableData
  init(_ data: NSData) {
    self._data = data.mutableCopy() as! NSMutableData
  }
}
```

If we copy a struct variable, a shallow bitwise copy is made. This means that the reference to the object, and not the object itself, will get copied:

```
let theData = NSData(base64Encoded: "wAEP/w==", options: [])!
let x = MyData(theData)
let y = x
x._data===y._data
```

We can add an append function, which delegates to the underlying _data property, and again, we can see that we've created a struct without value semantics:

```
extension MyData {
```

```
  func append(_ other: MyData) {
    _data.append(other._data as Data)
  }
}
```

```
x.append(x)
y // <c0010fff c0010fff>
```

Because we're only modifying the object _data is referring to, we don't even have to mark append as mutating. After all, the reference stays constant, and the struct too. Therefore, we were able to declare x and y using let, even though they were mutable.

Copy-On-Write (The Expensive Way)

To implement copy-on-write, we can make _data a private property of the struct. Instead of mutating _data directly, we access it through a computed property, _dataForWriting. This computed property always makes a copy and returns it:

```
struct MyData {
  fileprivate var _data: NSMutableData
  var _dataForWriting: NSMutableData {
    mutating get {
      _data = _data.mutableCopy() as! NSMutableData
      return _data
    }
  }
  init(_ data: NSData) {
    self._data = data.mutableCopy() as! NSMutableData
  }
}
```

Because _dataForWriting mutates the struct (it assigns a new value to the _data property), the getter has to be marked as mutating. This means we can only use it on variables declared with var.

We can use _dataForWriting in our append method, which now also needs to be marked as mutating:

```
extension MyData {
  mutating func append(_ other: MyData) {
    _dataForWriting.append(other._data as Data)
```

```
    }
}
```

Our struct now has value semantics. If we assign the value of x to the variable y, both variables are still pointing to the same underlying NSMutableData object. However, the moment we use append on either one of the variables, a copy gets made:

```
let theData = NSData(base64Encoded: "wAEP/w==", options: [])!
var x = MyData(theData)
let y = x
x._data===y._data
x.append(x)
y // <c0010fff>
x._data===y._data
```

This strategy works, but it's not very efficient if we mutate the same variable multiple times. For example, consider the following example:

```
var buffer = MyData(NSData())
for _ in 0..<5 {
    buffer.append(x)
}
```

Each time we call append, the underlying _data object gets copied. Because we're not sharing the buffer variable, it'd have been a lot more efficient to mutate it in place.

Copy-On-Write (The Efficient Way)

To provide efficient copy-on-write behavior, we need to know whether an object (e.g. the NSMutableData instance) is uniquely referenced. If it's a unique reference, we can modify the object in place. Otherwise, we create a copy of the object before modifying it. In Swift, we can use the isKnownUniquelyReferenced function to find out the uniqueness of a reference. If you pass in an instance of a Swift class to this function, and if no one else has a strong reference to the object, the function returns true. If there are other strong references, it returns false. It also returns false for Objective-C classes. Therefore, it doesn't make sense to use the function with NSMutableData directly. We can write a simple Swift class that wraps any Objective-C object into a Swift object:

```
final class Box<A> {
```

```
  var unbox: A
  init(_ value: A) { self.unbox = value }
}
```

```
var x = Box(NSMutableData())
isKnownUniquelyReferenced(&x) // true
```

If we have multiple references to the same object, the function will return false:

```
var y = x
isKnownUniquelyReferenced(&x) // false
```

This also works when the references are inside a struct, instead of just global variables. Using this knowledge, we can now write a variant of MyData, which checks whether _data is uniquely referenced before mutating it. We also add a print statement to quickly see during debugging how often we make a copy:

```
struct MyData {
  fileprivate var _data: Box<NSMutableData>
  var _dataForWriting: NSMutableData {
    mutating get {
      if !isKnownUniquelyReferenced(&_data) {
        _data = Box(_data.unbox.mutableCopy() as! NSMutableData)
        print("Making a copy")
      }
      return _data.unbox
    }
  }
  init(_ data: NSData) {
    self._data = Box(data.mutableCopy() as! NSMutableData)
  }
}
```

In the append method, we need to call unbox on the _data property of other. The logic for making a copy of the value we're appending to is already wrapped inside the _dataForWriting computed property:

To test out our code, let's write the loop again:

```
let someBytes = MyData(NSData(base64Encoded: "wAEP/w==", options: [])!)
```

```
var empty = MyData(NSData())
var emptyCopy = empty
```

```
for _ in 0..<5 {
  empty.append(someBytes)
}
empty // <c0010fff c0010fff c0010fff c0010fff c0010fff>
emptyCopy // <>
```

If we run the code above, we can see that our debug statement only gets printed once: when we call append for the first time. In subsequent iterations, the uniqueness is detected and no copy gets made.

This technique allows you to create custom structs that are value types while still being just as efficient as you would be working with objects or pointers. As a user of the struct, you don't need to worry about copying these structs manually — the implementation will take care of it for you. Because copy-on-write is combined with optimizations done by the compiler, many unnecessary copy operations can be removed.

When you define your own structs and classes, it's important to pay attention to the expected copying and mutability behavior. Structs are expected to have value semantics. When using a class inside a struct, we need to make sure that it's truly immutable. If this isn't possible, we either need to take extra steps (like above), or just use a class, in which case consumers of our data don't expect it to behave like a value.

Most data structures in the Swift standard library are value types using copy-on-write. For example, arrays, dictionaries, sets, and strings are all structs. This makes it simpler to understand code that uses those types. When we pass an array to a function, we know the function can't modify the original array: it only works on a copy of the array. Also, the way arrays are implemented, we know that no unnecessary copies will be made. Contrast this with the Foundation data types, where it's best practice to always manually copy types like NSArray and NSString. When working with Foundation data types, it's easy to forget to manually copy the object and instead accidentally write unsafe code.

Even when you could create a struct, there might still be very good reasons to use a class. For example, you might want an immutable type that only has a single instance, or maybe you're wrapping a reference type and don't want to implement copy-on-write. Or, you might need to interface with Objective-C, in which case, structs might not work either. By defining a restrictive interface for your class, it's still very possible to make it immutable.

It might also be interesting to wrap existing types in enums. In the chapter on wrapping CommonMark, we'll provide an enum-based interface to a reference type.

Copy-On-Write Gotchas

Unfortunately, it's all too easy to introduce accidental copies. To see this behavior, we'll create a very simple struct that contains a reference to an empty Swift class. The struct has a single mutating method, change, which checks whether or not the reference should be copied. Rather than copying, it just returns a string indicating whether or not a copy would have occurred:

```
final class Empty { }

struct COWStruct {
  var ref = Empty()

  mutating func change() -> String {
    if isKnownUniquelyReferenced(&ref) {
      return "No copy"
    } else {
      return "Copy"
    }
    // Perform actual change
  }
}
```

For example, if we create a variable and immediately mutate it, the variable isn't shared. Therefore, the reference is unique and no copy is necessary:

```
var s = COWStruct()
s.change() // No copy
```

As we'd expect, when we create a second variable, the reference is shared, and a copy is necessary the moment we call change:

```
var original = COWStruct()
var copy = original
original.change() // Copy
```

When we put one of our structs in an array, we can mutate the array element directly, and no copy is necessary. This is because the array subscript that we're using has direct access to the memory location:

```
var array = [COWStruct()]
array[0].change() // No copy
```

If we go through an intermediate variable, though, a copy is made:

```
var otherArray = [COWStruct()]
var x = array[0]
x.change() // Copy
```

Somewhat surprisingly, all other types — including dictionaries, sets, and your own types — behave very differently. For example, the dictionary subscript looks up the value in the dictionary and then returns the value. Because we're dealing with value semantics, a copy is returned. Therefore, calling change() on that value will make a copy, as the COWStruct is no longer uniquely referenced:

```
var dict = ["key": COWStruct()]
dict["key"]?.change() // Optional("Copy")
```

If you want to avoid making copies when you put a copy-on-write struct inside a dictionary, you can wrap the value inside a class box, effectively giving the value reference semantics.

When you're working with your own structs, you need to keep this in mind. For example, if we create a container that simply stores a value, we can either modify the storage property directly, or we can access it indirectly, such as through a subscript. When we directly access it, we get the copy-on-write optimization, but when we access it indirectly through a subscript, a copy is made:

```
struct ContainerStruct<A> {
  var storage: A
  subscript(s: String) -> A {
    get { return storage }
    set { storage = newValue }
  }
}
```

```
var d = ContainerStruct(storage: COWStruct())
d.storage.change() // No copy
d["test"].change() // Copy
```

The implementation of the Array subscript uses a special technique to make copy-on-write work, but unfortunately, no other types currently use this. The Swift team mentioned that they hope to generalize it to dictionaries.

The way Array implements the subscript is by using *addressors*. An addressor allows for direct access to memory. Instead of returning the element, an array subscript returns an addressor for the element. This way, the element memory can be modified in place, and unnecessary copies can be eliminated. You can use addressors in your own code, but as they're not officially documented, they're bound to change. For more information, see the Accessors.rst[1] document in the Swift repository.

Closures and Mutability

In this section, we'll look at how closures store data.

For example, consider a function that generates a unique integer every time it gets called (until it reaches Int.max). It works by moving the state outside of the function. In other words, it *closes* over the variable i:

```
var i = 0
func uniqueInteger() -> Int {
  i += 1
  return i
}
```

Every time we call this function, the shared variable i will change, and a different integer will be returned. Functions are reference types as well — if we assign uniqueInteger to another variable, the compiler won't copy the function (or i). Instead, it'll create a reference to the same function:

```
let otherFunction: () -> Int = uniqueInteger
```

Calling otherFunction will have exactly the same effect as calling uniqueInteger. This is true for all closures and functions: if we pass them around, they always get passed by reference, and they always share the same state.

Recall the function-based fibsIterator example from the collection protocols chapter, where we saw this behavior before. When we used the iterator, the

---

1 https://github.com/apple/swift/blob/73841a643c087e854a2f62c7e073317bd43af310/docs/proposals/Accessors.rst

iterator itself (being a function) was mutating its state. In order to create a fresh iterator for each iteration, we had to wrap it in an AnySequence.

If we want to have multiple different unique integer providers, we can use the same technique: instead of returning the integer, we return a closure that captures the mutable variable. The returned closure is a reference type, and passing it around will share the state. However, calling uniqueIntegerProvider repeatedly returns a fresh function that starts at zero every time:

```swift
func uniqueIntegerProvider() -> () -> Int {
  var i = 0
  return {
    i += 1
    return i
  }
}
```

Instead of returning a closure, we can also wrap the behavior in an AnyIterator. That way, we can even use our integer provider in a for loop:

```swift
func uniqueIntegerProvider() -> AnyIterator<Int> {
  var i = 0
  return AnyIterator {
    i += 1
    return i
  }
}
```

Swift structs are commonly stored on the stack rather than on the heap. However, this is an optimization: by default, a struct is stored on the heap, and in almost all cases, the optimization will store the struct on the stack. When a struct variable is closed over by a function, the optimization doesn't apply, and the struct is stored on the heap. Because the i variable is closed over by the function, the struct exists on the heap. That way, it persists even when the scope of uniqueIntegerProvider exits. Likewise, if a struct is too large, it's also stored on the heap.

Memory

Value types are very common in Swift, and memory management for them is very easy. Because they have a single owner, the memory needed for them is created and freed automatically. When using value types, you can't create cyclic references. For example, consider the following snippet:

```
struct Person {
  let name: String
  var parents: [Person]
}
```

```
var john = Person(name: "John", parents: [])
john.parents = [john]
john // John, parents: [John, parents: []]
```

Because of the way value types work, the moment we put john in an array, a copy is created. It'd be more precise to say: "we put the value of john in an array." If Person were a class, we'd now have a cycle. With the struct version, john now has a single parent, which is the initial value of john with an empty parents array.

For classes, Swift uses automated reference counting (ARC) to manage memory. In most cases, this means that things will work as expected. Every time you create a new reference to an object (for example, when you assign a value to a class variable), the reference count gets increased by one. Once you let go of that reference (for example, the variable goes out of scope), the reference count decreases by one. When the reference count goes to zero, the object is deallocated. A variable that behaves in this manner is also called a *strong reference* (compared to weak or unowned references, which we'll discuss in a bit).

For example, consider the following code:

```
class View {
  var window: Window
  init(window: Window) {
    self.window = window
  }
}
```

```
class Window {
  var rootView: View?
}
```

We can now allocate and initialize a window and assign the instance to a variable. After the first line, the reference count is one. The moment we set the variable to nil, the reference count of our Window instance is zero, and the instance gets deallocated:

```
var myWindow: Window? = Window()
myWindow = nil
```

When comparing Swift to a garbage-collected language, at first glance it looks like things are very similar when it comes to memory management. Most times, you don't even think about it. However, consider the following example:

```
var window: Window? = Window()
var view: View? = View(window: window!)
window?.rootView = view
view = nil
window = nil
```

First, the window gets created, and the reference count for the window will be one. The view gets created and holds a strong reference to the window, so the window's reference count will be two, and the view's reference count will be one. Then, assigning the view as the window's rootView will increase the view's reference count by one. Now, both the view and the window have a reference count of two. After setting both variables to nil, they still have a reference count of one. Even though they're no longer accessible from a variable, they strongly reference each other. This is called a *reference cycle*, and when dealing with graph-like data structures, we need to be very aware of this. Because of the reference cycle, these two objects will never be deallocated during the lifetime of the program.

Weak References

To break the reference cycle, we need to make sure that one of the references is either weak or unowned. When you mark a variable as weak, assigning a value to it doesn't change the reference count. A weak reference also means that the reference will be nil once the referred object gets deallocated. For example, we could make the rootView property weak, which means it won't be strongly referenced by the window and automatically becomes nil once the view is deallocated. When you're dealing with a weak variable, you have to make it optional. To debug the memory behavior, we can add a deinitializer, which gets called just before the class deallocates:

```
class View {
```

```
  var window: Window
  init(window: Window) {
    self.window = window
  }
  deinit {
    print("Deinit View")
  }
}

class Window {
  weak var rootView: View?
  deinit {
    print("Deinit Window")
  }
}
```

In the code below, we create a window and a view. The view strongly references the window, but because the window's rootView is declared as weak, the window doesn't strongly reference the view. This way, we have no reference cycle, and after setting both variables to nil, both views get deallocated:

```
var window: Window? = Window()
var view: View? = View(window: window!)
window?.rootView = view!
window = nil
view = nil
/*
Deinit View
Deinit Window
*/
```

A weak reference is very useful when working with delegates. The object that calls the delegate methods shouldn't own the delegate. Therefore, a delegate is usually marked as weak, and another object is responsible for making sure the delegate stays around for as long as needed.

Unowned References

Weak references must always be optional types because they can become nil, but sometimes we may not want this. For example, maybe we know that our views will always have a window (so the property shouldn't be optional), but we don't want a view to strongly reference the window. In other words, assigning to property should leave the reference count unchanged. For these cases, there's the unowned keyword, which assumes the reference is always valid:

```swift
class View {
  unowned var window: Window
  init(window: Window) {
    self.window = window
  }
  deinit {
    print("Deinit View")
  }
}

class Window {
  var rootView: View?
  deinit {
    print("Deinit Window")
  }
}
```

Now we can create a window, create views, and set the window's root view. There's no reference cycle, but we're responsible for ensuring that the window outlives the view. If the window is deallocated and the unowned variable is accessed, there'll be a runtime crash. In the code below, we can see that both objects get deallocated:

```swift
var window: Window? = Window()
var view: View? = View(window: window!)
window?.rootView = view
view = nil
window = nil
/*
Deinit Window
Deinit View
*/
```

The Swift runtime keeps a second reference count in the object to keep track of unowned references. When all strong references are gone, the object will release all of its resources (for example, any references to other objects). However, the memory of the object itself will still be there until all unowned references are gone too. The memory is marked as invalid (sometimes also called *zombie* memory), and any time we try to access an unowned reference, a runtime error will occur.

Note that this isn't the same as undefined behavior. There's a third option, unowned(unsafe), which doesn't have this runtime check. If we access an invalid reference that's marked as unowned(unsafe), we get undefined behavior.

When you don't need weak, it's recommended that you use unowned. A weak variable always needs to be defined using var, whereas an unowned variable can be defined using let and be immutable. However, only use unowned in situations where you know that the reference will always be valid.

Personally, we often find ourselves using weak, even when unowned could be used. We might want to refactor some code at a later point, and our assumptions about the lifetime of an object might not be valid anymore. When using weak, the compiler forces us to deal with the possibility that a reference might become nil.

Closures and Memory

Classes aren't the only kind of reference type in Swift. Functions are reference types too, and this includes closures. As we saw in the section on closures and mutability, a closure can capture variables. If these variables are reference types, the closure will maintain a strong reference to them. For example, if you have a variable handle that's a FileHandle object and you access it within a callback, the callback will increment the reference count for that handle:

```
let handle = FileHandle(forWritingAtPath: "out.html")
let request = URLRequest(url: URL(string: "http://www.objc.io")!)
URLSession.shared.dataTask(with: request) { (data, _, _) in
    guard let theData = data else { return }
    handle?.write(theData)
}
```

Once the callback is done, the closure gets released, and the variables it closes over (in the example above, just handle) will have their reference counts decremented. This strong reference to the closed-over variables is necessary, otherwise the variable could already be deallocated when you access it within the callback.

Only closures that can *escape* need to keep strong references to their variables. In the chapter on functions, we'll look into more detail at escaping vs. non-escaping functions.

Reference Cycles with Closures

One of the issues with closures capturing their variables is the (accidental) introduction of reference cycles. The usual pattern is like this: object A references object B, but object B references a callback that references object A. Let's consider our example from before, where a view references its window, and the window has a weak reference back to its root view. Additionally, the window now has an onRotate callback, which is optional and has an initial value of nil:

```
class View {
  var window: Window
  init(window: Window) {
    self.window = window
  }
  deinit {
    print("Deinit View")
  }
}

class Window {
  weak var rootView: View?
  deinit {
    print("Deinit Window")
  }

  var onRotate: (() -> ())?
}
```

If we create a view and set up the window like before, all is well, and we don't have a reference cycle yet:

```
var window: Window? = Window()
var view: View? = View(window: window!)
window?.rootView = view!
```

The view has a strong reference to the window, but the window has a weak reference to the view, so there's no cycle. However, if we configure the onRotate callback and use the view in there, we've introduced a reference cycle:

```
window?.onRotate = {
  print("We now also need to update the view: \(view)")
}
```

The view references the window, the window references the callback, and the callback references the view: a cycle.

In a diagram, it looks like this:

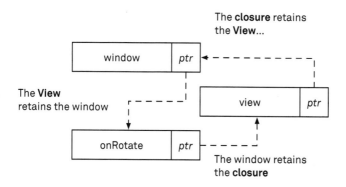

Figure 5.1: A retain cycle between the view, window, and closure

We need to find a way to break this cycle. There are three places where we could break the cycle (each corresponding to an arrow in the diagram):

→ We could make the reference to the Window weak. Unfortunately, this would make the Window disappear, because there are no other references keeping it alive.

→ We could change the Window to make the onRotate closure weak. This wouldn't work either, as closures can't be marked as weak. And even if weak closures were possible, all users of the Window would need to know this and somehow manually reference the closure.

→ We could make sure the closure doesn't reference the view by using a capture list. This is the only correct option in the above example.

In the case of the (constructed) example above, it's not too hard to figure out that we have a reference cycle. However, it's not always this easy. Sometimes the number of objects involved might be much larger, and the reference cycle might be harder to spot. And to make matters even worse, your code might be correct the first time you write it, but a refactoring might introduce a reference cycle without you noticing.

Capture Lists

To break the cycle above, we want to make sure the closure won't reference the view. We can do this by using a *capture list* and marking the captured variable (view) as either weak or unowned:

```
window?.onRotate = { [weak view] in
  print("We now also need to update the view: \(view)")
}
```

Capture lists can also be used to initialize new variables. For example, if we wanted to have a weak variable that refers to the window, we could initialize it in the capture list, or we could even define completely unrelated variables, like so:

```
window?.onRotate = { [weak view, weak myWindow=window, x=5*5] in
  print("We now also need to update the view: \(view)")
  print("Because the window \(myWindow) changed")
}
```

This is almost the same as defining the variable just above the closure, except that with capture lists, the scope of the variable is just the scope of the closure; it's not available outside of the closure.

Conclusion

We've looked at the differences between structs and classes in Swift. For entities (needing identity), classes are a better choice. For value types, structs are a better choice. When building structs that contain objects, we often need to take extra steps to ensure that they're really value types — for example, by implementing copy-on-write. We've looked at how to prevent reference cycles when dealing with classes. Often, a problem can be solved with either structs or classes, and what you choose depends on your needs. However, even problems that are classically solved using references can often benefit from values.

Functions

To open this chapter, let's recap some main points regarding functions. If you're already very familiar with first-class functions, feel free to skip ahead to the next section. But if you're even slightly hazy, skim through what's below.

To understand functions and closures in Swift, you really need to understand three things, in roughly this order of importance:

1. Functions can be assigned to variables and passed in and out of other functions as arguments, just as an Int or a String can be.

2. Functions can *capture* variables that exist outside of their local scope.

3. There are two ways of creating functions — either with the func keyword, or with { }. Swift calls the latter *closure expressions*.

Sometimes people new to the topic of closures come at it in reverse order and maybe miss one of these points, or conflate the terms *closure* and *closure expression* — and this can cause a lot of confusion. It's a three-legged stool, and if you miss one of the three points above, you'll fall over when you try to sit down.

1. Functions can be assigned to variables and passed in and out of other functions as arguments.

In Swift, as in many modern languages, functions are referred to as "first-class objects." You can assign functions to variables, and you can pass them in and out of other functions to be called later.

This is *the most important thing* to understand. "Getting" this for functional programming is akin to "getting" pointers in C. If you don't quite grasp this part, everything else will just be noise.

Let's start with a function that simply prints an integer:

```
func printInt(i: Int) {
    print("you passed \(i)")
}
```

To assign the function to a variable, funVar, we just use the function name as the value. Note the absence of parentheses after the function name:

```
let funVar = printInt
```

Now we can call the printInt function using the funVar variable. Note the use of parentheses after the variable name:

```
funVar(2) // you passed 2
```

We can also write a function that takes a function as an argument:

```
func useFunction(function: (Int) -> () ) {
  function(3)
}

useFunction(function: printInt) // you passed 3
useFunction(function: funVar) // you passed 3
```

Why is being able to treat functions like this such a big deal? Because it allows you to easily write "higher-order" functions, which take functions as arguments and apply them in useful ways, as we saw in the chapter on built-in collections.

You can also return functions from other functions:

```
func returnFunc() -> (Int) -> String {
  func innerFunc(i: Int) -> String {
    return "you passed \(i)"
  }
  return innerFunc
}
let myFunc = returnFunc()
myFunc(3) // you passed 3
```

2. Functions can *capture* variables that exist outside of their local scope.

When a function references variables outside the function's scope, those variables are *captured* and stick around after they would otherwise fall out of scope and be destroyed.

To see this, let's revisit our returnFunc function but add a counter that increases each time we call it:

```
func counterFunc() -> (Int) -> String {
  var counter = 0
  func innerFunc(i: Int) -> String {
```

```
    counter += i  // counter is captured
    return "running total: \(counter)"
  }
  return innerFunc
}
```

Normally counter, being a local variable of counterFunc, would go out of scope just after the return statement, and it'd be destroyed. Instead, because it's captured by innerFunc, it'll be kept alive. As we discussed in structs and classes, counter will exist on the heap rather than on the stack. We can call the inner function multiple times, and we see that the running total increases:

```
let f = counterFunc()
f(3) // running total: 3
f(4) // running total: 7
```

If we call counterFunc() again, a fresh counter variable will be created and captured:

```
let g = counterFunc()
g(2) // running total: 2
g(2) // running total: 4
```

This doesn't affect our first function, which still has its own captured version of counter:

```
f(2) // running total: 9
```

Think of these functions combined with their captured variables as similar to instances of classes with a single method (the function) and some member variables (the captured variables).

In programming terminology, a combination of a function and an environment of captured variables is called a *closure*. So f and g above are examples of closures, because they capture and use a non-local variable (counter) that was declared outside of them.

3. Functions can be declared using the { } syntax for closure expressions.

In Swift, you can declare functions in two ways. One is with the func keyword demonstrated above. The other way is to use a *closure expression*. Consider this simple function to double a number:

```
func doubler(i: Int) -> Int {
  return i * 2
}
[1, 2, 3, 4].map(doubler) // [2, 4, 6, 8]
```

And here's the same function written using the closure expression syntax. Just like before, we can pass it to map:

```
let doublerAlt = { (i: Int) -> Int in return i*2 }
[1, 2, 3, 4].map(doublerAlt) // [2, 4, 6, 8]
```

Functions declared as closure expressions can be thought of as *function literals* in the same way that 1 and "hello" are integer and string literals. They're also anonymous — they aren't named, unlike with the func keyword. The only way they can be used is if you assign them to a variable when they're created (as we do here with doubler), or if you pass them to another function or method.

The doubler declared using the closure expression, and the one declared earlier using the func keyword, are completely equivalent. They even exist in the same "namespace," unlike in some languages.

Why is the { } syntax useful then? Why not just use func every time? Well, it can be a lot more compact, especially when writing quick functions to pass into other functions, such as map. Here's our doubler map example written in a much shorter form:

```
[1, 2, 3].map { $0 * 2 } // [2, 4, 6]
```

This looks very different because we've leveraged several features of Swift to make code more concise. Here they are one by one:

1. If you're passing the closure in as an argument and that's all you need it for, there's no need to store it in a local variable first. Think of this like passing in a numeric expression, such as 5*i, to a function that takes an Int as a parameter.

2. If the compiler can infer a type from the context, you don't need to specify it. In our example, the function passed to map takes an Int (inferred from the type of the array elements) and returns an Int (inferred from the type of the multiplication expression).

3. If the closure expression's body contains just a single expression, it'll automatically return the value of the expression, and you can leave off the return.

4. Swift automatically provides shorthand names for the arguments to the function — $0 for the first, $1 for the second, etc.

5. If the last argument to a function is a closure expression, you can move the expression outside the parentheses of the function call. This *trailing closure syntax* is nice if you have a multi-line closure expression, as it more closely resembles a regular function definition or other block statement such as if (expr) { }.

6. Finally, if a function has no arguments other than a closure expression, you can leave off the parentheses after the function name altogether.

Using each of these rules, we can boil down the expression below to the form shown above:

```
[1, 2, 3].map({ (i: Int) -> Int in return i * 2 })
[1, 2, 3].map({ i in return i * 2 })
[1, 2, 3].map({ i in i * 2 })
[1, 2, 3].map({ $0 * 2 })
[1, 2, 3].map() { $0 * 2 }
[1, 2, 3].map { $0 * 2 }
```

If you're new to Swift's syntax, and to functional programming in general, these compact function declarations might seem daunting at first. But as you get more comfortable with the syntax and the functional programming style, they'll start to feel more natural, and you'll be grateful for the ability to remove the clutter so you can see more clearly what the code is doing. Once you get used to reading code written like this, it'll be much clearer to you at a glance than the equivalent code written with a conventional for loop.

Sometimes, Swift needs a helping hand with inferring the types. And sometimes, you may get something wrong and the types aren't what you think they should be. If ever you get a mysterious error when trying to supply a closure expression, it's a good idea to write out the full form (first version above), complete with types. In many cases, that will help clear up where things are going wrong. Once you have the long form compiling, take the types out again one by one until the compiler complains. And if the error was yours, you'll have fixed your code in the process.

Swift will also insist you be more explicit sometimes. For example, you can't completely ignore input parameters. Suppose you wanted an array of random numbers. A quick way to do this is to map a range with a function that just generates random numbers. But you must supply an argument nonetheless. You can use _ in such a case to indicate to the compiler that you acknowledge there's an argument but that you don't care what it is:

```
(0..<3).map { _ in arc4random() } // [1893808271, 1763543443, 4155238688]
```

When you need to explicitly type the variables, you don't have to do it inside the closure expression. For example, try defining isEven without any types:

```
let isEven = { $0 % 2 == 0 }
```

Above, the type of isEven is inferred to be (Int) -> Bool in the same way that let i = 1 is inferred to be Int — because Int is the default type for integer literals.

> This is because of a typealias, IntegerLiteralType, in the standard library:
>
> ```
> protocol ExpressibleByIntegerLiteral {
>   associatedtype IntegerLiteralType
>   /// Create an instance initialized to `value`.
>   init(integerLiteral value: Self.IntegerLiteralType)
> }
> ```
>
> ```
> /// The default type for an otherwise unconstrained integer literal.
> typealias IntegerLiteralType = Int
> ```
>
> If you were to define your own typealias, it would override the default one and change this behavior:
>
> ```
> typealias IntegerLiteralType = UInt32
> let i = 1 // i will be of type UInt32.
> ```
>
> This is almost certainly a bad idea.

If, however, you needed a version of isEven for a different type, you could type the argument and return value inside the closure expression:

```
let isEvenAlt = { (i: Int8) -> Bool in i % 2 == 0 }
```

But you could also supply the context from *outside* the closure:

```
let isEvenAlt2: (Int8) -> Bool = { $0 % 2 == 0 }
let isEvenAlt3 = { $0 % 2 == 0 } as (Int8) -> Bool
```

Since closure expressions are most commonly used in some context of existing input or output types, adding an explicit type isn't often necessary, but it's useful to know.

Of course, it would've been much better to define a generic version of isEven that works on *any* integer as a computed property:

```
extension Integer {
  var isEven: Bool { return self % 2 == 0 }
}
```

Alternatively, we could have chosen to define an isEven variant for all Integer types as a free function:

```
func isEven<T: Integer>(i: T) -> Bool {
  return i % 2 == 0
}
```

If you want to assign that free function to a variable, this is also when you'd have to lock down which specific types it's operating on. A variable can't hold a generic function — only a specific one:

```
let int8isEven: (Int8) -> Bool = isEven
```

One final point on naming. It's important to keep in mind that functions declared with func can be closures, just like ones declared with {}. Remember, a closure is a function combined with any captured variables. While functions created with {} are called *closure expressions*, people often refer to this syntax as just *closures*. But don't get confused and think that functions declared with the closure expression syntax are different from other functions — they aren't. They're both functions, and they can both be closures.

Flexibility through Functions

In the built-in collections chapter, we talked about parameterizing behavior by passing functions as arguments. Let's look at another example of this: sorting.

If you want to sort an array in Objective-C using Foundation, you're met with a long list of different options. These provide a lot of flexibility and power, but at the cost of complexity — even for the simplest method, you probably need to read the documentation in order to know how to use it.

Sorting collections in Swift is simple:

```
let myArray = [3, 1, 2]
myArray.sorted() // [1, 2, 3]
```

There are really four sort methods: the non-mutating variant sorted(by:), and the mutating sort(by:), times two for the overloads that default to sorting comparable things in ascending order. But the overloading means that when you want the simplest case, sorted() is all you need. If you want to sort in a different order, just supply a function:

```
myArray.sorted(by: >) // [3, 2, 1]
```

You can also supply a function if your elements don't conform to Comparable but *do* have a < operator, like tuples:

```
var numberStrings = [(2, "two"), (1, "one"), (3, "three")]
numberStrings.sort(by: <)
numberStrings // [(1, "one"), (2, "two"), (3, "three")]
```

Or, you can supply a more complicated function if you want to sort by some arbitrary calculated criteria:

```
let animals = ["elephant", "zebra", "dog"]
animals.sorted { lhs, rhs in
    let l = lhs.characters.reversed()
    let r = rhs.characters.reversed()
    return l.lexicographicallyPrecedes(r)
}
// ["zebra", "dog", "elephant"]
```

It's this last ability — the ability to use any comparison function to sort a collection — that makes the Swift sort so powerful, and makes this one function able to replicate much (if not all) of the functionality of the various sorting methods in Foundation.

To demonstrate this, let's take a complex example inspired by the Sort Descriptor Programming Topics guide in Apple's documentation. The sortedArray(using:) method on NSArray is very flexible and a great example of the power of Objective-C's dynamic nature. Support for selectors and dynamic dispatch is still there in Swift, but the Swift standard library favors a more function-based approach instead. Later on, we'll show a few techniques where functions as arguments, and treating functions as data, can be used to get the same dynamic effects.

We'll start by defining a Person object. Because we want to show how Objective-C's powerful runtime system works, we'll have to make this object an NSObject subclass (in pure Swift, a struct might have been a better choice):

```
final class Person: NSObject {
  var first: String
  var last: String
  var yearOfBirth: Int
  init(first: String, last: String, yearOfBirth: Int) {
    self.first = first
    self.last = last
    self.yearOfBirth = yearOfBirth
  }
}
```

Let's also define an array of people with different names and birth years:

```
let people = [
  Person(first: "Jo", last: "Smith", yearOfBirth: 1970),
  Person(first: "Joe", last: "Smith", yearOfBirth: 1970),
  Person(first: "Joe", last: "Smyth", yearOfBirth: 1970),
  Person(first: "Joanne", last: "smith", yearOfBirth: 1985),
  Person(first: "Joanne", last: "smith", yearOfBirth: 1970),
  Person(first: "Robert", last: "Jones", yearOfBirth: 1970),
]
```

We want to sort this array first by last name, then by first name, and finally by birth year. We want to do this case insensitively and using the user's locale. An NSSortDescriptor object describes how to order objects, and we can use them to express the individual sorting criteria:

```
let lastDescriptor = NSSortDescriptor(key: #keyPath(Person.last),
```

```
    ascending: true,
    selector: #selector(NSString.localizedCaseInsensitiveCompare(_:)))
let firstDescriptor = NSSortDescriptor(key: #keyPath(Person.first),
    ascending: true,
    selector: #selector(NSString.localizedCaseInsensitiveCompare(_:)))
let yearDescriptor = NSSortDescriptor(key: #keyPath(Person.yearOfBirth),
    ascending: true)
```

To sort the array, we can use the sortedArray(using:) method on NSArray. This takes a list of sort descriptors. To determine the order of two elements, it starts by using the first sort descriptor and uses that result. However, if two elements are equal according to the first descriptor, it uses the second descriptor, and so on:

```
let descriptors = [lastDescriptor, firstDescriptor, yearDescriptor]
(people as NSArray).sortedArray(using: descriptors)
/*
[Robert Jones (1970), Jo Smith (1970), Joanne smith (1970), Joanne smith (1985),
Joe Smith (1970), Joe Smyth (1970)]
*/
```

A sort descriptor uses two runtime features of Objective-C: the key is a key path, and key-value coding is used to look up the value of that key at runtime. The selector parameter takes a selector (which is really just a String describing a method name). At runtime, the selector is turned into a comparison function, and when comparing two objects, the values for the key are compared using that comparison function.

This is a pretty cool use of runtime programming, especially when you realize the array of sort descriptors can be built at runtime, based on, say, a user clicking a column heading.

How can we replicate this functionality using Swift's sort? It's simple to replicate *parts* of the sort — for example, if you want to sort an array using localizedCaseInsensitiveCompare:

```
var strings = ["Hello", "hallo", "Hallo", "hello"]
strings.sort { $0.localizedCaseInsensitiveCompare($1) == .orderedAscending}
strings // ["hallo", "Hallo", "Hello", "hello"]
```

If you want to sort using just a single property of an object, that's also simple:

```
people.sorted { $0.yearOfBirth < $1.yearOfBirth }
/*
```

*[Jo Smith (1970), Joe Smith (1970), Joe Smyth (1970), Joanne smith (1970),
 Robert Jones (1970), Joanne smith (1985)]*
*/

This approach doesn't work so great when optional properties are combined
with methods like localizedCaseInsensitiveCompare, though — it gets ugly fast.
For example, consider sorting an array of filenames by file extension (using the
fileExtension property from the optionals chapter):

```
var files = ["one", "file.h", "file.c", "test.h"]
files.sort { l, r in r.fileExtension.flatMap {
  l.fileExtension?.localizedCaseInsensitiveCompare($0)
} == .orderedAscending }
files // ["one", "file.c", "file.h", "test.h"]
```

Later on, we'll make it easier to use optionals when sorting. However, for now,
we haven't even tried sorting by multiple properties. To sort by last name and
then first name, we can use the standard library's lexicographicalCompare
method. This takes two sequences and performs a phonebook-style
comparison by moving through each pair of elements until it finds one that
isn't equal. So we can build two arrays of the elements and use
lexicographicalCompare to compare them. It also takes a function to perform
the comparison, so we'll put our use of localizedCaseInsensitiveCompare in the
function:

```
people.sorted { p0, p1 in
  let left  = [p0.last, p0.first]
  let right = [p1.last, p1.first]

  return left.lexicographicallyPrecedes(right) {
    $0.localizedCaseInsensitiveCompare($1) == .orderedAscending
  }
}
/*
[Robert Jones (1970), Jo Smith (1970), Joanne smith (1985), Joanne smith (1970),
 Joe Smith (1970), Joe Smyth (1970)]
*/
```

At this point, we've almost replicated the functionality of the original sort in
roughly the same number of lines. But there's still a lot of room for
improvement: the building of arrays on every comparison is very inefficient,
the comparison is hardcoded, and we can't really sort by yearOfBirth using this
approach.

Functions as Data

Rather than writing an even more complicated function that we can use to sort, let's take a step back. So far, the sort descriptors were much clearer, but they use runtime programming. The functions we wrote don't use runtime programming, but they're not so easy to write (and read).

A sort descriptor is a way of describing the ordering of objects. Instead of storing that information as a class, we can define a function to describe the ordering of objects. The simplest possible definition takes two objects and returns true if they're ordered correctly. This is also exactly the type that the standard library's sort(by:) and sorted(by:) methods take as an argument. It's helpful to define a generic typealias to describe sort descriptors:

```
typealias SortDescriptor<Value> = (Value, Value) -> Bool
```

As an example, we could define a sort descriptor that compares two Person objects by year of birth, or a sort descriptor that sorts by last name:

```
let sortByYear: SortDescriptor<Person> = { $0.yearOfBirth < $1.yearOfBirth }
let sortByLastName: SortDescriptor<Person> = {
    $0.last.localizedCaseInsensitiveCompare($1.last) == .orderedAscending
}
```

Rather than writing the sort descriptors by hand, we can write a function that generates them. It's not nice that we have to write the same property twice: in sortByLastName, we could have easily made a mistake and accidentally compared $0.last with $1.first. Also, it's tedious to write these sort descriptors; to sort by first name, it's probably easiest to copy and paste the sortByLastName definition and modify it.

Instead of copying and pasting, we can define a function with an interface that's a lot like NSSortDescriptor, but without the runtime programming. This function takes a key and a comparison method, and it returns a sort descriptor (the function, not the class NSSortDescriptor). Here, key isn't a string, but a function. To compare two keys, we use a function, areInIncreasingOrder. Finally, the result type is a function as well, even though this fact is slightly obscured by the typealias:

```
func sortDescriptor<Value, Key>(
    key: @escaping (Value) -> Key,
    _ areInIncreasingOrder: @escaping (Key, Key) -> Bool)
    -> SortDescriptor<Value>
```

```
{
  return { areInIncreasingOrder(key($0), key($1)) }
}
```

This allows us to define sortByYear in a different way:

```
let sortByYearAlt: SortDescriptor<Person> =
  sortDescriptor(key: { $0.yearOfBirth }, <)
people.sorted(by: sortByYearAlt)
/*
[Jo Smith (1970), Joe Smith (1970), Joe Smyth (1970), Joanne smith (1970),
 Robert Jones (1970), Joanne smith (1985)]
*/
```

We can even define an overloaded variant that works for all Comparable types:

```
func sortDescriptor<Value, Key>(key: @escaping (Value) -> Key)
  -> SortDescriptor<Value> where Key: Comparable
{
  return { key($0) < key($1) }
}
let sortByYearAlt2: SortDescriptor<Person> =
  sortDescriptor(key: { $0.yearOfBirth })
```

Both sortDescriptor variants above work with functions that return a boolean value. The NSSortDescriptor class has an initializer that takes a comparison function such as localizedCaseInsensitiveCompare, which returns a three-way value instead (ordered ascending, descending, or equal). Adding support for this is easy as well:

```
func sortDescriptor<Value, Key>(
  key: @escaping (Value) -> Key,
  ascending: Bool = true,
  _ comparator: @escaping (Key) -> (Key) -> ComparisonResult)
  -> SortDescriptor<Value>
{
  return { lhs, rhs in
    let order: ComparisonResult = ascending
      ? .orderedAscending
      : .orderedDescending
    return comparator(key(lhs))(key(rhs)) == order
  }
}
```

This allows us to write sortByFirstName in a much shorter and clearer way:

```
let sortByFirstName: SortDescriptor<Person> =
  sortDescriptor(key: { $0.first }, String.localizedCaseInsensitiveCompare)
people.sorted(by: sortByFirstName)
/*
[Jo Smith (1970), Joanne smith (1985), Joanne smith (1970), Joe Smith (1970),
Joe Smyth (1970), Robert Jones (1970)]
*/
```

This SortDescriptor is just as expressive as its NSSortDescriptor variant, but it's type safe, and it doesn't rely on runtime programming.

Currently, we can only use a single SortDescriptor function to sort arrays. If you recall, we used the NSArray.sortedArray(using:) method to sort an array with a number of comparison operators. We could easily add a similar method to Array, or even to the Sequence protocol. However, we'd have to add it twice: once for the mutating variant, and once for the non-mutating variant of sort.

We take a different approach so that we don't have to write more extensions. Instead, we write a function that combines multiple sort descriptors into a single sort descriptor. It works just like the sortedArray(using:) method: first it tries the first descriptor and uses that comparison result. However, if the result is equal, it uses the second descriptor, and so on, until we run out of descriptors:

```
func combine<Value>
  (sortDescriptors: [SortDescriptor<Value>]) -> SortDescriptor<Value> {
  return { lhs, rhs in
    for areInIncreasingOrder in sortDescriptors {
      if areInIncreasingOrder(lhs,rhs) { return true }
      if areInIncreasingOrder(rhs,lhs) { return false }
    }
    return false
  }
}
```

Using our new sort descriptors, we can now finally replicate the initial example:

```
let combined: SortDescriptor<Person> = combine(
  sortDescriptors: [sortByLastName,sortByFirstName,sortByYear]
)
people.sorted(by: combined)
/*
[Robert Jones (1970), Jo Smith (1970), Joanne smith (1970), Joanne smith (1985),
```

Joe Smith (1970), Joe Smyth (1970)]
*/

We ended up with the same behavior and functionality as the Foundation version, but it's safer and a lot more idiomatic in Swift. Because the Swift version doesn't rely on runtime programming, the compiler can also optimize it much better. Additionally, we can use it with structs or non-Objective-C objects.

This approach of using functions as data — storing them in arrays and building those arrays at runtime — opens up a new level of dynamic behavior, and it's one way in which a statically typed compile-time-oriented language like Swift can still replicate some of the dynamic behavior of languages like Objective-C or Ruby.

We also saw the usefulness of writing functions that combine other functions. For example, our combine(sortDescriptors:) function took an array of sort descriptors and combined them into a single sort descriptor. This is a very powerful technique with many different applications.

Alternatively, we could even have written a custom operator to combine two sort functions:

```
infix operator <||> : LogicalDisjunctionPrecedence
func <||><A>(lhs: @escaping (A,A) -> Bool, rhs: @escaping (A,A) -> Bool)
  -> (A,A) -> Bool
{
  return { x,y in
    if lhs(x,y) { return true }
    if lhs(y,x) { return false }

    // Otherwise, they're the same, so we check for the second condition
    if rhs(x,y) { return true }

    return false
  }
}
```

Most of the time, writing a custom operator is a bad idea. Custom operators are often harder to read than functions are, because the name isn't explicit. However, they can be very powerful when used sparingly. The operator above allows us to rewrite our combined sort example, like so:

```
let combinedAlt = sortByLastName <||> sortByFirstName <||> sortByYear
```

```
people.sorted(by: combinedAlt)
/*
[Robert Jones (1970), Jo Smith (1970), Joanne smith (1970), Joanne smith (1985),
Joe Smith (1970), Joe Smyth (1970)]
*/
```

This reads very clearly and perhaps also expresses the code's intent more succinctly than the alternative, but *only after* you (and every other reader of the code) have ingrained the meaning of the operator. We prefer the combine(sortDescriptors:) function over the custom operator. It's clearer at the call site and ultimately makes the code more readable. Unless you're writing highly domain-specific code, a custom operator is probably overkill.

The Foundation version still has one functional advantage over our version: it can deal with optionals without having to write any more code. For example, if we'd make the last property on Person an optional string, we wouldn't have to change anything in the sorting code that uses NSSortDescriptor.

The function-based version requires some extra code. You know what comes next: once again, we write a function that takes a function and returns a function. We can take a regular comparing function such as localizedCaseInsensitiveCompare, which works on two strings, and turn it into a function that takes two optional strings. If both values are nil, they're equal. If the left-hand side is nil, but the right-hand isn't, they're ascending, and the other way around. Finally, if they're both non-nil, we can use the compare function to compare them:

```
func lift<A>(_ compare: @escaping (A) -> (A) -> ComparisonResult) -> (A?) -> (A?)
    -> ComparisonResult
{
    return { lhs in { rhs in
        switch (lhs, rhs) {
        case (nil, nil): return .orderedSame
        case (nil, _): return .orderedAscending
        case (_, nil): return .orderedDescending
        case let (l?, r?): return compare(l)(r)
        default: fatalError() // Impossible case
        }
    }}
}
```

This allows us to "lift" a regular comparison function into the domain of optionals, and it can be used together with our sortDescriptor function. If you recall the files array from before, sorting it by fileExtension got really ugly because we had to deal with optionals. However, with our new lift function, it's very clean again:

```
let lcic = lift(String.localizedCaseInsensitiveCompare)
let result = files.sorted(by: sortDescriptor(key: { $0.fileExtension }, lcic))
result // ["one", "file.c", "file.h", "test.h"]
```

> We can write a similar version of lift for functions that return a Bool. As we saw in the optionals chapter, the standard library no longer provides comparison operators like > for optionals. They were removed because using them can lead to surprising results if you're not careful. A boolean variant of lift allows you to easily take an existing operator and make it work for optionals when you need the functionality.

One drawback of the function-based approach is that functions are opaque. We can take an NSSortDescriptor and print it to the console, and we get some information about the sort descriptor: the key path, the selector name, and the sort order. Our function-based approach can't do this. For sort descriptors, this isn't a problem in practice. If it's important to have that information, we could wrap the functions in a struct or class and store additional debug information.

This approach has also given us a clean separation between the sorting method and the comparison method. The algorithm that Swift's sort uses is a hybrid of multiple sorting algorithms — as of this writing, it's an introsort (which is itself a hybrid of a quicksort and a heapsort), but it switches to an insertion sort for small collections to avoid the upfront startup cost of the more complex sort algorithms.

Introsort isn't a "stable" sort. That is, it doesn't necessarily maintain relative ordering of values that are otherwise equal according to the comparison function. But if you implemented a stable sort, the separation of the sort method from the comparison would allow you to swap it in easily:

```
people.stablySorted(by: combine(
  sortDescriptors: [sortByLastName, sortByFirstName, sortByYear]
))
```

Local Functions and Variable Capture

If we wanted to implement such a stable sort, one choice might be a merge sort. The merge sort algorithm is made up of two parts: a division into sublists of one element, followed by a merge of those lists. Often, it's nice to define merge as a separate function. But this leads to a problem — merge requires some temporary scratch storage:

```
extension Array where Element: Comparable {
  private mutating func merge(lo: Int, mi: Int, hi: Int) {
    var tmp: [Element] = []
    var i = lo, j = mi
    while i != mi && j != hi {
      if self[j] < self[i] {
        tmp.append(self[j])
        j += 1
      } else {
        tmp.append(self[i])
        i += 1
      }
    }

    tmp.append(contentsOf: self[i..<mi])
    tmp.append(contentsOf: self[j..<hi])
    replaceSubrange(lo..<hi, with: tmp)
  }

  mutating func mergeSortInPlaceInefficient() {
    let n = count
    var size = 1

    while size < n {
      for lo in stride(from: 0, to: n-size, by: size*2) {
        merge(lo: lo, mi: (lo+size), hi: Swift.min(lo+size*2,n))
      }
      size *= 2
    }
  }
}
```

Note: because Array has a method named min() defined, we need to use Swift.min. This tells the compiler to explicitly use the standard library's free function named min (instead of the method on Array).

Of course, we could allocate this storage externally and pass it in as a parameter, but this is a little ugly. It's also complicated by the fact that arrays are value types — passing in an array we created outside wouldn't help. There's an optimization that replaces inout parameters with references, but the documentation tells us specifically not to rely on that.

As another solution, we can define merge as an inner function and have it capture the storage defined in the outer function's scope:

```
extension Array where Element: Comparable {
  mutating func mergeSortInPlace() {
    // Define the temporary storage for use by all merges
    var tmp: [Element] = []
    // and make sure it's big enough
    tmp.reserveCapacity(count)

    func merge(lo: Int, mi: Int, hi: Int) {
      // Wipe the storage clean while retaining its capacity
      tmp.removeAll(keepingCapacity: true)

      // The same code as before
      var i = lo, j = mi
      while i != mi && j != hi {
        if self[j] < self[i] {
          tmp.append(self[j])
          j += 1
        } else {
          tmp.append(self[i])
          i += 1
        }
      }

      tmp.append(contentsOf: self[i..<mi])
      tmp.append(contentsOf: self[j..<hi])
      replaceSubrange(lo..<hi, with: tmp)
    }

    let n = count
    var size = 1
```

```
    while size < n {
      for lo in stride(from: 0, to: n-size, by: size*2) {
        merge(lo: lo, mi: (lo+size), hi: Swift.min(lo+size*2,n))
      }
      size *= 2
    }
  }
}
```

Since closures (including inner functions) capture variables by reference, every call to merge within a single call to mergeSortInPlace will share this storage. But it's still a local variable — separate concurrent calls to mergeSortInPlace will use separate instances. Using this technique can give a significant speed boost to the sort without needing major changes to the original version.

Functions as Delegates

Delegates. They're everywhere. Drummed into the heads of Objective-C (and Java) programmers is this message: use protocols (interfaces) for callbacks. You define a protocol, the delegate implements that protocol, and it registers itself as the delegate so that it gets callbacks.

If a delegate has a simple method, it can mechanically be replaced by a function. However, there are a number of tradeoffs to keep in mind.

Delegates, Foundation-Style

Let's start off by defining a delegate protocol in the same way that Foundation defines its protocols. Most programmers who come from Objective-C have written code like this many times over:

```
protocol AlertViewDelegate: class {
  func buttonTapped(atIndex: Int)
}
```

It's defined as a class-only protocol, because in our AlertView class, we want to have a weak reference to the delegate. This way, we don't have to worry about reference cycles. An AlertView will never strongly retain its delegate, so even if the delegate strongly retains the alert view, all is well. If the delegate is deinitialized, the delegate property will automatically become nil:

```
class AlertView {
  var buttons: [String]
  weak var delegate: AlertViewDelegate?

  init(buttons: [String] = ["OK", "Cancel"]) {
    self.buttons = buttons
  }

  func fire() {
    delegate?.buttonTapped(atIndex: 1)
  }
}
```

This pattern works really well when we're dealing with classes. For example, we could create a ViewController class that initializes the alert view and sets itself as the delegate. Because the delegate is marked as weak, we don't need to worry about reference cycles:

```
class ViewController: AlertViewDelegate {
  init() {
    let av = AlertView(buttons: ["OK", "Cancel"])
    av.delegate = self
  }

  func buttonTapped(atIndex index: Int) {
    print("Button tapped: \(index)")
  }
}
```

It's common practice to always mark delegates as weak. This makes it very easy to reason about the memory management. Classes that implement the delegate protocol don't have to worry about creating a reference cycle.

Sometimes we might want to have a delegate protocol that's implemented by a struct. With the current definition of AlertViewDelegate, this is impossible, because it's a class-only protocol.

Delegates That Work with Structs

We can loosen the definition of AlertViewDelegate by not making it a class-only protocol. Also, we'll mark the buttonTapped(atIndex:) method as mutating. This way, a struct can mutate itself when the method gets called:

```
protocol AlertViewDelegate {
  mutating func buttonTapped(atIndex: Int)
}
```

We also have to change our AlertView because the delegate property can no longer be weak:

```
class AlertView {
  var buttons: [String]
  var delegate: AlertViewDelegate?

  init(buttons: [String] = ["OK", "Cancel"]) {
    self.buttons = buttons
  }

  func fire() {
    delegate?.buttonTapped(atIndex: 1)
  }
}
```

If we assign an object to the delegate property, the object will be strongly referenced. Especially when working with delegates, the strong reference means there's a very high chance that we'll introduce a reference cycle at some point. However, we can use structs now. For example, we could create a struct that logs all button taps:

```
struct TapLogger: AlertViewDelegate {
  var taps: [Int] = []
  mutating func buttonTapped(atIndex index: Int) {
    taps.append(index)
  }
}
```

At first, it might seem like everything works well. We can create an alert view and a logger and connect the two. Alas, if we look at logger.taps after an event is fired, the array is still empty:

```
let av = AlertView()
```

```
var logger = TapLogger()
av.delegate = logger
av.fire()
logger.taps // []
```

When we assigned to av.delegate, we assigned a copy of the struct. So the taps aren't recorded in logger, but rather in av.delegate. Even worse, when we assign the value, we lose the information that it was a struct. To get the information back out, we need a conditional type cast:

```
if let theLogger = av.delegate as? TapLogger {
    print(theLogger.taps)
}
```

Clearly this approach doesn't work well. When using classes, it's easy to create reference cycles, and when using structs, the original value doesn't get mutated. In short: delegate protocols don't make much sense when using structs.

Functions Instead of Delegates

If the delegate protocol only has a single method defined, we can simply replace the delegate property with a property that stores the callback function directly. In our case, this could be an optional buttonTapped property, which is nil by default. Unfortunately, we can't specify an argument label for the button index:

```
class AlertView {
    var buttons: [String]
    var buttonTapped: ((Int) -> ())?

    init(buttons: [String] = ["OK", "Cancel"]) {
        self.buttons = buttons
    }

    func fire() {
        buttonTapped?(1)
    }
}
```

Just like before, we can create a logger struct and then create an alert view instance and a logger variable:

```
struct TapLogger {
  var taps: [Int] = []

  mutating func logTap(index: Int) {
    taps.append(index)
  }
}

let av = AlertView()
var logger = TapLogger()
```

However, we can't simply assign the logTap method to the buttonTapped property. The Swift compiler tells us that "partial application of a 'mutating' method is not allowed":

```
av.buttonTapped = logger.logTap // Error
```

In the code above, it's not clear what should happen in the assignment. Does the logger get copied? Or should buttonTapped mutate the original variable (i.e. logger gets captured)?

To make this work, we have to wrap the right-hand side of the assignment in a closure. This has the benefit of making it very clear that we're now capturing the original logger variable (not the value) and that we're mutating it:

```
av.buttonTapped = { logger.logTap(index: $0) }
```

As an additional benefit, the naming is now decoupled: the callback property is called buttonTapped, but the function that implements it is called logTap. Rather than a method, we could also specify an anonymous function:

```
av.buttonTapped = { print("Button \($0) was tapped") }
```

When working with classes and callbacks, there are some caveats. We create a Test class that has a buttonTapped method:

```
class Test {
  func buttonTapped(atIndex: Int) {
    print(atIndex)
  }
}

let test = Test()
```

We can assign the buttonTapped instance method of Test to our alert view:

av.buttonTapped = test.buttonTapped

However, the alert view now has a strong reference to the test object (through the closure). In the example above, there's no reference cycle, because test doesn't reference the alert view. However, if we consider the view controller example from before, we can see that it's very easy to create reference cycles this way. To avoid a strong reference, it's often necessary to use a closure with a capture list:

```
av.buttonTapped = { [weak test] index in
  test?.buttonTapped(atIndex: index)
}
```

This way, the alert view doesn't have a strong reference to test. If the object that test is referring to gets deinitialized before the closure gets called, it'll be nil inside the closure, and the buttonTapped method won't be called.

As we've seen, there are definite tradeoffs between protocols and callback functions. A protocol adds some verbosity, but a class-only protocol with a weak delegate removes the need to worry about introducing reference cycles.

Replacing the delegate with a function adds a lot of flexibility and allows you to use structs and anonymous functions. However, when dealing with classes, you need to be careful not to introduce a reference cycle.

Also, when you need multiple callback functions that are closely related (for example, providing the data for a table view), it can be helpful to keep them grouped together in a protocol rather than having individual callbacks. When using a protocol, a single type has to implement all the methods.

To unregister a delegate or a function callback, we can simply set it to nil. What about when our type stores an array of delegates or callbacks? With class-based delegates, we can simply remove an object from the delegate list. With callback functions, this isn't so simple; we'd need to add extra infrastructure for unregistering, because functions can't be compared.

inout Parameters and Mutating Methods

The "&" that we use at the front of an inout argument in Swift might give you the impression — especially if you have a C or C++ background — that inout parameters are essentially pass-by-reference. But they aren't. inout is pass-by-value-and-copy-back, *not* pass-by-reference. To quote the official Swift Programming Language book:

> An inout parameter has a value that is passed in to the function, is modified by the function, and is passed back out of the function to replace the original value.

In the chapter on structs and classes, we wrote about inout parameters, and we looked at the similarities between mutating methods and methods that take an inout parameter.

In order to understand what kind of expressions can be passed as an inout parameter, we need to make the distinction between lvalues and rvalues. An *lvalue* describes a memory location. An *rvalue* describes a value. For example, array[0] is an lvalue, as it describes the memory location of the first element in the array. 2 + 2 is an rvalue, as it describes the value 4.

For inout parameters, you can only pass lvalues, because it doesn't make sense to mutate an rvalue. When you're working with inout parameters in regular functions and methods, you need to be explicit about passing them in: every lvalue needs to be prefixed with an &. For example, when we call the increment function (which takes an inout Int), we can pass in a variable by prefixing it with an ampersand:

```
func increment(value: inout Int) {
  value += 1
}

var i = 0
increment(value: &i)
```

If we define a variable using let, we can't use it as an lvalue. This makes sense, because we're not allowed to mutate let variables; we can only use "mutable" lvalues:

```
let y: Int = 0
```

```
increment(value: &y) // Error
```

We can pass in many more things in addition to variables. For example, we can also pass in an array subscript if the array is defined using var:

```
var array = [0, 1, 2]
increment(value: &array[0])
array // [1, 1, 2]
```

In fact, this works with every subscript (including your own custom subscripts), as long as they both have a get and a set defined. Likewise, we can use properties as lvalues, but again, only if they have both get and set defined:

```
struct Point {
    var x: Int
    var y: Int
}
var point = Point(x: 0, y: 0)
increment(value: &point.x)
point // Point(x: 1, y: 0)
```

If a property is read-only (that is, only get is available), we can't use it as an inout parameter:

```
extension Point {
    var squaredDistance: Int {
        return x*x + y*y
    }
}
increment(value: &point.squaredDistance) // Error
```

Operators can also take an inout value, but for the sake of simplicity, they don't require the ampersand when called; we just specify the lvalue. For example, let's add back the postfix increment operator, which was removed in SE-0004:

```
postfix func ++(x: inout Int) {
    x += 1
}
point.x++
```

A mutating operator can even be combined with optional chaining. This works with regular optionals, like below, but also with dictionary subscripts:

```
var dictionary = ["one": 1]
```

```
dictionary["one"]?++
```

Note that, in case the key lookup returns nil, the ++ operator won't get executed.

The compiler may optimize an inout variable to pass-by-reference, rather than copying in and out. However, it's explicitly stated in the documentation that we shouldn't rely on this behavior.

Nested Functions and inout

You can use an inout parameter with nested functions, but Swift will make sure that your usage is safe. For example, you can define a nested function (either using func or using a closure expression) and safely mutate an inout parameter:

```
func incrementTenTimes(value: inout Int) {
  func inc() {
    value += 1
  }
  for _ in 0..<10 {
    inc()
  }
}
```

```
var x = 0
incrementTenTimes(value: &x)
x // 10
```

However, you're not allowed to let that inout parameter escape (we'll talk more about escaping functions at the end of this chapter):

```
func escapeIncrement(value: inout Int) -> () -> () {
  func inc() {
    value += 1
  }
  return inc
}
```

This makes sense, given that the inout value is copied back just before the function returns. If we could somehow modify it later, what should happen? Should the value get copied back at some point? What if the source no longer exists? Having the compiler verify this is critical for safety.

When & Doesn't Mean inout

Speaking of unsafe functions, you should be aware of the other meaning of &: converting a function argument to an unsafe pointer.

If a function takes an UnsafeMutablePointer as a parameter, then you can pass a var into it using &, similar to an inout argument. But here you *really are* passing by reference — by pointer in fact.

Here's increment, written to take an unsafe mutable pointer instead of an inout:

```
func incref(pointer: UnsafeMutablePointer<Int>) -> () -> Int {
  // Store a copy of the pointer in a closure
  return {
    pointer.pointee += 1
    return pointer.pointee
  }
}
```

As we'll discuss in later chapters, Swift arrays implicitly decay to pointers to make C interoperability nice and painless. Now, suppose you pass in an array that goes out of scope before you call the resulting function:

```
let fun: () -> Int
do {
  var array = [0]
  fun = incref(pointer: &array)
}
fun()
```

This opens up a whole exciting world of undefined behavior. In testing, the above code printed different values on each run: sometimes 0, sometimes 1, sometimes 140362397107840 — and sometimes it produced a runtime crash.

The moral here is: know what you're passing in to. When appending an &, you could be invoking nice safe Swift inout semantics, or you could be casting your poor variable into the brutal world of unsafe pointers. When dealing with unsafe pointers, be very careful about the lifetime of variables. We'll go into more detail on this in the chapter on interoperability.

Properties and Subscripts

There are two special kinds of methods that differ from regular methods: computed properties and subscripts. A computed property looks like a regular property, but it doesn't use any memory to store its value. Instead, the value is computed on the fly every time the property is accessed. A computed property is really just a method with unusual defining and calling conventions.

Let's look at the various ways to define properties. We'll start with a struct that represents a GPS track. It stores all the recorded points in a stored property called record:

```
struct GPSTrack {
    var record: [(CLLocation, Date)] = []
}
```

We could also have defined record using let instead of var, in which case it'd be a constant stored property and couldn't be mutated anymore.

If we want to make the record property available as read-only to the outside, but read-write internally, we can use the private(set) or fileprivate(set) modifiers:

```
struct GPSTrack {
    private(set) var record: [(CLLocation, Date)] = []
}
```

To access all the dates in a GPS track, we create a computed property:

```
extension GPSTrack {
    /// Returns all the dates for the GPS track.
    /// - Complexity: O(*n*), where *n* is the number of points recorded.
    var dates: [Date] {
        return record.map { $0.1 }
    }
}
```

Because we didn't specify a setter, the dates property is read-only. The result isn't cached; each time you access the dates property, it computes the result. The Swift API Design Guidelines recommend that you document the complexity of every computed property that isn't $O(1)$, because callers might assume that computing a property takes constant time.

Lazy Stored Properties

Initializing a value lazily is such a common pattern that Swift has a special lazy keyword to define a lazy property. Note that a lazy property is automatically mutating and therefore must be declared as var. The lazy modifier is a very specific form of memoization.

For example, if we have a view controller that displays a GPSTrack, we might want to have a preview image of the track. By making the property for that lazy, we can defer the expensive generation of the image until the property is accessed for the first time:

```
class GPSTrackViewController: UIViewController {
  var track: GPSTrack = GPSTrack()

  lazy var preview: UIImage = {
    for point in self.track.record {
      // Do some expensive computation
    }
    return UIImage()
  }()
}
```

Notice how we defined the lazy property: it's a closure expression that returns the value we want to store — in our case, an image. When the property is first accessed, the closure is executed (note the parentheses at the end), and its return value is stored in the property. This is a common pattern for lazy properties that require more than a one-liner to be initialized.

Because a lazy variable needs storage, we're required to define the lazy property in the definition of GPSTrackViewController. Unlike computed properties, stored properties and stored lazy properties can't be defined in an extension. Also, we're required to use self. inside the closure expression when we want to access instance members (in this case, we need to write self.track).

If the track property changes, the preview won't automatically get invalidated. Let's look at an even simpler example to see what's going on. We have a Point struct, and we store distanceFromOrigin as a lazy computed property:

```
struct Point {
  var x: Double = 0
  var y: Double = 0
  lazy var distanceFromOrigin: Double = self.x*self.x + self.y*self.y
```

```
init(x: Double, y: Double) {
  self.x = x
  self.y = y
 }
}
```

When we create a point, we can access the distanceFromOrigin property, and it'll compute the value and store it for reuse. However, if we then change the x value, this won't be reflected in distanceFromOrigin:

```
var point = Point(x: 3, y: 4)
point.distanceFromOrigin // 25.0
point.x += 10
point.distanceFromOrigin // 25.0
```

It's important to be aware of this. One way around it would be to recompute distanceFromOrigin in the didSet property observers of x and y, but then distanceFromOrigin isn't really lazy anymore: it'll get computed each time x or y changes. Of course, in this example, the solution is easy: we should have made distanceFromOrigin a regular (non-lazy) computed property from the beginning.

As we saw in the chapter on structs and classes, we can also implement the willSet and didSet callbacks for properties and variables. These get called before and after the setter, respectively. One useful case is when working with Interface Builder: we can implement didSet to know when an IBOutlet gets connected, and then we can configure our views there. For example, if we want to set a label's text color once it's available, we can do the following:

```
class SettingsController: UIViewController {
  @IBOutlet weak var label: UILabel? {
    didSet {
      label?.textColor = .black
    }
  }
}
```

Overloading Subscripts with Different Arguments

We've already seen subscripts in Swift. For example, we can perform a dictionary lookup like so: dictionary[key]. These subscripts are very much a hybrid between functions and computed properties, with their own special syntax. Like functions, they take arguments. Like computed properties, they can be either read-only (using get) or read-write (using get set). Just like normal functions, we can overload them by providing multiple variants with different types — something that isn't possible with properties. For example, arrays have two subscripts by default — one to access a single element, and one to get at a slice:

```
let fibs = [0, 1, 1, 2, 3, 5]
let first = fibs[0] // 0
fibs[1..<3] // [1, 1]
```

We can add subscripting support to our own types, and we can also extend existing types with new subscript overloads. As an example, let's define a Collection subscript that takes a *half-bounded* interval, i.e. a range where there's only one end specified (either the lowerBound or the upperBound).

In Swift, the Range type represents bounded intervals: every Range has a lower bound and an upper bound. As we demonstrated above, we can use this to find a subsequence of an array (or to be more precise: of any Collection). We'll extend Collection to support half-bounded intervals using a similar operator. Using suffix(from:) and prefix(upTo:), we can already access these subsequences.

To represent half-bounded intervals, we'll create two new structs:

```
struct RangeStart<I> { let start: I }
struct RangeEnd<I> { let end: I }
```

We can define two convenience operators to write these intervals. These are prefix and postfix operators, and they only have one operand. This will allow us to write RangeStart(x) as x..< and RangeEnd(x) as ..<x:

```
postfix operator ..<
postfix func ..<<I>(lhs: I) -> RangeStart<I> {
  return RangeStart(start: lhs)
}

prefix operator ..<
prefix func ..<<I>(rhs: I) -> RangeEnd<I> {
  return RangeEnd(end: rhs)
}
```

Finally, we can extend Collection to support half-bounded ranges by adding two new subscripts:

```
extension Collection {
  subscript(r: RangeStart<Index>) -> SubSequence {
    return suffix(from: r.start)
  }
  subscript(r: RangeEnd<Index>) -> SubSequence {
    return prefix(upTo: r.end)
  }
}
```

This allows us to write half-bounded subscripts like so:

```
fibs[2..<] // [1, 2, 3, 5]
```

Using the suffix(from:) and prefix(upTo:) methods directly would save a lot of effort, and adding a custom operator for this is probably overkill. However, it's a nice example of prefix and postfix operators and custom subscripts.

Advanced Subscripts

Now that we've seen how to add simple subscripts, we can take things a bit further. Instead of taking a single parameter, subscripts can also take more than one parameter (just like functions). The following extension allows for dictionary lookup (and updating) with a default value. During a lookup, when the key isn't present, we return the default value (instead of nil, as the default dictionary subscript would). In the setter, we ignore it (because newValue isn't optional):

```
extension Dictionary {
  subscript(key: Key, or defaultValue: Value) -> Value {
    get {
      return self[key] ?? defaultValue
    }
    set(newValue) {
      self[key] = newValue
    }
  }
}
```

This allows us to write a very short computed property for the frequencies in a sequence. We start with an empty dictionary, and for every element we encounter, we increment the frequency. If the element wasn't present in the dictionary before, the default value of 0 is returned during lookup:

```
extension Sequence where Iterator.Element: Hashable {
    var frequencies: [Iterator.Element: Int] {
        var result: [Iterator.Element: Int] = [:]
        for x in self {
            result[x, or: 0] += 1
        }
        return result
    }
}

"hello".characters.frequencies // ["e": 1, "o": 1, "l": 2, "h": 1]
```

Automatic Closures

We're all familiar with the short-circuiting of the && operator. It takes two operands: first, the left operand is evaluated. Only if the left operand evaluates to true is the right operand evaluated. After all, if the left operand evaluates to false, there's no way the entire expression can evaluate to true. Therefore, we can short-circuit and we don't have to evaluate the right operand. For example, if we want to check if a condition holds for the first element of an array, we could write the following code:

```
let evens = [2,4,6]
if !evens.isEmpty && evens[0] > 10 {
    // Perform some work
}
```

In the snippet above, we rely on short-circuiting: the array lookup happens only if the first condition holds. Without short-circuiting, this code would crash on an empty array.

In almost all languages, short-circuiting is built into the language for the && and || operators. However, it's often not possible to define your own operators or functions that have short-circuiting. If a language supports closures, we can fake short-circuiting by providing a closure instead of a value. For example, let's say we wanted to define an and function in Swift with the same behavior as the && operator:

```
func and(_ l: Bool, _ r: () -> Bool) -> Bool {
```

```
  guard l else { return false }
  return r()
}
```

The function above first checks the value of l and returns false if l evaluates to false. Only if l is true does it return the value that comes out of the closure r. Using it is a little bit uglier than using the && operator, though, because the right operand now has to be a function:

```
if and(!evens.isEmpty, { evens[0] > 10 }) {
  // Perform some work
}
```

Swift has a nice feature to make this prettier. We can use the @autoclosure attribute to automatically create a closure around an argument. The definition of and is almost the same as above, except for the added @autoclosure annotation:

```
func and(_ l: Bool, _ r: @autoclosure () -> Bool) -> Bool {
  guard l else { return false }
  return r()
}
```

However, the usage of and is now much simpler, as we don't need to wrap the second parameter in a closure. Instead, we can just call it as if it took a regular Bool parameter:

```
if and(!evens.isEmpty, evens[0] > 10) {
  // Perform some work
}
```

This allows us to define our own functions and operators with short-circuiting behavior. For example, operators like ?? and !? (as defined in the chapter on optionals) are now straightforward to write. In the standard library, functions like assert and fatalError also use autoclosures in order to only evaluate the arguments when really needed. By deferring the evaluation of assertion conditions from the call sites to the body of the assert function, these potentially expensive operations can be stripped completely in optimized builds where they're not needed.

Autoclosures can also come in handy when writing logging functions. For example, here's how you could write your own log function, which only evaluates the log message if the condition is true:

```
func log(condition: Bool,
      message: @autoclosure () -> (String),
      file: String = #file, line function: String = #function, line: Int = #line) {
   if condition { return }
   print("myAssert failed: \(message()), \(file):\(function) (line \(line))")
}

log(condition: true, message: "This is a test")
```

The log function also uses the debugging identifiers #file, #function, and #line. They're especially useful when used as a default argument to a function, because they'll get the values of the filename, function name, and line number at the call site.

The @escaping Annotation

As we saw in the previous chapter, we need to be careful about memory when dealing with functions. Recall the capture list example, where we needed to mark view as weak in order to prevent a reference cycle:

```
window?.onRotate = { [weak view] in
   print("We now also need to update the view: \(view)")
}
```

However, we never marked anything as weak when we used functions like map. Since map is executed synchronously and the closure isn't referenced anywhere, this isn't necessary, because no reference cycle will be created. The difference between the closure we store in onRotate and the closure we pass to map is that the first closure *escapes*.

A closure that's stored somewhere to be called later (for example, after a function returns) is said to be *escaping*. The closure that gets passed to map only gets used directly within map. This means that the compiler doesn't need to change the reference count of the captured variables.

In Swift 3, closures are non-escaping by default. If you want to store a closure for later use, you need to mark the closure argument as @escaping. The compiler will verify this: unless you mark the closure argument as @escaping, it won't allow you to store the closure (or return it to the caller, for example). In the sort descriptors example, there were multiple function parameters that required the @escaping attribute:

```
func sortDescriptor<Value, Key>(
    key: @escaping (Value) -> Key,
    _ areInIncreasingOrder: @escaping (Key, Key) -> Bool)
    -> SortDescriptor<Value>
{
    return { areInIncreasingOrder(key($0), key($1)) }
}
```

> Before Swift 3, it was the other way around: you had the option to mark a closure as @noescape, and escaping was the default. The behavior in Swift 3 is better because it's safe by default: a function argument now needs to be explicitly annotated to signal the potential for reference cycles. The @escaping annotation serves as a warning to the developer using the function. Non-escaping closures can also be optimized much better by the compiler, making the fast path the norm you have to explicitly deviate from if necessary.

Note that the non-escaping-by-default rule only applies to function types in *immediate parameter position*. This means stored properties that have a function type are always escaping (which makes sense). Surprisingly, the same is true for closures that *are* used as parameters, but are wrapped in some other type, such as a tuple or an optional. Since the closure is no longer an *immediate* parameter in this case, it automatically becomes escaping. As a consequence, you can't write a function that takes a function argument where the parameter is both optional and non-escaping. In many situations, you can avoid making the argument optional by prodiving a default value for the closure. If that's not possible, a workaround is to use overloading to write two variants of the function, one with an optional (escaping) function parameter and one with a non-optional, non-escaping parameter:

```
func transform(_ input: Int, with f: ((Int) -> Int)?) -> Int {
    print("Using optional overload")
    guard let f = f else { return input }
    return f(input)
}
```

```
func transform(_ input: Int, with f: (Int) -> Int) -> Int {
    print("Using non-optional overload")
    return f(input)
}
```

This way, calling the function with a nil argument (or a variable of optional type) will use the optional variant, whereas passing a literal closure expression will invoke the non-escaping, non-optional overload.

```
transform(10, with: nil) // Using optional overload
transform(10) { $0 * $0 } // Using non-optional overload
```

Conclusion

Functions are first-class objects in Swift. Treating functions as data can make our code more flexible. We've seen how we can replace runtime programming with simple functions. We've compared different ways to implement delegates. We've looked at mutating functions and inout parameters, as well as computed properties (which really are a special kind of function). Finally, we've discussed the @autoclosure and @escaping attributes. In the chapters on generics and protocols, we'll come up with more ways to use functions in Swift to gain even more flexibility.

Strings

No More Fixed Width

Things used to be so simple. ASCII strings were a sequence of integers between 0 and 127. If you stored them in an 8-bit byte, you even had a bit to spare! Since every character was of a fixed size, ASCII strings could be random access.

But this is only if you were writing in English for a U.S. audience; other countries and languages needed other characters (even English-speaking Britain needed a £ sign). Most of them needed more characters than would fit into seven bits. ISO/IEC 8859 takes the extra bit and defines 16 different encodings above the ASCII range, such as Part 1 (ISO/IEC 8859-1, aka Latin-1), covering several Western European languages; and Part 5, covering languages that use the Cyrillic alphabet.

But this is still limiting. If you want use ISO/IEC 8859 to write in Turkish about Ancient Greek, you're out of luck, since you'd need to pick either Part 7 (Latin/Greek) or Part 9 (Turkish). And eight bits is still not enough to encode many languages. For example, Part 6 (Latin/Arabic) doesn't include the characters needed to write Arabic-script languages such as Urdu or Persian. Meanwhile, Vietnamese — which is based on the Latin alphabet but with a large number of diacritic combinations — only fits into eight bits by replacing a handful of ASCII characters from the lower half. And this isn't even an option for other East Asian languages.

When you run out of room with a fixed-width encoding, you have a choice: either increase the size, or switch to variable-width encoding. Initially, Unicode was defined as a 2-byte fixed-width format, now called UCS-2. This was before reality set in, and it was accepted that even two bytes would not be sufficient, while four would be horribly inefficient for most purposes.

So today, Unicode is a variable-width format, and it's variable in two different senses: in the combining of code units into code points, and in the combining of code points into characters.

Unicode data can be encoded with many different widths of "code unit," most commonly 8 (UTF-8) or 16 (UTF-16) bits. UTF-8 has the added benefit of being backwardly compatible with 8-bit ASCII — something that's helped it overtake ASCII as the most popular encoding on the web.

A "code point" in Unicode is a single value in the Unicode code space with a possible value from 0 to 0x10FFFF. Only about 128,000 of the 1.1 million code points possible are currently in use, so there's a lot of room for more emoji. A given code point might take a single code unit if you're using UTF-32, or it might take between one and four if you're using UTF-8. The first 256 Unicode code points match the characters found in Latin-1.

Unicode "scalars" are another unit. They're all the code points *except* the "surrogate" code points, i.e. the code points used for the leading and trailing codes that indicate pairs in UTF-16 encoding. Scalars are represented in Swift string literals as "\u{xxxx}", where xxxx represents hex digits. So the euro sign, €, can be written in Swift as "\u{20AC}".

But even when encoded using 32-bit code units, what a user might consider "a single character" — as displayed on the screen — might require multiple code points composed together. Most string manipulation code exhibits a certain level of denial about Unicode's variable-width nature. This can lead to some unpleasant bugs.

Swift's string implementation goes to heroic efforts to be as Unicode-correct as possible, or at least when it's not, to make sure you acknowledge the fact. This comes at a price. String in Swift isn't a collection. Instead, it's a type that presents multiple ways of viewing the string: as a collection of Character values; or as a collection of UTF-8, UTF-16, or Unicode scalars.

The Swift Character type is unlike the other views, in that it can encode an arbitrary number of code points, composed together into a single "grapheme cluster." We'll see some examples of this shortly.

For all but the UTF-16 view, these views do *not* support random access, i.e. measuring the distance between two indices or advancing an index by some number of steps is generally not an $O(1)$ operation. Even the UTF-16 view is only random access when you import Foundation (more on that below). Some of the views can also be slower than others when performing heavy text processing. In this chapter, we'll look at the reasons behind this, as well as some techniques for dealing with both functionality and performance.

Grapheme Clusters and Canonical Equivalence

A quick way to see the difference between Swift.String and NSString in handling Unicode data is to look at the two different ways to write é. Unicode defines U+00E9, "LATIN SMALL LETTER E WITH ACUTE," as a single value. But you can also write it as the plain letter e, followed by U+0301,

"COMBINING ACUTE ACCENT." In both cases, what's displayed is é, and a user probably has a reasonable expectation that two strings displayed as "résumé" would not only be equal to each other but also have a "length" of six characters, no matter which technique was used to produce the é in either one. They would be what the Unicode specification describes as "canonically equivalent."

And in Swift, this is exactly the behavior you get:

```
let single = "Pok\u{00E9}mon"
let double = "Pok\u{0065}\u{0301}mon"
```

They both display identically:

```
(single, double) // ("Pokémon", "Pokémon")
```

And both have the same character count:

```
single.characters.count // 7
double.characters.count // 7
```

Only if you drop down to a view of the underlying representation can you see that they're different:

```
single.utf16.count // 7
double.utf16.count // 8
```

Contrast this with NSString: the two strings aren't equal, and the length property — which many programmers probably use to count the number of characters to be displayed on the screen — gives different results:

```
let nssingle = NSString(characters: [0x0065,0x0301], length: 2)
nssingle.length // 2
let nsdouble = NSString(characters: [0x00e9], length: 1)
nsdouble.length // 1
nssingle == nsdouble // false
```

Here, == is defined as the version for comparing two NSObjects:

```
extension NSObject: Equatable {
  static func ==(lhs: NSObject, rhs: NSObject) -> Bool {
    return lhs.isEqual(rhs)
  }
}
```

In the case of NSString, this will do a literal comparison, rather than one accounting for equivalent but differently composed characters. NSString.isEqualToString will do the same, and most string APIs in other languages work this way too. If you really want to perform a canonical comparison, you must use NSString.compare. Didn't know that? Enjoy your future undiagnosable bugs and grumpy international user base.

Of course, there's one big benefit to just comparing code units: it's a lot faster! This is an effect that can still be achieved with Swift strings, via the utf16 view:

```
single.utf16.elementsEqual(double.utf16) // false
```

Why does Unicode support multiple representations at all? The existence of precomposed characters is what enables the opening range of Unicode code points to be compatible with Latin-1, which already had characters like é and ñ. While they might be a pain to deal with, it makes conversion between the two quick and simple.

Ditching them wouldn't have helped, because composition doesn't just stop at pairs; you can compose more than one diacritic together. For example, Yoruba has the character ´, which could be written three different ways: by composing ó with a dot, or by composing o̩ with an acute, or by composing o with both an acute and a dot. And for that last one, the two diacritics can be in either order! So these are all equal:

```
let chars: [Character] = [
  "\u{1ECD}\u{300}",    // □
  "\u{F2}\u{323}",      // □
  "\u{6F}\u{323}\u{300}", // □
  "\u{6F}\u{300}\u{323}" // □
]
chars.dropFirst().all { $0 == chars.first } // true
```

(The all method checks if the condition is true for all elements in a sequence and is defined in the chapter on built-in collections.)

In fact, some diacritics can be added ad infinitum:

```
let zalgo = "s̸o̤̓ͤ̄o̤̽n̦̈́"
```

In the above, zalgo.characters.count returns 4, while zalgo.utf16.count returns 36. And if your code doesn't work correctly with Internet memes, then what good is it, really?

Strings containing emoji can also be a little surprising. For example, a row of emoji flags is considered a single character:

```
let flags = "🇸🇪🇬🇧"
flags.characters.count // 1
// The scalars are the underlying ISO country codes:
flags.unicodeScalars.map { String($0) }.joined(separator: ",")
// N ,L ,G ,B
```

On the other hand, "👋".characters.count returns 2 (one for the generic character, one for the skin tone), and "👨‍👨‍👧‍👦".characters.count returns 4 in Swift 3.0, as the multi-person groupings are composed from individual member emoji joined with the zero-width joiner:

```
"👨\u{200D}👩\u{200D}👧\u{200D}👦" == "👨‍👩‍👧‍👦"
```

While counting the concatenated flags as one character is a weird but expected behavior, these emoji should really be treated as a single character. Expect these results to change as soon as Swift updates its rules for grapheme cluster boundaries to Unicode 9.0, which was released in June 2016.

Strings and Collections

Strings in Swift have an Index associated type, startIndex and endIndex properties, a subscript that takes the index to fetch a specific character, and an index(after:) method that advances an index by one.

This means that String meets all the criteria needed to qualify as conforming to Collection. Yet String is *not* a collection. You can't use it with for...in, nor does it inherit all the protocol extensions of Collection or Sequence.

In theory, you can change this yourself by extending String:

```
extension String: Collection {
    // Nothing needed here – it already has the necessary implementations
}

var greeting = "Hello, world!"
```

```
greeting.dropFirst(7) // "world!"
```

However, this is probably not wise. Strings aren't collections for a reason —
this isn't just because the Swift team forgot. When Swift 2.0 introduced
protocol extensions, this had the huge benefit of granting all collections and
sequences method-like access to dozens of useful algorithms. But this also led
to some concerns that collection-processing algorithms presenting themselves
as methods on strings would give the implicit indication that such methods
are completely safe and Unicode-correct, which wouldn't necessarily be true.
Even though Character does its best to present combining character sequences
as single values, as seen above, there are still some cases where processing a
string character by character can result in incorrect results.

To this end, the collection-of-characters view of strings was moved to a
property, characters, which put it on a footing similar to the other collection
views: unicodeScalars, utf8, and utf16. Picking a specific view prompts you to
acknowledge that you're moving into a "collection-processing" mode and that
you should consider the consequences of the algorithm you're about to run.

CharacterView, however, has a special place among those views. String.Index is
actually just a type alias for CharacterView.Index. This means that once you've
found an index into the character view, you can then index directly into the
string with it.

But for reasons that should be clear from the examples in the previous section,
the characters view isn't a random-access collection. How could it be, when
knowing where the nth character of a particular string is involves evaluating
just how many code points precede that character?

For this reason, CharacterView conforms only to BidirectionalCollection. You
can start at either end of the string, moving forward or backward, and the code
will look at the composition of the adjacent characters and skip over the
correct number of bytes. However, you need to iterate up and down one
character at a time.

Like all collection indices, string indices conform to Comparable. You might
not know how many characters lie between two indices, but you do at least
know that one lies before the other.

You can automate iterating over multiple characters in one go via the
index(_:offsetBy:) method:

```
let s = "abcdef"
// Advance 5 from the start
let idx = s.index(s.startIndex, offsetBy: 5)
s[idx] // f
```

If there's a risk of advancing past the end of the string, you can add a limitedBy: parameter. The method returns nil if it hits the limit before reaching the target index:

```
let safeIdx = s.index(s.startIndex, offsetBy: 400, limitedBy: s.endIndex)
safeIdx // nil
```

This behavior is new in Swift 3.0. The corresponding method in Swift 2.2, advancedBy(_:limit:), didn't differentiate between hitting the limit and going beyond it — it returned the end value in both situations. By returning an optional, the new API is more expressive.

Now, you might look at this and think, "I know! I can use this to give strings integer subscripting!" So you might do something like this:

```
extension String {
  subscript(idx: Int) -> Character {
    guard let strIdx = index(startIndex, offsetBy: idx, limitedBy: endIndex)
      else { fatalError("String index out of bounds") }
    return self[strIdx]
  }
}
s[5] // returns "f"
```

However, just as is the case with extending String to make it a collection, this kind of extension is best avoided. You might otherwise be tempted to start writing code like this:

```
for i in 0..<5 {
  print(s[i])
}
```

As simple as this code looks, it's horribly inefficient. Every time s is accessed with an integer, an $O(n)$ function to advance its starting index is run. Running a linear loop inside another linear loop means this for loop is accidentally $O(n^2)$ — as the length of the string increases, the time this loop takes increases quadratically.

To someone used to dealing with fixed-width characters, this seems challenging at first — how will you navigate without integer indices? And indeed, some seemingly simple tasks like extracting the first four characters of a string can turn into monstrosities like this one:

```
s[s.startIndex..<s.index(s.startIndex, offsetBy: 4)] // abcd
```

But thankfully, String providing access to characters via a collection also means you have several helpful techniques at your disposal. Many of the methods that operate on Array also work on String.characters. Using the prefix method, the same thing looks much clearer (note that this returns a CharacterView; to convert it back into a String, we need to wrap it in a String.init):

```
String(s.characters.prefix(4)) // abcd
```

Iterating over characters in a string is easy without integer indices; just use a for loop. If you want to number each character in turn, use enumerated():

```
for (i, c) in "hello".characters.enumerated() {
   print("\(i): \(c)")
}
```

Or say you want to find a specific character. In that case, you can use index(of:):

```
var hello = "Hello!"
if let idx = hello.characters.index(of: "!") {
   hello.insert(contentsOf: ", world".characters, at: idx)
}
hello // Hello, world!
```

Note here that while the index was found using characters.index(of:), the insert(contentsOf:) method is called directly on the string, because String.Index is just an alias for Character.Index. The insert(contentsOf:) method inserts another collection of the same element type (e.g. Character for strings) after a given index. This doesn't have to be another String; you could insert an array of characters into a string just as easily.

Just like Array, String meets all the criteria to conform to RangeReplaceableCollection — but again, it doesn't conform to it. You could add the conformance manually, but we once more advise against it because it falsely implies that all collection operations are Unicode-safe in every situation:

```
extension String: RangeReplaceableCollection { }

if let comma = greeting.index(of: ",") {
  print(greeting[greeting.startIndex..<comma])
  greeting.replaceSubrange(greeting.startIndex..<greeting.endIndex,
    with: "How about some original example strings?")
}
```

One collection-like feature strings do *not* provide is that of MutableCollection. This protocol adds one feature to a collection — that of the single-element subscript set — in addition to get. This isn't to say strings aren't mutable — they have several mutating methods. But what you can't do is replace a single character using the subscript operator. The reason comes back to variable-length characters. Most people can probably intuit that a single-element subscript update would happen in constant time, as it does for Array. But since a character in a string may be of variable width, updating a single character could take linear time in proportion to the length of the string, because changing the width of a single element might require shuffling all the later elements up or down in memory. Moreover, indices that come after the replaced index would become invalid through the shuffling, which is equally unintuitive. For these reasons, you have to use replaceSubrange, even if the range you pass in is only a single element.

Strings and Slicing

A good sign that a collection function will work well with strings is if the result is a SubSequence of the input. Performing slicing operations on arrays is a bit awkward, as the value you get back isn't an Array, but rather an ArraySlice. This makes writing recursive functions that slice up their input especially painful.

String's collection views have no such trouble. They define their SubSequence to be an instance of Self, so the generic functions that take a sliceable type and return a subsequence work very well with strings. For example, world here will be of type String.CharacterView:

```
let world = "Hello, world!".characters.suffix(6).dropLast()
String(world) // world
```

split, which returns an array of subsequences, is also useful for string processing. It's defined like so:

```
extension Collection {
  func split(maxSplits: Int = default,
    omittingEmptySubsequences: Bool = default,
    whereSeparator isSeparator: (Self.Iterator.Element) throws -> Bool)
    rethrows -> [AnySequence<Self.Iterator.Element>]
}
```

You can use its simplest form like this:

```
let commaSeparatedArray = "a,b,c".characters.split { $0 == "," }
commaSeparatedArray.map(String.init) // ["a", "b", "c"]
```

This can serve a function similar to the components(separatedBy:) method
String inherits from NSString, but with added configurations for whether or
not to drop empty components. But since it takes a closure, it can do more
than just compare characters. Here's an example of a primitive word wrap,
where the closure captures a count of the length of the line thus far:

```
extension String {
  func wrapped(after: Int = 70) -> String {
    var i = 0
    let lines = self.characters.split(omittingEmptySubsequences: false) {
      character in
      switch character {
      case "\n",
        " " where i >= after:
        i = 0
        return true
      default:
        i += 1
        return false
      }
    }.map(String.init)
    return lines.joined(separator: "\n")
  }
}
```

```
let paragraph = "The quick brown fox jumped over the lazy dog."
paragraph.wrapped(after: 15)
/*
The quick brown
fox jumped over
the lazy dog.
*/
```

The map on the end of the split is necessary because we want an array of String, not an array of String.CharacterView.

That said, chances are that you'll want to split things by character most of the time, so you might find it convenient to use the variant of split that takes a single separator:

```
extension Collection where Iterator.Element: Equatable {
  public func split(separator: Self.Iterator.Element,
    maxSplits: Int = default,
    omittingEmptySubsequences: Bool = default)
    -> [Self.SubSequence]
}
```

```
"1,2,3".characters.split(separator: ",").map(String.init) // ["1", "2", "3"]
```

Or, consider writing a version that takes a sequence of multiple separators:

```
extension Collection where Iterator.Element: Equatable {
  func split<S: Sequence>(separators: S) -> [SubSequence]
    where Iterator.Element == S.Iterator.Element
  {
    return split { separators.contains($0) }
  }
}
```

This way, you can write the following:

```
"Hello, world!".characters.split(separators: ",! ".characters).map(String.init)
// ["Hello", "world"]
```

A Simple Regular Expression Matcher

To demonstrate how useful it is that string slices are also strings, we'll implement a simple regular expression matcher based on a similar matcher written in C in Brian W. Kernighan and Rob Pike's *The Practice of Programming*. The original code, while beautifully compact, made extensive use of C pointers, so it often doesn't translate well to other languages. But with Swift, through use of optionals and slicing, you can almost match the C version in simplicity.

First, let's define a basic regular expression type:

```swift
/// A simple regular expression type, supporting ^ and $ anchors,
/// and matching with . and *
public struct Regex {
  fileprivate let regexp: String

  /// Construct from a regular expression String
  public init(_ regexp: String) {
    self.regexp = regexp
  }
}
```

Since this regular expression's functionality is going to be so simple, it's not really possible to create an "invalid" regular expression with its initializer. If the expression support were more complex (for example, supporting multi-character matching with []), you'd possibly want to give it a failable initializer.

Next, we extend Regex to support a match function, which takes a string and returns true if it matches the expression:

```swift
extension Regex {
  /// Returns true if the string argument matches the expression.
  public func match(_ text: String) -> Bool {

    // If the regex starts with ^, then it can only match the
    // start of the input
    if regexp.characters.first == "^" {
      return Regex.matchHere(regexp: regexp.characters.dropFirst(),
        text: text.characters)
    }

    // Otherwise, search for a match at every point in the input
    // until one is found
    var idx = text.startIndex
    while true {
      if Regex.matchHere(regexp: regexp.characters,
        text: text.characters.suffix(from: idx))
      {
        return true
      }
      guard idx != text.endIndex else { break }
      text.characters.formIndex(after: &idx)
    }

    return false
```

```
    }
}
```

The matching function doesn't do much except iterate over every possible substring of the input, from the start to the end, checking if it matches the regular expression from that point on. But if the regular expression starts with a ^, then it need only match from the start of the text.

matchHere is where most of the regular expression processing logic lies:

```
extension Regex {
  /// Match a regular expression string at the beginning of text.
  fileprivate static func matchHere(
    regexp: String.CharacterView, text: String.CharacterView) -> Bool
  {
    // Empty regexprs match everything
    if regexp.isEmpty {
      return true
    }

    // Any character followed by * requires a call to matchStar
    if let c = regexp.first, regexp.dropFirst().first == "*" {
      return matchStar(character: c, regexp: regexp.dropFirst(2), text: text)
    }

    // If this is the last regex character and it's $, then it's a match iff the
    // remaining text is also empty
    if regexp.first == "$" && regexp.dropFirst().isEmpty {
      return text.isEmpty
    }

    // If one character matches, drop one from the input and the regex
    // and keep matching
    if let tc = text.first, let rc = regexp.first, rc == "." || tc == rc {
      return matchHere(regexp: regexp.dropFirst(), text: text.dropFirst())
    }

    // If none of the above, no match
    return false
  }

  /// Search for zero or more `c`'s at beginning of text, followed by the
  /// remainder of the regular expression.
  fileprivate static func matchStar
    (character c: Character, regexp: String.CharacterView,
```

```
      text: String.CharacterView)
    -> Bool
  {
    var idx = text.startIndex
    while true {  // a * matches zero or more instances
      if matchHere(regexp: regexp, text: text.suffix(from: idx)) {
        return true
      }
      if idx == text.endIndex || (text[idx] != c && c != ".") {
        return false
      }
      text.formIndex(after: &idx)
    }
  }
}
```

The matcher is very simple to use:

```
Regex("^h..lo*!$").match("hellooooo!") // true
```

This code makes extensive use of slicing (both with range-based subscripts and with the dropFirst method) and optionals — especially the ability to equate an optional with a non-optional value. So, for example, if regexp.characters.first == "^" will work, even with an empty string, because "".characters.first returns nil. However, you can still equate that to the non-optional "^", and when nil, it'll return false.

The ugliest part of the code is probably the while true loop. The requirement is that this loops over every possible substring, *including* an empty string at the end. This is to ensure that expressions like Regex("$").match("abc") return true. If strings worked similarly to arrays, with an integer index, we could write something like this:

```
// ... means up to _and including_ the endIndex
for idx in text.startIndex...text.endIndex {
  // Slice string between idx and the end
  if Regex.matchHere(regexp: _regexp, text: text[idx..<text.endIndex]) {
    return true
  }
}
```

The final time around the for, idx would equal text.endIndex, so text[idx..<text.endIndex] would be an empty string.

So why doesn't the for loop work? We mentioned in the built-in collection chapter that ranges are neither sequences nor collections by default. So we can't iterate over a range of string indices because the range isn't a sequence. And we can't use the character view's indices collection either, because it doesn't include its endIndex. As a result, we're stuck with using the C-style while loop.

ExpressibleByStringLiteral

Throughout this chapter, we've been using String("blah") and "blah" pretty much interchangeably, but they're different. "" is a string literal, just like the array literals covered in the collection protocols chapter. You can make your types initializable from a string literal by conforming to ExpressibleByStringLiteral.

String literals are slightly more work to implement than array literals because they're part of a hierarchy of three protocols: ExpressibleByStringLiteral, ExpressibleByExtendedGraphemeClusterLiteral, and ExpressibleByUnicodeScalarLiteral. Each defines an init for creating a type from each kind of literal, so you have to implement all three. But unless you really need fine-grained logic based on whether or not the value is being created from a single scalar/cluster, it's probably easiest to implement them all in terms of the string version, like so:

```
extension Regex: ExpressibleByStringLiteral {
  public init(stringLiteral value: String) {
    regexp = value
  }
  public init(extendedGraphemeClusterLiteral value: String) {
    self = Regex(stringLiteral: value)
  }
  public init(unicodeScalarLiteral value: String) {
    self = Regex(stringLiteral: value)
  }
}
```

Once defined, you can begin using string literals to create the regex matcher by explicitly naming the type:

```
let r: Regex = "^h..lo*!$"
```

Or even better is when the type is already named for you, because the compiler can then infer it:

```
func findMatches(in strings: [String], regex: Regex) -> [String] {
  return strings.filter { regex.match($0) }
}
findMatches(in: ["foo","bar","baz"], regex: "^b..") // ["bar", "baz"]
```

By default, string literals create the String type because of this typealias in the standard library:

```
typealias StringLiteralType = String
```

But if you wanted to change this default specifically for your application (perhaps because you had a different kind of string that was faster for your particular use case — say it implemented a small-string optimization where a couple of characters were held directly in the string itself), you could change this by re-aliasing the value:

```
typealias StringLiteralType = StaticString

let what = "hello"
what is StaticString // true
```

Internal Structure of String

(Note: this section describes the internal organization of Swift.String. While it's correct as of Swift 3.0, it should never be relied on for production use, as it could change at any time. It's presented more to help you understand the performance characteristics of Swift strings. If you want to follow along, check out the source code in String.swift and StringCore.swift.)

A string's internal storage is made up of something that looks like this:

```
struct String {
  var _core: _StringCore
}
struct _StringCore {
  var _baseAddress: UnsafeMutableRawPointer?
  var _countAndFlags: UInt
  var _owner: AnyObject?
}
```

The _core property is currently public and therefore easily accessible. But even if that were to change in a future release, you'd still be able to bitcast any string to _StringCore:

```
let hello = "hello"
let bits = unsafeBitCast(hello, to: _StringCore.self)
```

(While strings really aggregate an internal type, because they're structs and thus have no overhead other than their members, you can just bitcast the outer container without a problem.)

That's enough to print out the contents using print(bits), but you'll notice that you can't access the individual fields, such as _countAndFlags, because they're private. To work around this, we can duplicate the _StringCore struct in our own code and do another bitcast:

```
/// A clone of Swift._StringCore to work around access control
struct StringCoreClone {
  var _baseAddress: UnsafeMutableRawPointer?
  var _countAndFlags: UInt
  var _owner: AnyObject?
}

let clone = unsafeBitCast(bits, to: StringCoreClone.self)
clone._countAndFlags // 5
```

You'll see that _countAndFlags is 5, the length of the string. The base address is a pointer to memory holding the sequence of ASCII characters. You can print out this buffer using the C puts function. puts expects an Int8 pointer, so you have to convert the untyped pointer to UnsafePointer<Int8> first:

```
if let pointer = clone._baseAddress?.assumingMemoryBound(to: Int8.self) {
  puts(pointer)
}
```

The above will print out hello. Or it might print out hello, followed by a bunch of garbage, because the buffer isn't necessarily null-terminated like a regular C string.

So, does this mean Swift uses a UTF-8 representation to store strings internally? You can find out by storing a non-ASCII string instead:

```
let emoji = "Hello, 🌏"
let emojiBits = unsafeBitCast(emoji, StringCoreClone.self)
```

If you do this, you'll see two differences from before. One is that the _countAndFlags property is now a huge number. This is because it isn't just holding the length. The high-order bits are used to store a flag indicating that this string includes non-ASCII values (there's also another flag indicating the string points to the buffer of an NSString). Conveniently, _StringCore has a public count property that returns the length in code units:

```
emoji._core.count // 9
```

The second change is that the _baseAddress now points to 16-bit characters. This is reflected in the elementWidth property:

```
emoji._core.elementWidth // 2
```

Now that one or more of the characters is no longer ASCII, it triggers String to start storing the buffer as UTF-16. It does this no matter which non-ASCII characters you store in the string — even if they require 32 bits to store, there isn't a third mode where UTF-32 is used.

The last _StringCore property, _owner, will be a null pointer:

```
emojiBits._owner // nil
```

This is because all the strings thus far have been initialized via a string literal, so the buffer points to a constant string in memory in the read-only data part of the binary. Let's see what happens when we create a non-constant string:

```
var greeting = "hello"
greeting.append(" world")
let greetingBits = unsafeBitCast(greeting, to: StringCoreClone.self)
greetingBits._owner
// Optional(Swift._HeapBufferStorage<Swift._StringBufferIVars, Swift.UInt16>)
```

This string's _owner field contains a value. This will be a pointer to an ARC-managed class reference, used in conjunction with a function like isKnownUniquelyReferenced, to give strings value semantics with copy-on-write behavior.

This _owner manages the memory allocated to hold the string. The picture we've built up so far looks something like this:

*Additional memory
allocated on the heap*

let s = "hello"

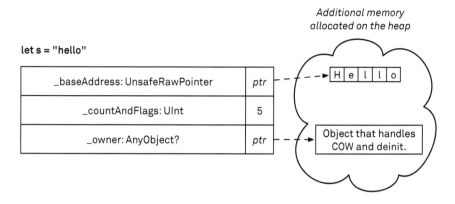

Figure 7.1: Memory of a String value

Since the owner is a class, this means it can have a deinit method, which, when triggered, frees the memory:

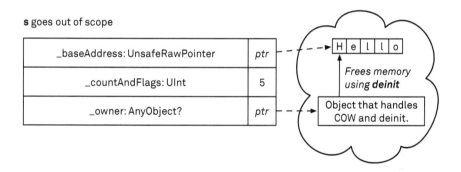

Figure 7.2: When a String goes out of scope

Strings, like arrays and other standard library collection types, are copy-on-write. When you assign a string to a second string variable, the string buffer isn't copied immediately. Instead, as with any copy assignment of a struct, a shallow copy of only the immediate fields takes place, and they initially share that storage:

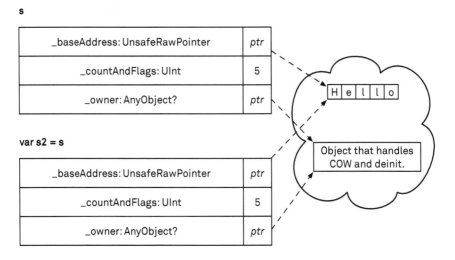

Figure 7.3: Two Strings share the same memory

Then, when one of the strings mutates its contents, the code detects this sharing by checking whether or not the _owner is uniquely referenced. If it isn't, it first copies the shared buffer before mutating it, at which point the buffer is no longer shared:

s2.append("!")

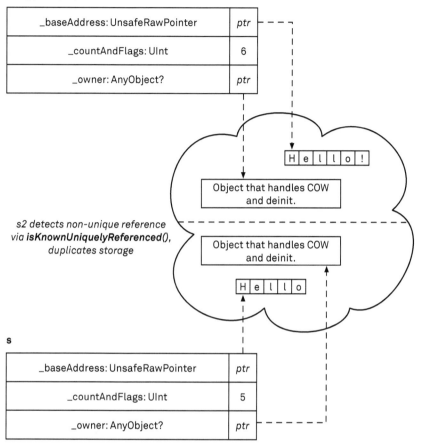

Figure 7.4: String Mutation

For more on copy-on-write, see the chapter on structs and classes.

One final benefit of this structure returns us to slicing. If you take a string and create slices from it, the internals of these slices look like this:

"hello, world" split

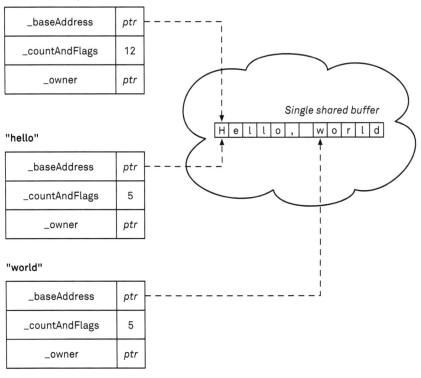

"hello"

"world"

Figure 7.5: String Slices

This means that when calling split on a string, what you're essentially creating is an array of starting/ending pointers to within the original string buffer, as opposed to making numerous copies. This comes at a cost, though — a single slice of a string keeps the whole string in memory. Even if that slice is just a few characters, it could be keeping a string of several megabytes alive.

If you create a String from an NSString, then another optimization means the _owner reference used will actually be a reference to the original NSString, and the buffer will point to that NSString's storage. This can be shown by extracting the owner reference *as* an NSString, so long as the string was originally an NSString:

```
let ns = "hello" as NSString
let s = ns as String
let nsBits = unsafeBitCast(s, to: StringCoreClone.self)
nsBits._owner is NSString // true
```

nsBits._owner === ns // *true*

Internal Organization of Character

As we've seen, Swift.Character represents a sequence of code points that might be arbitrarily long. How does Character manage this? If you look at the source code, you'll find that Character is essentially defined like this:

```
struct Character {
  enum Representation {
    case large(Buffer)
    case small(Builtin.Int63)
  }

  var _representation: Representation
}
```

This technique — holding a small number of elements internally and switching to a heap-based buffer — is sometimes called the "small string optimization." Since characters are almost always just a handful of bytes, it works particularly well here.

Builtin.Int63 is an internal LLVM type that's only available to the standard library. The unusual size of 63 bits indicates another possible optimization. Since one bit is needed to discriminate between the two enum cases, 63 is the maximum available width to fit the entire struct in a single machine word. This currently has no effect though, because the associated value for the large case is a pointer that occupies the full 64 bits. Pointer alignment rules mean that some bits of a valid object pointer will always be zero, and these could potentially be used as storage for the enum case tag, but this particular optimization isn't implemented in Swift 3.0[1]. As a result, a Character is nine bytes long:

MemoryLayout<Character>.size // *9*

---

1 https://lists.swift.org/pipermail/swift-dev/Week-of-Mon-20160822/002747.html

Code Unit Views

Sometimes it's necessary to drop down to a lower level of abstraction and operate directly on Unicode code units instead of characters. There are a few common reasons for this.

Firstly, maybe you actually need the code units, perhaps for rendering into a UTF-8-encoded webpage, or for interoperating with a non-Swift API that takes them.

For an example of an API that requires code units, let's look at using CharacterSet from the Foundation framework in combination with Swift strings. The CharacterSet API is mostly defined in terms of Unicode scalars. So if you wanted to use CharacterSet to split up a string, you could do it via the unicodeScalars view:

```
extension String {
  func words(with charset: CharacterSet = .alphanumerics) -> [String] {
    return self.unicodeScalars.split {
      !charset.contains($0)
    }.map(String.init)
  }
}

let s = "Wow! This contains _all_ kinds of things like 123 and \"quotes\"?"
s.words()
/*
["Wow", "This", "contains", "all", "kinds", "of", "things", "like", "123",
 "and", "quotes"]
*/
```

This will break the string apart at every non-alphanumeric character, giving you an array of String.UnicodeScalarView slices. They can be turned back into strings via map with the String initializer that takes a UnicodeScalarView.

The good news is, even after going through this fairly extensive pipeline, the string slices in words will *still* just be views onto the original string; this property isn't lost by going via the UnicodeScalarView and back again.

A second reason for using these views is that operating on code units rather than fully composed characters can be much faster. This is because to compose grapheme clusters, you must look ahead of every character to see if it's followed by combining characters. To see just how much faster these views can be, take a look at the performance section later on.

Finally, the UTF-16 view has one benefit the other views don't have: it can be random access. This is possible for just this view type because, as we've seen, this is how strings are held internally within the String type. What this means is the nth UTF-16 code unit is always at the nth position in the buffer (even if the string is in "ASCII buffer mode" – it's just a question of the width of the entries to advance over).

The Swift team made the decision *not* to conform String.UTF16View to RandomAccessCollection in the standard library, though. Instead, they moved the conformance into Foundation, so you need to import Foundation to take advantage of it. A comment in the Foundation source code explains why:

// Random access for String.UTF16View, only when Foundation is
// imported. Making this API dependent on Foundation decouples the
// Swift core from a UTF16 representation.
...
extension String.UTF16View : RandomAccessCollection {}

Nothing would break if a future String implementation used a different internal representation. Existing code that relied on the random-access conformance could take advantage of the option for a String to be backed by an NSString, like we discussed above. NSString also uses UTF-16 internally.

That said, it's probably rarer than you think to need random access. Most practical string use cases just need serial access. But some processing algorithms rely on random access for efficiency. For example, the Boyer-Moore search algorithm relies on the ability to skip along the text in jumps of multiple characters.

So you could use the UTF-16 view with algorithms that require such a characteristic. Another example is the search algorithm we define in the generics chapter:

```
let helloWorld = "Hello, world!"
if let idx = helloWorld.utf16.search(for: "world".utf16)?
   .samePosition(in: helloWorld)
{
   print(helloWorld[idx..<helloWorld.endIndex])
}
```

But beware! These convenience or efficiency benefits come at a price, which is that your code may no longer be completely Unicode-correct. So unfortunately, the following search will fail:

```
let text = "Look up your Pok\u{0065}\u{0301}mon in a Pokédex."
text.utf16.search(for: "Pokémon".utf16) // nil
```

Unicode defines diacritics that are used to combine with alphabetic characters as being alphanumeric, so this fares a little better:

```
let nonAlphas = CharacterSet.alphanumerics.inverted
text.unicodeScalars.split(whereSeparator: nonAlphas.contains).map(String.init)
// ["Look", "up", "your", "Pokemon", "in", "a", "Pokédex"]
```

CustomStringConvertible and CustomDebugStringConvertible

Functions like print, String(describing:), and string interpolation are written to take any type, no matter what. Even without any customization, the results you get back might be acceptable because structs print their properties by default:

```
print(Regex("colou?r"))
// prints out Regex(regexp: "colou?r")
```

Then again, you might want something a little prettier, especially if your type contains private variables you don't want displayed. But never fear! It only takes a minute to give your custom class a nicely formatted output when it's passed to print:

```
extension Regex: CustomStringConvertible {
  public var description: String {
    return "/\(regexp)/"
  }
}
```

Now, if someone converts your custom type to a string through various means — using it with a streaming function like print, passing it to String(describing:), or using it in some string interpolation — it'll print out as /expression/:

```
let regex = Regex("colou?r")
```

print(regex) // /colou?r/

There's also CustomDebugStringConvertible, which you can implement when someone calls String(reflecting:), in order to provide more debugging output than the pretty-printed version:

```
extension Regex: CustomDebugStringConvertible {
  public var debugDescription: String {
    return "{expression: \(regexp)}"
  }
}
```

String(reflecting:) falls back to using CustomStringConvertible if CustomDebugStringConvertible isn't implemented, and vice versa. So often, CustomDebugStringConvertible isn't worth implementing if your type is simple. However, if your custom type is a container, it's probably polite to conform to CustomDebugStringConvertible in order to print the debug versions of the elements the type contains. So we can extend the FIFOQueue example from the collection protocols chapter:

```
extension FIFOQueue: CustomStringConvertible,
  CustomDebugStringConvertible
{
  public var description: String {
    // Print contained elements using String(describing:), which favors
    // CustomStringConvertible
    let elements = map { String(describing: $0) }.joined(separator: ", ")
    return "[\(elements)]"
  }

  public var debugDescription: String {
    // Print contained elements using String(reflecting:), which favors
    // CustomDebugStringConvertible
    let elements = map { String(reflecting: $0) }.joined(separator: ", ")
    return "FIFOQueue: [\(elements)]"
  }
}
```

Note the word "favors" there — String(describing:) falls back to CustomDebugStringConvertible if CustomStringConvertible isn't available — so if you do anything out of the ordinary when printing for debug, be sure to implement CustomStringConvertible as well. But if your implementations for description and debugDescription are identical, you can pick either one and omit the other.

By the way, Array always prints out the debug description of its elements, even when invoked via String(describing:). The reason given on the swift-dev mailing list[2] was that an array's description should never be presented to the user, so debugging is the only use case. And an array of empty strings would look wrong without the enclosing quotes, which String.description omits.

Given that conforming to CustomStringConvertible implies that a type has a pretty print output, you may be tempted to write something like the following generic function:

```
func doSomethingAttractive<T: CustomStringConvertible>(with value: T) {
    // Print out something incorporating value, safe in the knowledge
    // it will print out sensibly.
}
```

But you're not supposed to use CustomStringConvertible in this manner. Instead of poking at types to establish whether or not they have a description property, you should use String(describing:) regardless and live with the ugly output if a type doesn't conform to the protocol. This will never fail for any type. And it's a good reason to implement CustomStringConvertible whenever you write more than a very simple type. It only takes a handful of lines.

Text Output Streams

The print and dump functions in the standard library log text to the standard output. How does that work? The default versions of these functions forward to overloads named print(_:to:) and dump(_:to:). The to: argument is the output target; it can be any type that conforms to the TextOutputStream protocol:

```
public func print<Target: TextOutputStream>
    (_ items: Any..., separator: String = " ",
    terminator: String = "\n", to output: inout Target)
)
```

The standard library maintains an internal text output stream that writes everything that's streamed to it to the standard output. What else can you write to? Well, String is the only type in the standard library that's an output stream:

---

2 https://lists.swift.org/pipermail/swift-dev/Week-of-Mon-20151207/000272.html

```
var s = ""
let numbers = [1,2,3,4]
print(numbers, to: &s)
s // [1, 2, 3, 4]
```

This is useful if you want to reroute the output of the print and dump functions into a string. Incidentally, the standard library also harnesses output streams to allow Xcode to capture all stdout logging. Take a look at this global variable declaration in the standard library:

```
public var _playgroundPrintHook: ((String) -> Void)?
```

If this is non-nil, print will use a special output stream that routes everything that's printed both to the standard output *and* to this function. Since the declaration is public, you can even use this for your own shenanigans:

```
var printCapture = ""
_playgroundPrintHook = { text in
   printCapture += text
}
print("This is supposed to only go to stdout")
printCapture // This is supposed to only go to stdout
```

But don't rely on it! It's totally undocumented, and we don't know what functionality in Xcode will break when you reassign this.

We can also make our own output streams. The protocol has only one requirement: a write method that takes a string and writes it to the stream. For example, this output stream buffers writes to an array:

```
struct ArrayStream: TextOutputStream {
   var buffer: [String] = []
   mutating func write(_ string: String) {
      buffer.append(string)
   }
}

var stream = ArrayStream()
print("Hello", to: &stream)
print("World", to: &stream)
stream.buffer // ["", "Hello", "\n", "", "World", "\n"]
```

The documentation explicitly allows functions that write their output to an output stream to call write(_:) multiple times per writing operation. That's why the array buffer in the example above contains separate elements for line breaks and even some empty strings. This is an implementation detail of the print function that may change in future releases.

Another possibility is to extend Data so that it takes a stream, writing it as UTF-8-encoded output:

```
extension Data: TextOutputStream {
  mutating public func write(_ string: String) {
    string.utf8CString.dropLast().withUnsafeBufferPointer {
      append($0)
    }
  }
}
```

The source of an output stream can be any type that conforms to the TextOutputStreamable protocol. This protocol requires a generic method, write(to:), which accepts any type that conforms to TextOutputStream and writes self to it.

In the standard library, String, Character, and UnicodeScalar conform to TextOutputStreamable, but you can also add conformance to your own types. One way to do this is with print(_:to:). However, it's very easy to make a mistake here by accidentally forgetting the to: parameter. Unless you test with a target that's not the standard output, you might not even notice the oversight. Another option is to call the target stream's write method directly. This is how our queue could adopt TextOutputStreamable:

```
extension FIFOQueue: TextOutputStreamable {
  func write<Target: TextOutputStream>(to target: inout Target) {
    target.write("[")
    target.write(map { String(describing: $0) }.joined(separator: ","))
    target.write("]")
  }
}
```

```
var textRepresentation = ""
let queue: FIFOQueue = [1,2,3]
queue.write(to: &textRepresentation)
textRepresentation // [1,2,3]
```

This isn't very different from saying
let textRepresentation = String(describing: queue), though, aside from being more complicated. One interesting aspect of output streams is that a source

can call write multiple times and the stream will process each write immediately. You can see this if you write the following rather silly sample:

```
struct SlowStreamer: TextOutputStreamable, ExpressibleByArrayLiteral {
  let contents: [String]

  init(arrayLiteral elements: String...) {
    contents = elements
  }

  func write<Target: TextOutputStream>(to target: inout Target) {
    for x in contents {
      target.write(x)
      target.write("\n")
      sleep(1)
    }
  }
}

let slow: SlowStreamer = [
  "You'll see that this gets",
  "written slowly line by line",
  "to the standard output",
]
print(slow)
```

As new lines are printed to target, the output appears; it doesn't wait for the call to complete.

As we've seen, internally, print is using some TextOutputStream-conforming wrapper on the standard output. You could write something similar for standard error, like this:

```
struct StdErr: TextOutputStream {
  mutating func write(_ string: String) {
    guard !string.isEmpty else { return }

    // Strings can be passed directly into C functions that take a
    // const char* - see the interoperability chapter for more!
    fputs(string, stderr)
  }
}

var standarderror = StdErr()
print("oops!", to: &standarderror)
```

Streams can also hold state and potentially transform their output. Additionally, you can chain them together. The following output stream replaces all occurrences of the specified phrases with the given alternatives. Like String, it also conforms to TextOutputStreamable, making it both a target and a source of text-streaming operations:

```
struct ReplacingStream: TextOutputStream, TextOutputStreamable {
    let toReplace: DictionaryLiteral<String, String>

    private var output = ""

    init(replacing toReplace: DictionaryLiteral<String, String>) {
        self.toReplace = toReplace
    }

    mutating func write(_ string: String) {
        let toWrite = toReplace.reduce(string) { partialResult, pair in
            partialResult.replacingOccurrences(of: pair.key, with: pair.value)
        }
        print(toWrite, terminator: "", to: &output)
    }

    func write<Target: TextOutputStream>(to target: inout Target) {
        output.write(to: &target)
    }
}

var replacer = ReplacingStream(replacing: [
    "in the cloud": "on someone else's computer"
])

let source = "People find it convenient to store their data in the cloud."
print(source, terminator: "", to: &replacer)

var output = ""
print(replacer, terminator: "", to: &output)
output
// People find it convenient to store their data on someone else's computer.
```

DictionaryLiteral is used in the above code instead of a regular dictionary. This is useful when you want to be able to use the [key: value] literal syntax, but you don't want the two side effects you'd get from using a Dictionary: elimination of duplicate keys and reordering of the keys. If this indeed isn't what you want, then DictionaryLiteral is a nice alternative to an array of pairs (i.e. [(key, value)]) while allowing the caller to use the more convenient [:] syntax.

String Performance

There's no denying that coalescing multiple variable-length UTF-16 values into extended grapheme clusters is going to be more expensive than just ripping through a buffer of 16-bit values. But what's the cost? One way to test performance would be to adapt the regular expression matcher above to work against all of the different collection views.

However, this presents a problem. Ideally, you'd write a generic regex matcher with a placeholder for the view. But this doesn't work — the four different views don't all implement a common "string view" protocol. Also, in our regex matcher, we need to represent specific character constants like * and ^ to compare against the regex. In the UTF16View, these would need to be UInt16, but with the character view, they'd need to be characters. Finally, we want the regex matcher initializer itself to still take a String. How would it know which method to call to get the appropriate view out?

One technique is to bundle up all the variable logic into a single type and then parameterize the regex matcher on that type. First, we define a protocol that has all the necessary information:

```
protocol StringViewSelector {
  associatedtype View: Collection

  static var caret: View.Iterator.Element { get }
  static var asterisk: View.Iterator.Element { get }
  static var period: View.Iterator.Element { get }
  static var dollar: View.Iterator.Element { get }

  static func view(from s: String) -> View
}
```

This information includes an associated type for the view we're going to use, getters for the four constants needed, and a function to extract the relevant view from a string.

Given this, you can implement concrete versions like so:

```
struct UTF8ViewSelector: StringViewSelector {
```

```
  static var caret: UInt8 { return UInt8(ascii: "^") }
  static var asterisk: UInt8 { return UInt8(ascii: "*") }
  static var period: UInt8 { return UInt8(ascii: ".") }
  static var dollar: UInt8 { return UInt8(ascii: "$") }

  static func view(from s: String) -> String.UTF8View { return s.utf8 }
}

struct CharacterViewSelector: StringViewSelector {
  static var caret: Character { return "^" }
  static var asterisk: Character { return "*" }
  static var period: Character { return "." }
  static var dollar: Character { return "$" }

  static func view(from s: String) -> String.CharacterView { return s.characters }
}
```

You can probably guess what UTF16ViewSelector and UnicodeScalarViewSelector look like.

These are what some people call "phantom types" — types that only exist at compile time and that don't actually hold any data. Try calling MemoryLayout<CharacterViewSelector>.size — it'll return zero. It contains no data. All we're using these types for is to parameterize behavior of another type: the regex matcher. It'll use them like so:

```
struct Regex<V: StringViewSelector>
  where V.View.Iterator.Element: Equatable,
  V.View.SubSequence == V.View
{
  let regexp: String
  /// Construct from a regular expression String.
  init(_ regexp: String) {
    self.regexp = regexp
  }
}

extension Regex {
  /// Returns true if the string argument matches the expression.
  func match(text: String) -> Bool {
    let text = V.view(from: text)
    let regexp = V.view(from: self.regexp)

    // If the regex starts with ^, then it can only match the start
    // of the input.
```

```
  if regexp.first == V.caret {
    return Regex.matchHere(regexp: regexp.dropFirst(), text: text)
  }

  // Otherwise, search for a match at every point in the input until
  // one is found.
  var idx = text.startIndex
  while true {
    if Regex.matchHere(regexp: regexp, text: text.suffix(from: idx)) {
      return true
    }
    guard idx != text.endIndex else { break }
    text.formIndex(after: &idx)
  }
  return false
}


/// Match a regular expression string at the beginning of text.
fileprivate static func matchHere(regexp: V.View, text: V.View) -> Bool {
  // ...
}
// ...
}
```

Once the code is rewritten like this, it's easy to write some benchmarking code that measures the time taken to process some arbitrary regular expression across very large input:

```
func benchmark<V: StringViewSelector>(_: V.Type)
  where V.View.Iterator.Element: Equatable, V.View.SubSequence == V.View
{
  let r = Regex<V>("h..a*")
  var count = 0

  let startTime = CFAbsoluteTimeGetCurrent()
  while let line = readLine() {
    if r.match(text: line) { count = count &+ 1 }
  }
  let totalTime = CFAbsoluteTimeGetCurrent() - startTime
  print("\(V.self): \(totalTime) s")
}


func ~=<T: Equatable>(lhs: T, rhs: T?) -> Bool {
  return lhs == rhs
}
```

```
switch CommandLine.arguments.last {
case "ch": benchmark(CharacterViewSelector.self)
case "8": benchmark(UTF8ViewSelector.self)
case "16": benchmark(UTF16ViewSelector.self)
case "sc": benchmark(UnicodeScalarViewSelector.self)
default: print("unrecognized view type")
}
```

The results show the following speeds for the different views in processing the regex on a large corpus of English text (128,000 lines, 1 million words):

View	Time
UTF16	0.3 seconds
UnicodeScalars	0.3 seconds
UTF8	0.4 seconds
Characters	4.2 seconds

Only you can know if your use case justifies choosing your view type based on performance. It's almost certainly the case that these performance characteristics only matter when you're doing extremely heavy string manipulation, but if you're certain that what you're doing would be correct when operating on UTF-16, Unicode scalar, or UTF-8 data, this can give you a decent speedup.

Outlook

When Chris Lattner outlined the goals for Swift 4[3] in July 2016, improvements to string handling were among the handful of primary objectives:

> String is one of the most important fundamental types in the language. The standard library leads have numerous ideas of how to improve the programming model for it, without jeopardizing the goals

---

3 https://lists.swift.org/pipermail/swift-evolution/Week-of-Mon-20160725/025676.html

> of providing a unicode-correct-by-default model. Our goal is to be better at string processing than Perl!

The Swift team has also expressed on numerous occasions its desire to provide native language support for regular expressions, though it remains to be seen if there's time for such an additive feature in the Swift 4 timeframe. Whatever the case may be, expect string handling to change in the future.

Error Handling

Swift provides multiple ways for dealing with errors and even allows us to build our own mechanisms. In the chapter on optionals, we looked at two of them: optionals and assertions. An optional indicates that a value may or may not be there; we have to inspect the optional and unwrap the value before we can use it. An assertion validates that a condition is true; if the condition doesn't hold, the program crashes.

Looking at the interfaces of types in the standard library can give us a good feel for when to use an optional and when not to. Optionals are used for operations that have a clear and commonly used "not found" or "invalid input" case. For instance, consider the failable initializer for Int that takes a string: it returns nil if the input isn't a valid integer. Another example: when you look up a key in a dictionary, it's often expected that the key might not be present. Therefore, a dictionary lookup returns an optional result.

Contrast this with arrays: when looking up an element at a specific index, the element is returned directly and isn't wrapped in an optional. This is because the programmer is expected to know if an array index is valid. Accessing an array with an index that's out of bounds is considered a programmer error, and consequently, this will crash your application. If you're unsure whether or not an index is within bounds, you need to check beforehand.

Assertions are a great tool for identifying bugs in your code. Used correctly, they show you at the earliest possible moment when your program is in a state you didn't expect. They should never be used to signal *expected errors* such as a network error.

Note that arrays also have accessors that return optionals. For example, the first and last properties on Collection return nil when called on an empty collection. The developers of Swift's standard library deliberately designed the API this way because it's common to access these values in situations when the collection might be empty.

An alternative to returning an optional from a function that can fail is to mark the function as throws. Besides a different syntax for how the caller must handle the success and failure cases, the key difference to returning an optional is that throwing functions can return a rich error value that carries information about the error that occurred.

This difference is a good guideline for when to use one approach over the other. Consider the first and last properties on Collection again. They have exactly one error condition (the collection is empty) — returning a rich error wouldn't give the caller more information than what's already present in the optional value. Compare this to a function that executes a network request: many things can fail, from the network being down, to being unable to parse the server's response. Rich error information is necessary to allow the caller to react differently to different errors (or just to show the user what exactly went wrong).

The Result Type

Before we look at Swift's built-in error handling in more detail, let's discuss the Result type, which will help clarify how Swift's error handling works when you take away the syntactic sugar. A Result type is very similar to an optional. Recall that an optional is just an enumeration with two cases: a .none or nil case, with no associated value; and a .some case, which has an associated value. The Result type is an enum with two cases as well: a failure case, which carries an associated error value; and a success case, also with an associated value. Just like optionals, Result has one generic parameter:

```
enum Result<A> {
    case failure(Error)
    case success(A)
}
```

The failure case constrains its associated value to the Error protocol. We'll come back to this shortly.

Let's suppose we're writing a function to read a file from disk. As a first try, we could define the interface using an optional. Because reading a file might fail, we want to be able to return nil:

```
func contentsOrNil(ofFile filename: String) -> String?
```

The interface above is very simple, but it doesn't tell us anything about why reading the file failed. Does the file not exist? Or do we not have the right permissions? This is another example where the failure reason matters. Let's define an enum for the possible error cases:

```
enum FileError: Error {
    case fileDoesNotExist
    case noPermission
}
```

Now we can change the type of our function to return either an error or a valid result:

```
func contents(ofFile filename: String) -> Result<String>
```

Now the caller of the function can look at the result cases and react differently based on the error. In the code below, we try to read the file, and in case reading succeeds, we print the contents. If the file doesn't exist, we print that, and we handle any remaining errors in a different way:

```
let result = contents(ofFile: "input.txt")
switch result {
case let .success(contents):
  print(contents)
case let .failure(error):
  if let fileError = error as? FileError,
    fileError == .fileDoesNotExist
  {
    print("File not found")
  } else {
    // Handle error
  }
}
```

Throwing and Catching

Swift's built-in error handling is implemented almost like in the above example, only with a different syntax. Instead of giving a function a Result return type to indicate that it can fail, we mark it as throws. Note that Result applies to types, whereas throws applies to functions (we'll come back to this difference later in this chapter). For every throwing function, the compiler will verify that the caller either catches the error or propagates it to its caller. In the case of contents(ofFile:), the function signature including throws looks like this:

```
func contents(ofFile filename: String) throws -> String
```

From now on, our code won't compile unless we annotate every call to contents(ofFile:) with try. The try keyword serves two purposes: first, it signals to the compiler that we know we're calling a function that can throw an error. Second, and more importantly, it immediately makes clear to readers of the code which functions can throw.

Calling a throwing function also forces us to make a decision about how we want to deal with possible errors. We can either handle an error by using do/catch, or we can have it propagate up the call stack by marking the calling function as throws. We can use pattern matching to catch specific errors or catch all errors. In the example below, we explicitly catch a fileDoesNotExist case and then handle all other errors in a catch-all case. Within the catch-all case, the compiler automatically makes a variable, error, available (much like the implicit newValue variable in a property's willSet handler):

```
do {
    let result = try contents(ofFile: "input.txt")
    print(result)
} catch FileError.fileDoesNotExist {
    print("File not found")
} catch {
    print(error)
    // Handle any other error
}
```

The error handling syntax in Swift probably looks familiar to you. Many other languages use the same try, catch, and throw keywords for exception handling. Despite the resemblance, error handling in Swift doesn't incur the runtime cost that's often associated with exceptions. The compiler treats throw like a regular return, making both code paths very fast.

If we want to expose more information in our errors, we can use an enum with associated values. (We could've also used a struct or class instead; any type that conforms to the Error protocol can be used as an error in a throwing function.) For example, a file parser could choose to model the possible errors like this:

```
enum ParseError: Error {
    case wrongEncoding
    case warning(line: Int, message: String)
}
```

Now, if we want to parse a string, we can again use pattern matching to distinguish between the cases. In the case of .warning, we can bind the line number and warning message to a variable:

```
do {
```

```
  let result = try parse(text: "{ \"message\": \"We come in peace\" }")
  print(result)
} catch ParseError.wrongEncoding {
  print("Wrong encoding")
} catch let ParseError.warning(line, message) {
  print("Warning at line \(line): \(message)")
} catch {
}
```

Something about the above code doesn't feel quite right. Even if we're absolutely sure that the only error that could happen is of type `ParseError` (which we handled exhaustively), we still need to write a final catch case to convince the compiler that we caught all possible errors. In a future Swift version, the compiler might be able to check exhaustiveness within a module, but across modules, this problem can't be solved. The reason is that Swift errors are untyped: we can only mark a function as throws, but we can't specify *which* errors it'll throw. This was a deliberate design decision — most of the time, you only care about whether or not an error was present. If we needed to specify the types of all errors, this could quickly get out of hand: it would make functions' type signatures quite complicated, especially for functions that call several other throwing functions and propagate their errors. Moreover, adding a new error case would be a breaking change for all clients of the API.

> That said, Swift will probably get typed errors someday; this topic is being actively discussed on the mailing lists. When typed errors come to Swift, we expect them to be an opt-in feature. You'll be able to specify the concrete error types your functions will throw, but you won't have to.
>
> Because errors in Swift are untyped, it's important to document the types of errors your functions can throw. Xcode supports a Throws keyword in documentation markup for this purpose. Here's an example:

```
/// Opens a text file and returns its contents.
///
/// - Parameter filename: The name of the file to read.
/// - Returns: The file contents, interpreted as UTF-8.
/// - Throws: `FileError` if the file does not exist or
///     the process doesn't have read permissions.
func contents(ofFile filename: String) throws -> String
```

> The Quick Help popover that appears when you Option-click on the function name will now include an extra section for the thrown errors.

Typed Errors

It can sometimes be useful to take advantage of the type system to specify the concrete errors a function can throw. If we care about this, we can come up with a slightly altered Result type, which has an additional generic parameter for the error type:

```
enum Result<A, ErrorType: Error> {
  case failure(ErrorType)
  case success(A)
}
```

This way, we can declare functions using an explicit error type. The following parseFile function will return either an array of strings or a ParseError. We don't have to handle any other cases when calling it, and the compiler knows this:

```
func parse(text: String) -> Result<[String], ParseError>
```

In code where your errors have a significant semantic meaning, you can choose to use a typed Result type instead of Swift's built-in error handling. This way, you can let the compiler verify that you caught all possible errors. However, in most applications, using throws and do/try/catch will lead to simpler code. There's another big benefit to using the built-in error handling: the compiler will make sure you can't ignore the error case when calling a function that might throw. With the definition of parseFile above, we could write the following code:

```
let _ = parse(text: invalidData)
```

If the function were marked as throws, the compiler would force us to call it using try. The compiler would also force us to either wrap that call in a do/catch block or propagate the error.

Granted, the example above is unrealistic, because ignoring the parse function's return value doesn't make any sense, and the compiler *would* force you to consider the failure case when you unwrap the result. It's relevant when dealing with functions that don't have a meaningful return value, though, and in these situations, it can really help you not forget to catch the error. For example, consider the following function:

```
func setupServerConnection() throws
```

Because the function is marked as throws, we need to call it with try. If the server connection fails, we probably want to switch to a different code path or display an error. By having to use try, we're forced to think about this case. Had we chosen to return a Result<()> instead, it would be all too easy to ignore errors.

Bridging Errors to Objective-C

Objective-C has no mechanism that's similar to throws and try. (Objective-C *does* have exception handling that uses these same keywords, but exceptions in Objective-C should only be used to signal programmer errors. You rarely catch an Objective-C exception in a normal app.)

Instead, the common pattern in Cocoa is that a method returns NO or nil when an error occurs. In addition, failable methods take a reference to an NSError pointer as an extra argument; they can use this pointer to pass concrete error information to the caller. For example, the contents(ofFile:) method would look like this in Objective-C:

```
- (NSString *)contentsOfFile(NSString *)filename error:(NSError **)error;
```

Swift automatically translates methods that follow this pattern to the throws syntax. The error parameter gets removed since it's no longer needed, and BOOL return types are changed to Void. This is extremely helpful when dealing with existing frameworks in Objective-C. The method above gets imported like this:

```
func contents(ofFile filename: String) throws -> String
```

Other NSError parameters — for example, in asynchronous APIs that pass an error back to the caller in a completion block — are bridged to the Error protocol, so you don't generally need to interact with NSError directly. Error has only one property, localizedDescription. For pure Swift errors that don't override this, the runtime will generate a default text derived from the type name, but if you intend your error values to be presented to the user, it's good practice to provide a meaningful description.

If you pass a pure Swift error to an Objective-C method, it'll similarly be bridged to NSError. Since all NSError objects must have a domain string and an integer error code, the runtime will again provide default values, using the type name as the domain and numbering the enum cases from zero for the error code. Optionally, you can provide better implementations by conforming your type to the CustomNSError protocol.

For example, we could extend our ParseError like this:

```
extension ParseError: CustomNSError {
  static let errorDomain = "io.objc.parseError"
  var errorCode: Int {
    switch self {
    case .wrongEncoding: return 100
    case .warning(_, _): return 200
    }
  }
  var errorUserInfo: [String: Any] {
    return [:]
  }
}
```

In a similar manner, you can add conformance to one or both of the following protocols to make your errors more meaningful and provide better interoperability with Cocoa conventions:

→ **LocalizedError** — provides localized messages describing why the error occurred (failureReason), tips for how to recover (recoverySuggestion), and additional help text (helpAnchor).

→ **RecoverableError** — describes an error the user can recover from by presenting one or more recoveryOptions and performing the recovery when the user requests it.

Errors and Function Parameters

In the following example, we'll write a function that checks a list of files for validity. The checkFile function can return three possible values. If it returns true, the file is valid. If it returns false, the file is invalid. If it throws an error, something went wrong when checking the file:

```
func checkFile(filename: String) throws -> Bool
```

As a first step, we can write a simple function that loops over a list of filenames and makes sure that checkFile returns true for every file. If checkFile returns false, we want to make sure to exit early, avoiding any unnecessary work. Since we don't catch any errors that checkFile throws, the first error would propagate to the caller and thus also exit early:

```
func checkAllFiles(filenames: [String]) throws -> Bool {
    for filename in filenames {
        guard try checkFile(filename: filename) else { return false }
    }
    return true
}
```

Checking whether all the elements in an array conform to a certain condition is something that might happen more often in our app. For example, consider the function checkPrimes, which checks whether all numbers in a given list are prime numbers. It works in exactly the same way as checkAllFiles. It loops over the array and checks all elements for a condition (isPrime), exiting early when one of the numbers doesn't satisfy the condition:

```
func checkPrimes(_ numbers: [Int]) -> Bool {
    for number in numbers {
        guard number.isPrime else { return false }
    }
    return true
}
```

```
checkPrimes([2,3,7,17]) // true
checkPrimes([2,3,4,5]) // false
```

Both functions mix the process of iterating over a sequence (the for loops) with the actual logic that decides if an element meets the condition. This is a good opportunity to create an abstraction for this pattern, similar to map or filter. To do that, we can add a function named all to Sequence. Like filter, all takes a function that performs the condition check as an argument. The difference to filter is the return type. all returns true if all elements in the sequence satisfy the condition, whereas filter returns the elements themselves:

```
extension Sequence {
    /// Returns `true` iff all elements satisfy the predicate
    func all(condition: (Iterator.Element) -> Bool) -> Bool {
        for element in self {
            guard condition(element) else { return false }
        }
```

```
        return true
    }
}
```

This allows us to rewrite checkPrimes in a single line, which makes it easier to read once you know what all does, and it helps us focus on the essential parts:

```
func checkPrimes2(_ numbers: [Int]) -> Bool {
    return numbers.all { $0.isPrime }
}
```

However, we can't rewrite checkAllFiles to use all, because checkFile is marked as throws. We could easily rewrite all to accept a throwing function, but then we'd have to change checkPrimes too, either by annotating checkPrimes as throwing, by using try!, or by wrapping the call to all in a do/catch block. Alternatively, we could define two versions of all: one that throws and one that doesn't. Except for the try call, their implementations would be identical.

Rethrows

Fortunately, there's a better way. By marking all as rethrows, we can write both variants in one go. Annotating a function with rethrows tells the compiler that this function will only throw an error when its function parameter throws an error. This allows the compiler to waive the requirement that call must be called with try when the caller passes in a non-throwing check function:

```
extension Sequence {
    func all(condition: (Iterator.Element) throws -> Bool) rethrows
        -> Bool {
        for element in self {
            guard try condition(element) else { return false }
        }
        return true
    }
}
```

The implementation of checkAllFiles is now very similar to checkPrimes, but because the call to all can now throw an error, we need to insert an additional try:

```
func checkAllFiles(filenames: [String]) throws -> Bool {
    return try filenames.all(condition: checkFile)
}
```

Almost all sequence and collection functions in the standard library that take a function argument are annotated with rethrows. For example, the map function is only throwing if the transformation function is a throwing function itself.

Cleaning Up Using defer

Let's go back to the contents(ofFile:) function from the beginning of this chapter for a minute and have a look at the implementation. In many languages, it's common to have a try/finally construct, where the block marked with finally is always executed when the function returns, regardless of whether or not an error was thrown. The defer keyword in Swift has a similar purpose but works a bit differently. Like finally, a defer block is always executed when a scope is exited, regardless of the reason of exiting — whether it's because a value is successfully returned, because an error happened, or any other reason. Unlike finally, a defer block doesn't require a leading try or do block, and it's more flexible in terms of where you place it in your code:

```
func contents(ofFile filename: String) throws -> String
{
    let file = open("test.txt", O_RDONLY)
    defer { close(file) }
    let contents = try process(file: file)
    return contents
}
```

While defer is often used together with error handling, it can be useful in other contexts too — for example, when you want to keep the code for initialization and cleanup of a resource close together. Putting related parts of the code close to each other can make your code significantly more readable, especially in longer functions.

The standard library uses defer in multiple places where a function needs to increment a counter *and* return the counter's previous value. This saves creating a local variable for the return value; defer essentially serves as a replacement for the removed postfix increment operator. Here's a typical example from the implementation of EnumeratedIterator:

```
struct EnumeratedIterator<Base: IteratorProtocol>: IteratorProtocol, Sequence {
    internal var _base: Base
    internal var _count: Int
    ...
```

```
func next() -> Element? {
    guard let b = _base.next() else { return nil }
    defer { _count += 1 }
    return (offset: _count, element: b)
  }
}
```

If there are multiple defer blocks in the same scope, they're executed in reverse order; you can think of them as a stack. At first, it might feel strange that the defer blocks run in reverse order. However, if we look at an example, it should quickly make sense:

```
guard let database = openDatabase(...) else { return }
defer { closeDatabase(database) }
guard let connection = openConnection(database) else { return }
defer { closeConnection(connection) }
guard let result = runQuery(connection, ...) else { return }
```

If an error occurs — for example, during the runQuery call — we want to close the connection first and the database second. Because the defer is executed in reverse order, this happens automatically. The runQuery depends on openConnection, which in turn depends on openDatabase. Therefore, cleaning these resources up needs to happen in reverse order.

There are some cases in which defer blocks don't get executed: when your program segfaults, or when it raises a fatal error (e.g. using fatalError or by force-unwrapping a nil), all execution halts immediately.

Errors and Optionals

Errors and optionals are both very common ways for functions to signal that something went wrong. Earlier in this chapter, we gave you some advice on how to decide which pattern you should use for your own functions. You'll end up working a lot with both errors and optionals, and passing results to other APIs will often make it necessary to convert back and forth between throwing functions and optional values.

The try? keyword allows us to ignore the error of a throws function and convert the return value into an optional that tells us if the function succeeded or not:

```
if let result = try? parse(text: input) {
    print(result)
```

```
}
```

Using the try? keyword means we receive less information than before: we only know if the function returned a successful value or if it returned some error — any specific information about that error gets thrown away. To go the other way, from an optional to a function that throws, we have to provide the error value that gets used in case the optional is nil. Here's an extension on Optional that, given an error, does this:

```
extension Optional {
  /// Unwraps `self` if it is non-`nil`.
  /// Throws the given error if `self` is `nil`.
  func or(error: Error) throws -> Wrapped {
    switch self {
      case let x?: return x
      case nil: throw error
    }
  }
}
```

```
do {
  let int = try Int("42").or(error: ReadIntError.couldNotRead)
} catch {
  print(error)
}
```

This can be useful in conjunction with multiple try statements, or when you're working inside a function that's already marked as throws.

The existence of the try? keyword may appear contradictory to Swift's philosophy that ignoring errors shouldn't be allowed. However, you still have to explicitly write try? so that the compiler forces you to acknowledge your actions. In cases where you're not interested in the error message, this can be very helpful.

It's also possible to write equivalent functions for converting between Result and throws, or between throws and Result, or between optionals and Result.

Chaining Errors

Chaining multiple calls to functions that can throw errors becomes trivial with Swift's built-in error handling — there's no need for nested if statements or similar constructs; we simply place these calls into a single do/catch block (or wrap them in a throwing function). The first error that occurs breaks the chain and switches control to the catch block (or propagates the error to the caller):

```
func checkFilesAndFetchProcessID(filenames: [String]) -> Int {
  do {
    try filenames.all(condition: checkFile)
    let pidString = try contents(ofFile: "Pidfile")
    return try Int(pidString).or(error: ReadIntError.couldNotRead)
  } catch {
    return 42 // Default value
  }
}
```

Chaining Result

To see how well Swift's native error handling matches up against other error handling schemes, let's compare this to an equivalent example based on the Result type. Chaining multiple functions that return a Result — where the input to the second function is the result of the first — is a lot of work if you want to do it manually. To do so, you call the first function and unwrap its return value; if it's a .success, you can pass the wrapped value to the second function and start over. As soon as one function returns a .failure, the chain breaks and you short-circuit by immediately returning the failure to the caller.

To refactor this, we should turn the common steps of unwrapping the Result, short-circuiting in case of failure, and passing the value to the next transformation in case of success, into a separate function. That function is the flatMap operation. Its structure is identical to the existing flatMap for optionals that we covered in the optionals chapter:

```
extension Result {
  func flatMap<B>(transform: (A) -> Result<B>) -> Result<B> {
    switch self {
    case let .failure(m): return .failure(m)
    case let .success(x): return transform(x)
    }
  }
}
```

With this in place, the end result is quite elegant:

```
func checkFilesAndFetchProcessID(filenames: [String]) -> Result<Int> {
```

```
    return filenames
      .all(condition: checkFile)
      .flatMap { _ in contents(ofFile: "Pidfile") }
      .flatMap { contents in
        Int(contents).map(Result.success)
          ?? .failure(ReadIntError.couldNotRead)
    }
}
```

(We're using variants of all, checkFile, and contents(ofFile:) here that return Result values. The implementations aren't shown here.)

But you can also see that Swift's error handling stands up extremely well. It's shorter, and it's arguably more readable and easier to understand.

Higher-Order Functions and Errors

One domain where Swift's error handling unfortunately does *not* work very well is asynchronous APIs that need to pass errors to the caller in callback functions. Let's look at a function that asynchronously computes a large number and calls back our code when the computation has finished:

```
func compute(callback: (Int) -> ())
```

We can call it by providing a callback function. The callback receives the result as the only parameter:

```
compute { result in
  print(result)
}
```

If the computation can fail, we could specify that the callback receives an optional integer, which would be nil in case of a failure:

```
func computeOptional(callback: (Int?) -> ())
```

Now, in our callback, we must check whether the optional is non-nil, e.g. by using the ?? operator:

```
computeOptional { result in
  print(result ?? -1)
}
```

But what if we want to report specific errors to the callback, rather than just an optional? This function signature seems like a natural solution:

```
func computeThrows(callback: Int throws -> ())
```

Perhaps surprisingly, this type has a totally different meaning. Instead of saying that the computation might fail, it expresses that the callback itself could throw an error. This highlights the key difference that we mentioned earlier: optionals and Result work on types, whereas throws works only on function types. Annotating a function with throws means that the *function* might fail.

It becomes a bit clearer when we try to rewrite the wrong attempt from above using Result:

```
func computeResult(callback: Int -> Result<()>)
```

This isn't correct either. We need to wrap the Int argument in a Result, not the callback's return type. Finally, this is the correct solution:

```
func computeResult(callback: (Result<Int>) -> ())
```

Unfortunately, there's currently no clear way to write the variant above with throws. The best we can do is wrap the Int inside another throwing function. This makes the type more complicated:

```
func compute(callback: (() throws -> Int) -> ())
```

And using this variant becomes more complicated for the caller too. In order to get the integer out, the callback now has to call the throwing function. This is where the caller must perform the error checking:

```
compute { (resultFunc: () throws -> Int) in
  do {
    let result = try resultFunc()
    print(result)
  } catch {
    print("An error occurred: \(error)")
  }
}
```

This works, but it's definitely not idiomatic Swift; Result is the way to go for asynchronous error handling. It's unfortunate that this creates an impedance mismatch with synchronous functions that use throws. The Swift team has expressed interest in extending the throws model to other scenarios, but this will likely be part of the much greater task of adding native concurrency features to the language, and that won't happen until after Swift 4.

Until then, we're stuck with using our own custom Result types. Apple did consider adding a Result type to the standard library, but ultimately decided against it[1] on the grounds that it wasn't independently valuable enough outside the error handling domain and that the team didn't want to endorse it as an alternative to throws-style error handling. Luckily, using Result for asynchronous APIs is a pretty well established practice among the Swift developer community, so you shouldn't hesitate to use it in your APIs when the native error handling isn't appropriate. It certainly beats the Objective-C style of having completion handlers with two nullable arguments (a result object and an error object).

Conclusion

When Apple introduced its error handling model in Swift 2.0, a lot of people in the community were skeptical. People were rolling their own Result types in the Swift 1.x days, mostly with a typed error case. The fact that throws uses untyped errors was seen as a needless deviation from the strict typing in other parts of the language. Unsurprisingly, the Swift team had considered this very carefully and intentionally went for untyped errors. We were skeptical too, but in hindsight, we think the Swift team was proven correct, not least by the large acceptance of the error handling model in the developer community.

There's a good chance that typed error handling will be added as an opt-in feature in the future, along with better support for asynchronous errors and passing errors around as values. As it stands now, error handling is a good example of Swift being a pragmatic language that optimizes for the most common use case first. Keeping the syntax familiar for developers who are used to C-based languages is a more important goal than adhering to the "purer" functional style based on Result and flatMap.

In the meantime, we now have many possible choices for handling the unexpected in our code. When we can't possibly continue, we can use fatalError or an assertion. When we're not interested in the kind of error, or if there's only one kind of error, we can use optionals. When we need more than

---

1 https://lists.swift.org/pipermail/swift-evolution/Week-of-Mon-20151207/001433.html

one kind of error or want to provide additional information, we can use Swift's built-in errors or write our own Result type. When we want to write functions that take a function as a parameter, rethrows lets us write one variant for both throwing and non-throwing function parameters. Finally, the defer statement is very useful in combination with the built-in errors. defer statements provide us with a single place to put our cleanup code, regardless of how a scope exits normally or with an error.

Generics

9

Like most modern languages, Swift has a number of features that can all be grouped under *generic programming*. Generic code allows you to write reusable functions and data types that can work with any type that matches the constraints you define. For example, types such as Array and Set are generic over their elements. Generic functions are generic over their input and/or output types. The definition func identity<A>(input: A) -> A defines a function that works on any type, identified by the placeholder A. In a way, we can also think of protocols with an associated type as "generic protocols." The associated type allows us to abstract over specific implementations. IteratorProtocol is an example of such a protocol: it's generic over the Element type it produces.

The goal of generic programming is to express the *essential interface* an algorithm or data structure requires. For example, consider the last(where:) method we wrote in the built-in collections chapter. Writing this method as an extension on Array would've been the obvious choice, but an Array has lots of capabilities last(where:) doesn't need. By asking ourselves what the essential interface is — that is, the minimal set of features required to implement the desired functionality — we can make the function available to a much broader set of types. In this example, last(where:) has only one requirement: it needs to traverse a sequence of elements in reverse order. This makes an extension on Sequence the right place for this algorithm.

In this chapter, we'll look at how to write generic code. We'll start by talking about overloading because this concept is closely related to generics. We'll use generic programming to provide multiple implementations of an algorithm, each relying on a different set of assumptions. We'll also discuss some common difficulties you may encounter when writing generic algorithms for collections. We'll then look at how you can use generic data types to refactor code to make it testable and more flexible. Finally, we'll cover how the compiler handles generic code and what we can do to get the best performance for our own generic code.

Overloading

Overloaded functions, i.e. multiple functions that have the same name but different argument and/or return types, are not generic per se. But like generics, they allow us to make one interface available to multiple types.

Overload Resolution for Free Functions

For example, we could define a function named raise(_:to:) to perform exponentiation and provide separate overloads for Double and Float arguments. Based on the types, the right overload gets picked by the compiler:

```
func raise(_ base: Double, to exponent: Double) -> Double {
  return pow(base, exponent)
}

func raise(_ base: Float, to exponent: Float) -> Float {
  return powf(base, exponent)
}

let double = raise(2.0, to: 3.0) // 8.0
type(of: double) // Double
let float: Float = raise(2.0, to: 3.0) // 8.0
type(of: float) // Float
```

We used the pow and powf functions declared in Swift's Darwin module (or Glibc on Linux) for the implementations.

Swift has a complex set of rules for which overloaded function to pick, which is based on whether or not a function is generic and what kind of type is being passed in. While the rules are too long to go into here, they can be summarized as "pick the most specific one." This means that non-generic functions are picked over generic ones.

As an example, consider the following function that logs certain properties of a view. We provide a generic implementation for UIView that logs the view's class name and frame, and a specific overload for UILabel that prints the label's text:

```
func log<View: UIView>(_ view: View) {
  print("It's a \(type(of: view)), frame: \(view.frame)")
}

func log(_ view: UILabel) {
  let text = view.text ?? "(empty)"
  print("It's a label, text: \(text)")
}
```

Passing a UILabel will call the label-specific overload, whereas passing any other view will use the generic one:

```
let label = UILabel(frame: CGRect(x: 20, y: 20, width: 200, height: 32))
label.text = "Password"
log(label) // It's a label, text: Password

let button = UIButton(frame: CGRect(x: 0, y: 0, width: 100, height: 50))
log(button) // It's a UIButton, frame: (0.0, 0.0, 100.0, 50.0)
```

It's important to note that overloads are resolved statically at compile time. This means the compiler bases its decision of which overload to call on the static types of the variables involved, and not on the values' dynamic types at runtime. This is why the generic overload of log will be used for both views if we put the label and the button into an array and then call the log function in a loop over the array's elements:

```
let views = [label, button] // Type of views is [UIView]
for view in views {
    log(view)
}
/*
It's a UILabel, frame: (20.0, 20.0, 200.0, 32.0)
It's a UIButton, frame: (0.0, 0.0, 100.0, 50.0)
*/
```

This is because the static type of the view variable is UIView; it's irrelevant that the dynamic type UILabel would result in a different overload at runtime.

If instead you need runtime polymorphism — that is, you want the function to be picked based on what a variable points to and not what the type of the variable is — you should be using methods not functions, i.e. define log as a method on UIView and UILabel.

Overload Resolution for Operators

The compiler exhibits some surprising behavior when it comes to the resolution of overloaded operators. As Matt Gallagher points out[1], the type checker always favors non-generic overloads over generic variants, even when the generic version would be the better choice (and the one which would be chosen if we were talking about a normal function).

---

1 http://www.cocoawithlove.com/blog/2016/07/12/type-checker-issues.html

Going back to the exponentiation example from above, let's define a custom operator named ** for the same operation:

```
// Exponentiation has higher precedence than multiplication
precedencegroup ExponentiationPrecedence {
    associativity: left
    higherThan: MultiplicationPrecedence
}
infix operator **: ExponentiationPrecedence

func **(lhs: Double, rhs: Double) -> Double {
    return pow(lhs, rhs)
}
func **(lhs: Float, rhs: Float) -> Float {
    return powf(lhs, rhs)
}
```

```
2.0 ** 3.0 // 8.0
```

The above code is equivalent to the raise function we implemented in the previous section. Let's add another overload for integers next. We want exponentiation to work for all integer types, so we define a generic overload for all types conforming to SignedInteger (we'd need another overload for UnsignedInteger, not shown here):

```
func **<I: SignedInteger>(lhs: I, rhs: I) -> I {
    // Cast to IntMax, use Double overload to compute result,
    // then numericCast to return type.
    let result = Double(lhs.toIntMax()) ** Double(rhs.toIntMax())
    return numericCast(IntMax(result))
}
```

This looks like it should work, but if we now call ** with two integer literals, the compiler complains about an ambiguous use of the ** operator:

```
2 ** 3 // Error: Ambiguous use of operator '**'
```

The explanation for why this happens brings us back to what we said at the beginning of this section: when resolving overloaded operators, the type checker always favors non-generic over generic overloads. Apparently, the compiler ignores the generic overload for integers and then raises the error because it can't decide whether it should call the overload for Double or the one for Float — both are equally valid choices for two integer literal arguments. To convince the compiler to pick the correct overload, we have to explicitly cast at least one of the arguments to an integer type, or else provide an explicit result type:

```
let intResult: Int = 2 ** 3 // 8
```

The compiler only behaves in this manner for operators — a generic overload of the raise function for SignedInteger would work just fine without introducing ambiguities. The reason for this discrepancy comes down to performance: the Swift team considers the reduction of complexity the type checker has to deal with significant enough to warrant the use of this simpler but sometimes incorrect overload resolution model for operators.

Overloading with Generic Constraints

You'll often encounter overloading in conjunction with generic code when the same operation can be expressed with multiple algorithms that each require different constraints on their generic parameters. Suppose we want to determine if all the entries in one array are also contained in another. In other words, we want to find out if the first array is a *subset* of the second (keeping in mind that the element order is inconsequential). The standard library provides a method named isSubset(of:) that does this, but only for types that conform to the SetAlgebra protocol, such as Set.

If we wanted to write a version of isSubset(of:) that works with a broader set of types, it'd look something like this:

```
extension Sequence where Iterator.Element: Equatable {
  /// Returns true if all elements in `self` are also in `other`.
  func isSubset(of other: [Iterator.Element]) -> Bool {
    for element in self {
      guard other.contains(element) else {
        return false
      }
    }
    return true
  }
}

let oneToThree = [1,2,3]
let fiveToOne = [5,4,3,2,1]
oneToThree.isSubset(of: fiveToOne) // true
```

isSubset is defined as an extension on the Sequence protocol, where the elements of the sequence are Equatable. It takes an array of the same type to check against, and it returns true if every single element in the receiver is also a member of the argument array. The method doesn't care about what the elements are, just so long as they conform to Equatable, because only equatable types can be used with contains. The element type can be an Int, a String, or your own custom user-defined class, just so long as it's equatable.

This version of isSubset comes with a big downside, and that's performance. The algorithm has performance characteristics of $O(n * m)$, where n and m are the element counts of the two arrays. That is, as the input sizes grow, the worst-case time the function takes to run grows quadratically. This is because contains runs in linear time on arrays, i.e. $O(m)$. This makes sense if you think about what it needs to do: loop over the contents of the source sequence, checking if they match a given element. But our algorithm calls contains inside another loop — the one over the receiver's elements — which *also* runs in linear time in a similar fashion. And running an $O(m)$ loop inside an $O(n)$ loop results in an $O(n * m)$ function.

This is fine for small inputs, and perhaps you're only ever going to call this with arrays with entries in the hundreds. But call it with arrays with thousands or millions of elements and you'll be sorry.

We can write a better-performing version by tightening the constraints on the sequence's element type. If we require the elements to conform to Hashable, we can convert the other array into a Set, taking advantage of the fact that a set performs lookups in constant time:

```
extension Sequence where Iterator.Element: Hashable {
  /// Returns true iff all elements in `self` are also in `other`.
  func isSubset(of other: [Iterator.Element]) -> Bool {
    let otherSet = Set(other)
    for element in self {
      guard otherSet.contains(element) else {
        return false
      }
    }
    return true
  }
}
```

With the contains check taking $O(1)$ time (assuming a uniform distribution of the hashes), the entire for loop now becomes $O(n)$ — the time required grows linearly with the number of elements in the receiver. The additional cost of converting other into a set is $O(m)$, but we incur it only once, outside the loop. Thus, the total cost becomes $O(n + m)$, which is much better than the $O(n * m)$ for the Equatable version — if both arrays have 1,000 elements, it's the difference between 2,000 and one million iterations.

So now we have two versions of the algorithm, none of which is clearly better than the other — one is faster, and the other works with a wider range of types. The good news is that you don't have to pick one of these options. You can implement both overloads of isSubset and let the compiler select the most appropriate one based on the argument types. Swift is very flexible about overloading — you can overload not just by input type or return type, but also based on different constraints on a generic placeholder, as seen in this example.

The general rule that the type checker will pick the most specific overload it can find also applies here. Both versions of isSubset are generic, so the rule that non-generic variants are favored over generic ones is no help. But the version that requires the elements to be Hashable is more specific, because Hashable extends Equatable, and thus it imposes more constraints. Given that these constraints are probably there to make the algorithm more efficient — as they are in the case of isSubset — the more specific function is probably the better choice.

There's another way in which isSubset can be made more general. Up until now, it's only taken an array of elements to check against. But Array is a specific type. Really, isSubset doesn't need to be this specific. Across the two versions, there are only two function calls: contains in both, and Set.init in the Hashable version. In both cases, these functions only require an input type that conforms to the Sequence protocol:

```
extension Sequence where Iterator.Element: Equatable {
    /// Returns a Boolean value indicating whether the sequence contains the
    /// given element.
    func contains(_ element: Iterator.Element) -> Bool
}

struct Set<Element: Hashable>:
    SetAlgebra, Hashable, Collection, ExpressibleByArrayLiteral
{
    /// Creates a new set from a finite sequence of items.
    init<Source: Sequence>(_ sequence: Source)
        where Source.Iterator.Element == Element
```

```
}
```

Given this, the only thing isSubset needs is for other to be of some type that also conforms to Sequence. What's more is that the two sequence types — self and other — *don't have to be the same*. They just need to be sequences of the same element. So here's the Hashable version, rewritten to operate on any two kinds of sequence:

```
extension Sequence where Iterator.Element: Hashable {
  /// Returns true iff all elements in `self` are also in `other`.
  func isSubset<S: Sequence>(of other: S) -> Bool
    where S.Iterator.Element == Iterator.Element
  {
    let otherSet = Set(other)
    for element in self {
      guard otherSet.contains(element) else {
        return false
      }
    }
    return true
  }
}
```

Now that the two sequences don't have to be the same type, this opens up a lot more possibilities. For example, you could pass in a CountableRange of numbers to check against:

```
[5,4,3].isSubset(of: 1...10) // true
```

A similar change can be made to the version that requires the elements to be equatable (not shown here).

extension Sequence where Iterator.Element: Equatable { func isSubset<S: Sequence>(of other: S) -> Bool where S.Iterator.Element == Iterator.Element { for element in self { guard other.contains(element) else { return false } } return true } }

Parameterizing Behavior with Closures

The isSubset method is still not as general as it could be. What about sequences where the elements aren't equatable? Arrays, for example, aren't equatable, and if we use them as elements, it won't work with our current implementation. Arrays do have an == operator, defined like this:

/// Returns true if these arrays contain the same elements.
func ==<Element: Equatable>(lhs: [Element], rhs: [Element]) -> Bool

But that doesn't mean you can use them with isSubset:

// Error: Type of expression is ambiguous without more context
[[1,2]].isSubset(of: [[1,2], [3,4]])

This is because Array doesn't conform to Equatable. It can't, because the type
the array contains might not, itself, be equatable. Swift currently lacks support
for *conditional protocol conformance*, i.e. the ability to express the idea that
Array (or any Sequence) only conforms to a protocol when certain constraints
are met, such as Iterator.Element: Equatable. So Array *can* provide an
implementation of == for when the contained type is equatable, but it *can't*
conform to the protocol.

So how can we make isSubset work with non-equatable types? We can do this
by giving control of what equality means to the caller, requiring them to
supply a function to determine equality. For example, the standard library
provides a second version of contains that does this:

```
extension Sequence {
    /// Returns a Boolean value indicating whether the sequence contains an
    /// element that satisfies the given predicate.
    func contains(where predicate: (Iterator.Element) throws -> Bool)
        rethrows -> Bool
}
```

That is, it takes a function that takes an element of the sequence and performs
some check. It runs the check on each element, returning true as soon as the
check returns true. This version of contains is much more powerful. For
example, you can use it to check for any condition inside a sequence:

```
let isEven = { $0 % 2 == 0 }
(0..<5).contains(where: isEven) // true
[1, 3, 99].contains(where: isEven) // false
```

We can leverage this more flexible version of contains to write a similarly
flexible version of isSubset:

```
extension Sequence {
    func isSubset<S: Sequence>(of other: S,
        by areEquivalent: (Iterator.Element, S.Iterator.Element) -> Bool)
        -> Bool
```

```
  {
    for element in self {
      guard other.contains(where: { areEquivalent(element, $0) }) else {
        return false
      }
    }
    return true
  }
}
```

Now, we can use isSubset with arrays of arrays by supplying a closure expression that compares the arrays using ==:

```
[[1,2]].isSubset(of: [[1,2], [3,4]]) { $0 == $1 } // true
```

The two sequences' elements don't even have to be of the same type, so long as the supplied closure handles the comparison:

```
let ints = [1,2]
let strings = ["1","2","3"]
ints.isSubset(of: strings) { String($0) == $1 } // true
```

Operating Generically on Collections

Generic algorithms on collections often pose some special problems, particularly when it comes to working with indices and slices. In this section, we'd like to demonstrate how to deal with these problems by showing three examples that heavily rely on the correct handling of indices and slices.

A Binary Search

Suppose you find yourself in need of a binary search algorithm for collections. You reach for your nearest favorite reference[2], which happens to be written in Java, and port the code to Swift. Here's one example — albeit a boringly iterative, rather than recursive, one:

```
extension Array {
    /// Returns the first index where `value` appears in `self`, or `nil`,
    /// if `value` is not found.
```

---

2 http://algs4.cs.princeton.edu/home/

```
///
/// - Requires: `areInIncreasingOrder` is a strict weak ordering over the
/// elements in `self`, and the elements in the array are already
/// ordered by it.
/// - Complexity: O(log `count`)
func binarySearch
  (for value: Element, areInIncreasingOrder: (Element, Element) -> Bool)
  -> Int?
{
  var left = 0
  var right = count - 1

  while left <= right {
    let mid = (left + right) / 2
    let candidate = self[mid]

    if areInIncreasingOrder(candidate,value) {
      left = mid + 1
    } else if areInIncreasingOrder(value,candidate) {
      right = mid - 1
    } else {
      // If neither element comes before the other, they _must_ be
      // equal, per the strict ordering requirement of areInIncreasingOrder
      return mid
    }
  }
  // Not found
  return nil
}
}


extension Array where Element: Comparable {
  func binarySearch(for value: Element) -> Int? {
    return self.binarySearch(for: value, areInIncreasingOrder: <)
  }
}
```

For such a famous and seemingly simple algorithm, a binary search is notoriously hard to get right[a]. This one contains a bug that also existed in the Java implementation for two decades — one we'll fix in the generic version. But we also don't guarantee that it's the only bug!

a http://googleresearch.blogspot.com/2006/06/extra-extra-read-all-about-it-nearly.html

It's worth noting some of the conventions from the Swift standard library that this follows:

→ Similar to index(of:), it returns an optional index, with nil representing "not found."

→ It's defined twice — once with a user-supplied parameter to perform the comparison, and once relying on conformance to supply that parameter as a convenience to callers.

→ The ordering must be a strict weak ordering. This means that when comparing two elements, if neither is ordered before the other, they *must* be equal.

This works for arrays, but if you wanted to binary search a ContiguousArray or an ArraySlice, you're out of luck. The method should really be in an extension to RandomAccessCollection — the random access is necessary to preserve the logarithmic complexity, as you need to be able to locate the midpoint in constant time and also check the ordering of the indices using <=.

A shortcut might be to require the collection to have an Int index. This will cover almost every random-access collection in the standard library, and it means you can cut and paste the entire Array version as is:

```
extension RandomAccessCollection where Index == Int, IndexDistance == Int {
    public func binarySearch(for value: Iterator.Element,
        areInIncreasingOrder: (Iterator.Element, Iterator.Element) -> Bool)
        -> Index?
    {
        // Identical implementation to that of Array...
    }
}
```

Warning: If you do this, you'll introduce an *even worse* bug, which we'll come to shortly.

But this is still restricted to integer-indexed collections, and collections don't always have an integer index. Dictionary, Set, and the various String collection views have custom index types. The most notable random-access example in the standard library is ReversedRandomAccessCollection, which, as we saw in the collection protocols chapter, has an opaque index type that wraps the original index, converting it to the equivalent position in the reversed collection.

Generic Binary Search

If you lift the requirement for an Int index, you'll hit several compiler errors. The code needs some rewrites in order to be fully generic, so here's a fully generic version:

```
extension RandomAccessCollection {
  public func binarySearch(for value: Iterator.Element,
    areInIncreasingOrder: (Iterator.Element, Iterator.Element) -> Bool)
    -> Index?
  {
    guard !isEmpty else { return nil }
    var left = startIndex
    var right = index(before: endIndex)

    while left <= right {
      let dist = distance(from: left, to: right)
      let mid = index(left, offsetBy: dist/2)
      let candidate = self[mid]

      if areInIncreasingOrder(candidate, value) {
        left = index(after: mid)
      } else if areInIncreasingOrder(value, candidate) {
        right = index(before: mid)
      } else {
        // If neither element comes before the other, they _must_ be
        // equal, per the strict ordering requirement of areInIncreasingOrder
        return mid
      }
    }
    // Not found
    return nil
  }
}

extension RandomAccessCollection
  where Iterator.Element: Comparable
{
  func binarySearch(for value: Iterator.Element) -> Index? {
    return binarySearch(for: value, areInIncreasingOrder: <)
  }
}
```

The changes are small but significant. First, the left and right variables have changed type to no longer be integers. Instead, we're using the start and end index values. These might be integers, but they might also be opaque types like String's index type (or Dictionary's or Set's, not that these are random access).

But secondly, the simple statement (left + right) / 2 has been replaced by the slightly uglier index(left, offsetBy: dist/2), where let dist = distance(from: left, to: right). How come?

The key concept here is that there are actually two types involved in this calculation: Index and IndexDistance. These are *not necessarily the same thing*. When using integer indices, we happen to be able to use them interchangeably. But loosening that requirement breaks this.

The distance is the number of times you'd need to call index(after:) to get from one point in the collection to another. The end index must be "reachable" from the start index — there's always a finite integer number of times you need to call index(after:) to get to it. This means it must be an integer (though not necessarily an Int). So this is a constraint in the definition of Collection:

```
public protocol Collection: Indexable, Sequence {
    /// A type that can represent the number of steps between a pair of
    /// indices.
    associatedtype IndexDistance: SignedInteger = Int
}
```

This is also why we need an extra guard to ensure the collection isn't empty. When you're just doing integer arithmetic, there's no harm in generating a right value of -1 and then checking that it's less than zero. But when dealing with any kind of index, you need to make sure you don't move back through the start of the collection, which might be an invalid operation. (For example, what would happen if you tried to go back one from the start of a doubly linked list?)

Being integers, index distances can be added together or divided to find the remainder. What we *can't* do is add two indices of any kind together, because what would that mean? If you had the linked list from the collection protocols chapter, you obviously couldn't "add" the pointers to two nodes together. Instead, we must think only in terms of moving indices by some distance using index(after:), index(before:), or index(_:offsetBy:).

This way of thinking takes some getting used to if you're accustomed to thinking in terms of arrays. But think of many array index expressions as a kind of shorthand. For example, when we wrote let right = count - 1, what we really meant was right = index(startIndex, offsetBy: count - 1). It's just that when the index is an Int and startIndex is zero, this reduces to 0 + count - 1, which in turn reduces to count - 1.

This leads us to the serious bug in the implementation that took our Array code and just applied it to RandomAccessCollection: collections with integer indices don't necessarily start with an index of zero, the most common example being ArraySlice. A slice created via myArray[3..<5] will have a startIndex of three. Try and use our simplistic generic binary search on it, and it'll crash *at runtime*. While we were able to require that the index be an integer, the Swift type system has no good way of requiring that the collection be zero-based. And even if it did, in this case, it'd be a silly requirement to impose, since we know a better way. Instead of adding together the left and right indices and halving the result, we find half the distance between the two, and then we advance the left index by that amount to reach the midpoint.

> This version also fixes the bug in our initial implementation. If you didn't spot it, it's that if the array is extremely large, then adding two integer indices together might overflow before being halved (suppose count was approaching Int.max and the searched-for element was the last one in the array). On the other hand, when adding half the distance between the two indices, this doesn't happen. Of course, the chances of anyone ever hitting this bug is very low, which is why the bug in the Java standard library took so long to be discovered.

Now, we can use our binary search algorithm to search ReversedRandomAccessCollection:

```
let a = ["a", "b", "c", "d", "e", "f", "g"]
let r = a.reversed()

r.binarySearch(for: "g", areInIncreasingOrder: >) == r.startIndex // true
```

And we can also search slices, which aren't zero-based:

```
let s = a[2..<5]
s.startIndex // 2
s.binarySearch(for: "d") // Optional(3)
```

Shuffling Collections

To help cement this concept, here's another example, this time an implementation of the Fisher-Yates shuffling algorithm:

```
extension Array {
  mutating func shuffle() {
    for i in 0..<(count - 1) {
      let j = Int(arc4random_uniform(UInt32(count - i))) + i

      // Guard against the (slightly pedantic) requirement of swap that you
      // not try to swap an element with itself.
      guard i != j else { continue }

      swap(&self[i], &self[j])
    }
  }

  /// Non-mutating variant of `shuffle`
  func shuffled() -> [Element] {
    var clone = self
    clone.shuffle()
    return clone
  }
}
```

Again, we've followed a standard library practice: providing an in-place version, since this can be done more efficiently, and then providing a non-mutating version that generates a shuffled copy of the array, which can be implemented in terms of the in-place version.

So how can we write a generic version of this that doesn't mandate integer indices? Just like with binary search, we still need random access, but we also have a new requirement that the collection be mutable, since we want to be able to provide an in-place version. The use of count - 1 will definitely need to change in a way similar to the binary search.

Before we get to the generic implementation, there's an extra complication. We want to use arc4random_uniform to generate random numbers, but we don't know exactly what type of integer IndexDistance will be. We know it's an integer, but not necessarily that it's an Int.

> Swift's current integer APIs aren't well suited for generic programming. A proposal for revised integer protocols that would improve this considerably has been accepted, but it wasn't implemented in time for Swift 3.0.

To handle this, we need to use numericCast, which is a function for converting generically between different integer types. Using this, we can write a version of arc4random_uniform that works on any signed integer type (we could write a version for unsigned integer types too, but since index distances are always signed, we don't need to):

```
extension SignedInteger {
  static func arc4random_uniform(_ upper_bound: Self) -> Self {
    precondition(upper_bound > 0 &&
      upper_bound.toIntMax() < UInt32.max.toIntMax(),
      "arc4random_uniform only callable up to \(UInt32.max)")
    return numericCast(
      Darwin.arc4random_uniform(numericCast(upper_bound)))
  }
}
```

> You could write a version of arc4random that operates on ranges spanning negative numbers, or above the max of UInt32, if you wanted to. But to do so would require a lot more code. If you're interested, the definition of arc4random_uniform is actually open source and quite well commented, and it gives several clues as to how you might do this.

We then use the ability to generate a random number for every IndexDistance type in our generic shuffle implementation:

```
extension MutableCollection where Self: RandomAccessCollection {
  mutating func shuffle() {
    var i = startIndex
    let beforeEndIndex = index(before: endIndex)
    while i < beforeEndIndex {
      let dist = distance(from: i, to: endIndex)
      let randomDistance = IndexDistance.arc4random_uniform(dist)
      let j = index(i, offsetBy: randomDistance)
      guard i != j else { continue }
      swap(&self[i], &self[j])
```

```
        formIndex(after: &i)
      }
    }
}

extension Sequence {
  func shuffled() -> [Iterator.Element] {
    var clone = Array(self)
    clone.shuffle()
    return clone
  }
}

var numbers = Array(1...10)
numbers.shuffle()
numbers // [9, 1, 5, 2, 6, 4, 8, 3, 10, 7]
```

The shuffle method is significantly more complex and less readable than the non-generic version. This is partly because we had to replace simple integer math like count - 1 with index calculations such as index(before: endIndex). The other reason is that we switched from a for to a while loop. The alternative, iterating over the indices with for i in indices.dropLast(), has a potential performance problem that we already talked about in the collection protocols chapter: if the indices property holds a reference to the collection, mutating the collection while traversing the indices will defeat the copy-on-write optimizations and cause the collection to make an unnecessary copy.

Admittedly, the chances of this happening in our case are small, because most random-access collections likely use plain integer indices where the Indices type doesn't need to reference its base collection. For instance, Array.Indices is CountableRange<Int> instead of the default DefaultRandomAccessIndices. One example of a random-access collection that uses a back-referencing Indices type is String.UTF16View (which, if you recall from the strings chapter, conforms to RandomAccessCollection when you import Foundation). But that one isn't a MutableCollection and therefore doesn't meet the shuffling algorithm's requirements either.

Inside the loop, we measure the distance from the running index to the end and then use our new SignedInteger.arc4random method to compute a random index to swap with. The actual swap operation remains the same as in the non-generic version.

You might wonder why we didn't extend MutableCollection when implementing the non-modifying shuffle. Again, this is a pattern you see often in the standard library — for example, when you sort a ContiguousArray, you get back an Array and not a ContiguousArray.

In this case, the reason is that our immutable version relies on the ability to clone the collection and then shuffle it in place. This, in turn, relies on the collection having value semantics. But not all collections are guaranteed to have value semantics. If NSMutableArray conformed to MutableCollection (which it doesn't — probably because it's bad form for Swift collections to not have value semantics — but could), then shuffled and shuffle would have the same effect, since NSMutableArray has reference semantics. var clone = self just makes a copy of the reference, so a subsequent clone.shuffle would shuffle self — probably not what the user would expect. Instead, we take a full copy of the elements into an array and shuffle and return that.

There's a compromise approach. You could write a version of shuffle to return the same type of collection as the one being shuffled, so long as that type is also a RangeReplaceableCollection:

```
extension MutableCollection
  where Self: RandomAccessCollection,
    Self: RangeReplaceableCollection
{
  func shuffled() -> Self {
    var clone = Self()
    clone.append(contentsOf: self)
    clone.shuffle()
    return clone
  }
}
```

This relies on the two abilities of RangeReplaceableCollection: to create a fresh empty version of the collection, and to then append any sequence (in this case, self) to that empty collection, thus guaranteeing a full clone takes place. The standard library doesn't take this approach — probably because the consistency of always creating an array for any kind of non-in-place operation is preferred — but it's an option if you want it. However, remember to create the sequence version as well, so that you offer shuffling for non-mutable range-replaceable collections and sequences.

SubSequence and Generic Algorithms

Here's one final example to demonstrate a problem you'll encounter if you try and use slicing generically.

Say you want to write an algorithm that searches for a given subsequence — so similar to index(of:), but searching for a subsequence rather than an individual element. In theory, a naive solution to this is simple: return the first index where the slice from that index to the end of the collection starts with the pattern. We can use index(where:) for this. However, if you try it, you'll find you get a compiler error:

```
extension Collection where Iterator.Element: Equatable {
  func search<Other: Sequence>(for pattern: Other) -> Index?
    where Other.Iterator.Element == Iterator.Element
  {
    return indices.first { idx in
      // Error: Missing argument for parameter 'by'
      suffix(from: idx).starts(with: pattern)
    }
  }
}
```

The error message suggests that the compiler expects starts(with:by:) here, which takes an additional closure to determine if two elements are equivalent. This seems odd. The non-parameterized variant, starts(with:), should be available to sequences whose elements are Equatable, which is exactly what we specified for our extension (via Iterator.Element: Equatable).

We also constrained the elements of Other to be the same as our own elements (via Other.Iterator.Element == Iterator.Element), as is required by both starts(with:) overloads. Unfortunately, though, there's one thing that isn't guaranteed, which is that SubSequence.Iterator.Element — that is, the type of an element in a slice — is equal to the type of an element in the collection. Of course it should be! But as of Swift 3.0, the language isn't powerful enough to write this constraint. This makes the slice we create with suffix(from: idx) incompatible with Other in the eyes of the compiler.

Fixing this on the language level would require a redeclaration of the SubSequence associated type with the constraint that SubSequence.Iterator.Element must be equal to Iterator.Element, but where clauses on associated types are currently not supported. However, Swift will likely get this feature in the future.

Until then, you must constrain your protocol extension to ensure that any slices you use contain the same element as the collection. A first attempt might be to require the subsequence be the same as the collection:

```
extension Collection
  where Iterator.Element: Equatable, SubSequence == Self {
  // Implementation of search same as before
}
```

This would work when a subsequence has the same type as its collection, like in the case with strings. But as we saw in the built-in collections chapter, the slice type for arrays is ArraySlice, so you still couldn't search arrays. Therefore, we need to loosen the constraint a little and instead require that the subsequences' elements match:

```
extension Collection
  where Iterator.Element: Equatable,
    SubSequence.Iterator.Element == Iterator.Element
{
  // Implementation of search same as before
}
```

The compiler responds to this with another error message, this time regarding the trailing closure argument of the indices.first call: "Cannot convert value of type (Self.Index) -> Bool to expected argument type (_) -> Bool." What does this mean? It's essentially the same problem, but this time, it's for indices instead of elements. The type system can't express the idea that the element type of Indices (which itself is a collection) is always equal to the collection's index type — therefore, the idx parameter of the closure (which has the type Indices.Iterator.Element) is incompatible with the argument type suffix(from:) expects (which is Index).

Adding this constraint to the extension finally makes the code compile:

```
extension Collection
  where Iterator.Element: Equatable,
    SubSequence.Iterator.Element == Iterator.Element,
    Indices.Iterator.Element == Index
{
  func search<Other: Sequence>(for pattern: Other) -> Index?
    where Other.Iterator.Element == Iterator.Element
  {
    return indices.first { idx in
      suffix(from: idx).starts(with: pattern)
```

```
      }
    }
}
```

```
let text = "It was the best of times, it was the worst of times"
text.characters.search(for: ["b","e","s","t"])
/*
Optional(Swift.String.CharacterView.Index(_base: Swift.String.UnicodeScalarView.Index(_
11), _countUTF16: 1))
*/
```

Notice that throughout this entire process we haven't changed the actual code
once, only the constraints that specify the requirements types must meet to
use this functionality.

Overrides and Optimizations

Finally, it's often the case that you can provide a more efficient generic
algorithm if you tighten the constraints slightly. For example, you could
improve the speed of the search algorithm above if you knew that both the
searched collection and the pattern were random-access collections. That way,
you could avoid searching for the pattern in the part of the collection that was
too short to match it, and when the pattern was longer than the collection, you
could avoid searching completely.

For this to work, you need to guarantee that both Self and Other conform to
RandomAccessCollection. We then find ourselves with an algorithm that's
about as much constraint as it is code:

```
extension RandomAccessCollection
   where Iterator.Element: Equatable,
      Indices.Iterator.Element == Index,
      SubSequence.Iterator.Element == Iterator.Element,
      SubSequence.Indices.Iterator.Element == Index
{
   func search<Other: RandomAccessCollection>
      (for pattern: Other) -> Index?
      where Other.IndexDistance == IndexDistance,
         Other.Iterator.Element == Iterator.Element
   {
      // If pattern is longer, this cannot match, exit early.
      guard !isEmpty && pattern.count <= count else { return nil }
```

```
    // Otherwise, from the start up to the end
    // less space for the pattern ...
    let stopSearchIndex = index(endIndex, offsetBy: -pattern.count)

    // ... check if a slice from this point
    // starts with the pattern.
    return prefix(upTo: stopSearchIndex).indices.first { idx in
      suffix(from: idx).starts(with: pattern)
    }
  }
}
```

```
let numbers = 1..<100
numbers.search(for: 80..<90) // Optional(80)
```

We've added one other constraint here: the distance types of the two collections are the same. This keeps the code simple, though it does rule out the possibility that they might differ. This is pretty rare though — the type-erasing AnyCollection struct uses IntMax, which is different from Int on 32-bit systems. The alternative would be a light sprinkling of numericCasts — for example, guard numericCast(pattern.count) <= count else { return nil }. We also had to add SubSequence.Indices.Iterator.Element == Index to make sure that the element type of prefix(upTo: stopSearchIndex).indices is the collection's index type. Again, this should be trivially true, but we need to explicitly tell it to the compiler.

Designing with Generics

As we've seen, generics can be used to provide multiple implementations of the same functionality. We can write generic functions but provide specific implementations for certain types. Also, by using protocol extensions, we can write generic algorithms that operate on many types.

Generics can also be very helpful during the design of your program, in order to factor out shared functionality and reduce boilerplate. In this section, we'll refactor a normal piece of code, pulling out the common functionality by using generics. Not only can we make generic functions, but we can also make generic data types.

Let's write some functions to interact with a web service. For example, consider fetching a list of users and parsing it into the User datatype. We write a function named loadUsers, which loads the users from the network asynchronously and then calls the callback with the list of fetched users.

We start by implementing it in a naive way. First, we build the URL. Then, we load the data synchronously (this is just for the sake of the example; you should always do networking asynchronously in production code). Next, we parse the JSON response, which will give us arrays of dictionaries. Finally, we transform the plain JSON objects into User structs:

```
func loadUsers(callback: ([User]?) -> ()) {
    let usersURL = webserviceURL.appendingPathComponent("/users")
    let data = try? Data(contentsOf: usersURL)
    let json = data.flatMap {
        try? JSONSerialization.jsonObject(with: $0, options: [])
    }
    let users = (json as? [Any]).flatMap { jsonObject in
      jsonObject.flatMap(User.init)
    }
    callback(users)
}
```

This function has three possible error cases: the URL loading can fail, the JSON parsing can fail, and building user objects from the JSON array can fail. All three operations return nil upon failure. By using flatMap on the optional values, we ensure that subsequent operations are only executed if the previous ones succeeded. Otherwise, the nil value from the first failing operation will be propagated through the chain to the end, where we eventually call the callback either with a valid users array or nil.

Now, if we want to write the same function to load other resources, we'd need to duplicate most of the code. For example, if we consider a function to load blog posts, its type could look like this:

```
func loadBlogPosts(callback: ([BlogPost])? -> ())
```

The implementation would be almost the same. Not only would we have duplicated code, but both functions are hard to test: we need to make sure the test can access the web service or else find some way to fake the requests. And because the functions take a callback, we need to make the tests asynchronous too.

Extracting Common Functionality

A better approach is to try to move the User-specific parts outside the function in order to make the other parts reusable. For example, we could add the path and the conversion function that turns JSON objects into domain objects as parameters. We name this new function loadResource to indicate its universality. Because we want the conversion function to handle arbitrary types, we also make the function generic over A:

```
func loadResource<A>(at path: String,
    parse: (Any) -> A?,
    callback: (A?) -> ())
{
    let resourceURL = webserviceURL.appendingPathComponent(path)
    let data = try? Data(contentsOf: resourceURL)
    let json = data.flatMap {
        try? JSONSerialization.jsonObject(with: $0, options: [])
    }
    callback(json.flatMap(parse))
}
```

Now we can base our loadUsers function on loadResource:

```
func loadUsers(callback: ([User]?) -> ()) {
    loadResource(at: "/users", parse: jsonArray(User.init), callback: callback)
}
```

We use a helper function, jsonArray, to convert JSON into user objects. It first tries to convert an Any to an array of Anys, and then it tries to parse each element using the supplied function, returning nil if any of the steps fail:

```
func jsonArray<A>(_ transform: @escaping (Any) -> A?) -> (Any) -> [A]? {
    return { array in
        guard let array = array as? [Any] else {
            return nil
        }
        return array.flatMap(transform)
    }
}
```

To load the blog posts, we just change the path and the parsing function:

```
func loadBlogPosts(callback: ([BlogPost]?) -> ()) {
    loadResource(at: "/posts", parse: jsonArray(BlogPost.init), callback: callback)
```

```
}
```

This avoids a lot of duplication. And if we later decide to switch from synchronous to asynchronous networking, we don't need to update either loadUsers or loadBlogPosts. But even though these functions are now very short, they're still hard to test — they remain asynchronous and depend on the web service being accessible.

Creating a Generic Data Type

The path and parse parameters of the loadResource function are very tightly coupled; if you change one, you likely have to change the other too. Let's bundle them up in a struct that describes a resource. Just like functions, structs (and other types) can also be generic:

```
struct Resource<A> {
    let path: String
    let parse: (Any) -> A?
}
```

Now we can write an alternative version of loadResource as a method on Resource. It uses the resource's properties to determine what to load and how to parse the result, so the only remaining argument is the callback function:

```
extension Resource {
    func loadSynchronously(callback: (A?) -> ()) {
        let resourceURL = webserviceURL.appendingPathComponent(path)
        let data = try? Data(contentsOf: resourceURL)
        let json = data.flatMap {
            try? JSONSerialization.jsonObject(with: $0, options: [])
        }
        callback(json.flatMap(parse))
    }
}
```

The previous top-level functions to load a specific resource now become values of the Resource struct. This makes it very easy to add new resources without having to create new functions:

```
let usersResource: Resource<[User]> =
    Resource(path: "/users", parse: jsonArray(User.init))
let postsResource: Resource<[BlogPost]> =
    Resource(path: "/posts", parse: jsonArray(BlogPost.init))
```

Adding a variant that uses asynchronous networking is now possible with minimal duplication. We don't need to change any of our existing code describing the endpoints:

```
extension Resource {
  func loadAsynchronously(callback: @escaping (A?) -> ()) {
    let resourceURL = webserviceURL.appendingPathComponent(path)
    let session = URLSession.shared
    session.dataTask(with: resourceURL) { data, response, error in
      let json = data.flatMap {
        try? JSONSerialization.jsonObject(with: $0, options: [])
      }
      callback(json.flatMap(self.parse))
    }.resume()
  }
}
```

Aside from the usage of the asynchronous URLSession API, the only material difference to the synchronous version is that the callback argument must now be annotated with @escaping because the callback function escapes the method's scope. See the functions chapter if you want to learn more about escaping vs. non-escaping closures.

We've now completely decoupled our endpoints from the network calls. We boiled down usersResource and postsResource to their absolute minimums so that they only describe where the resource is located and how to parse it. The design is also extensible: adding more configuration options, such as the HTTP method or a way to add POST data to a request, is simply a matter of adding additional properties to the Resource type. (Specifying default values, e.g. GET for the HTTP method, helps keep the code clean.)

Testing has become much simpler. The Resource struct is fully synchronous and independent of the network, so testing whether a resource is configured correctly becomes trivial. The networking code is still harder to test, of course, because it's naturally asynchronous and depends on the network. But this complexity is now nicely isolated in the loadAsynchronously method; all other parts are simple and don't involve asynchronous code.

In this section, we started with a non-generic function for loading some data from the network. Next, we created a generic function with multiple parameters, significantly reducing duplicate code. Finally, we bundled up the parameters into a separate Resource data type. The domain-specific logic for the concrete resources is fully decoupled from the networking code. Changing the network stack doesn't require any change to the resources.

How Generics Work

How do generics work from the perspective of the compiler? To answer this question, consider the min function from the standard library (we took this example from the Optimizing Swift Performance[3] session at Apple's 2015 Worldwide Developers Conference):

```
func min<T: Comparable>(_ x: T, _ y: T) -> T {
    return y < x ? y : x
}
```

The only constraints for the arguments and return value of min are that all three must have the same type T and that T must conform to Comparable. Other than that, T could be anything — Int, Float, String, or even a type the compiler knows nothing about at compile time because it's defined in another module. This means that the compiler lacks two essential pieces of information it needs to emit code for the function:

→ The sizes of the variables of type T (including the arguments and return value).

→ The address of the specific overload of the < function that must be called at runtime.

Swift solves these problems by introducing a level of indirection for generic code. Whenever the compiler encounters a value that has a generic type, it boxes the value in a container. This container has a fixed size to store the value; if the value is too large to fit, Swift allocates it on the heap and stores a reference to it in the container.

The compiler also maintains a list of one or more *witness tables* per generic type parameter: one so-called *value witness table*, plus one *protocol witness table* for each protocol constraint on the type. The witness tables (also called *vtables*) are used to dynamically dispatch function calls to the correct implementations at runtime.

---

3 https://developer.apple.com/videos/play/wwdc2015/409/?time=992

The value witness table is always present for any generic type. It contains pointers to the fundamental operations of the type, such as allocation, copying, and destruction. These can be simple no-ops or memcopies for value types such as Int, whereas reference types include their reference counting logic here. The value witness table also records the size and alignment of the type.

The record for the generic type T in our example will include one protocol witness table because T has one protocol constraint, namely Comparable. For each method or property the protocol declares, the witness table contains a pointer to the implementation for the conforming type. Any calls to one of these methods in the body of the generic function are then dispatched at runtime through the witness table. In our example, the expression y < x is dispatched in this way.

The protocol witness tables provide a mapping between the protocols to which the generic type conforms (this is statically known to the compiler through the generic constraints) and the functions that implement that functionality for the specific type (these are only known at runtime). In fact, the only way to query or manipulate the value in any way is through the witness tables. We couldn't declare the min function with an unconstrained parameter <T> and then expect it to work with any type that has an implementation for <, regardless of Comparable conformance. The compiler wouldn't allow this because there wouldn't be a witness table for it to locate the correct < implementation. This is why generics are so closely related to protocols — you can't do much with unconstrained generics except write container types like Array<Element> or Optional<Wrapped>.

In summary, the code the compiler generates for the min function looks something like this (in pseudocode):

```
func min<T: Comparable>(_ x: TBox, _ y: TBox,
    valueWTable: VTable, comparableWTable: VTable)
    -> TBox
{
    let xCopy = valueWTable.copy(x)
    let yCopy = valueWTable.copy(y)
    let result = comparableWTable.lessThan(yCopy, xCopy) ? y : x
    valueWTable.release(xCopy)
    valueWTable.release(yCopy)
    return result
}
```

The layout of the container for generic parameters is similar but not identical to the *existential containers* used for protocol types that we'll cover in the next chapter. An existential container combines the storage for the value and the pointers to zero or more witness tables in one structure, whereas the container for a generic parameter only includes the value storage — the witness tables are stored separately so that they can be shared between all variables of the same type in the generic function.

Generic Specialization

The compile-once-and-dispatch-dynamically model we described in the previous section was an important design goal for Swift's generics system. Compared to how C++ templates work — where the compiler generates a separate instance of the templated function or class for every permutation of concrete types using the template — this leads to faster compilation times and potentially smaller binaries. Swift's model is also more flexible because, unlike C++, code that uses a generic API doesn't need to see the implementation of the generic function or type, only the declaration.

The downside is lower performance at runtime, caused by the indirection the code has to go through. This is likely negligible when you consider a single function call, but it does add up when generics are as pervasive as they are in Swift. The standard library uses generics everywhere, including for very common operations that must be as fast as possible, such as comparing values. Even if generic code is only slightly slower than non-generic code, chances are developers will try to avoid using it.

Luckily, the Swift compiler can make use of an optimization called *generic specialization* to remove this overhead. Generic specialization means that the compiler clones a generic type or function, such as min<T>, for a concrete parameter type, such as Int. This specialized function can then be optimized for Int, removing all the overhead. So the specialized version of min<T> for Int would look like this:

```
func min(_ x: Int, _ y: Int) -> Int {
  return y < x ? y : x
}
```

This not only eliminates the cost of the virtual dispatch, but it also enables further optimizations such as inlining, for which the indirection would otherwise be a barrier.

The optimizer uses heuristics to decide which generic types or functions it chooses to specialize, and for which concrete types it performs the specialization. This decision requires a balancing of compilation times, binary size, and runtime performance. If your code calls min with Int arguments very frequently, but only once with Float arguments, chances are only the Int variant will be specialized. Make sure to compile your release builds with optimizations enabled (swiftc -O on the command line) to take advantage of all available heuristics.

Regardless of how aggressive the compiler is with generic specialization, the generic version of the function will always exist, at least if the generic function is visible to other modules. This ensures that external code can always call the generic version, even if the compiler didn't know anything about the external types when it compiled the generic function.

Whole Module Optimization

Generic specialization only works if the compiler can see the full definition of the generic type or function it wants to specialize. Since Swift compiles source files individually by default, it can only perform specialization if the code that uses the generic code resides in the same file as the generic code.

Since this is a pretty big limitation, the compiler has a flag to enable *whole module optimization*. In this mode, all files in the current module are optimized together as if they were one file, allowing generic specializations across the full codebase. You can enable whole module optimization by passing -whole-module-optimization to swiftc. Be sure to do so in release builds (and possibly also in debug builds), because the performance gains can be huge. The drawback is longer compilation times.

Whole module optimization enables other important optimizations. For example, the optimizer will recognize when an internal class has no subclasses in the entire module. Since the internal modifier makes sure the class isn't visible outside the module, this means the compiler can replace dynamic dispatch with static dispatch for all methods of this class.

Generic specialization requires the definition of the generic type or function to be visible, and therefore can't be performed across module boundaries. This means your generic code will likely be faster for clients that reside in the same module where the code is defined than for external clients. The only exception to this is generic code in the standard library. Because the standard library is so important and used by every other module, definitions in the standard library are visible in all modules and thus available for specialization.

Swift includes a semi-official attribute[4] called @_specialize that allows you to make specialized versions of your generic code available to other modules. You must specify the list of types you want to specialize, so this only helps if you know your code will mostly be used with a limited number of types. Making specialized versions of our min function for integers and strings available to other modules would look like this:

```
@_specialize(Int)
@_specialize(String)
public func min<T: Comparable>(_ x: T, _ y: T) -> T {
  return y < x ? y : x
}
```

Notice we added public — it makes no sense to specify @_specialize for internal, fileprivate, or private APIs, since those are not visible outside the module anyway.

Conclusion

In the beginning of this chapter, we defined generic programming as identifying the essential interface an algorithm or data type requires. We achieved this for our isSubset method by starting with a non-generic version and then carefully removing constraints. Writing multiple overloads with different constraints allowed us to provide the function to the widest possible range of types and meet performance expectations at the same time, and we relied on the compiler to select the best variant for the types involved.

In the asynchronous networking example, we removed many assumptions about the network stack from our Resource struct. Concrete resource values make no assumptions about the server's root domain or how to load data —

4 https://lists.swift.org/pipermail/swift-dev/Week-of-Mon-20160314/001449.html

they're just inert representations of API endpoints. Here, generic programming helps keep the resources simple and decoupled from the networking code. This also makes testing easier.

If you're interested in the theoretical details behind generic programming and how different languages facilitate it, we recommend Ronald Garcia et al.'s 2007 paper titled "An Extended Comparative Study of Language Support for Generic Programming."

Finally, generic programming in Swift wouldn't be possible without protocols. This brings us to our next chapter.

Protocols

10

In previous chapters, we saw how functions and generics can help us write very dynamic programs. Protocols work together with functions and generics to enable even more dynamic behavior.

Swift protocols aren't unlike Objective-C protocols. They can be used for delegation, and they allow you to specify abstract interfaces (such as IteratorProtocol or Sequence). Yet, at the same time, they're very different from Objective-C protocols. For example, we can make structs and enums conform to protocols. Additionally, protocols can have associated types. We can even add method implementations to protocols using protocol extensions. We'll look at all these things in the section on protocol-oriented programming.

Protocols allow for dynamic dispatch: the correct method implementation is selected at runtime based on the type of the receiver. However, when a method is or isn't dynamically dispatched is sometimes unintuitive, and this can lead to surprising behavior. We'll look at this issue in the next section.

Regular protocols can be used either as type constraints or as standalone types. Protocols with associated types and protocols with Self requirements, however, are special: we can't use them as standalone types; we can only use them as type constraints. This may sound like a small limitation, but it makes protocols with associated types almost entirely different things in practice. We'll take a closer look at this later. We'll also discuss type erasers (such as AnyIterator) as a way of making it easier to work with protocols with associated types.

In object-oriented programming, subclassing is a powerful way to share code among multiple classes. A subclass inherits all the methods from its superclass and can choose to override some of the methods. For example, we could have an AbstractSequence class and subclasses such as Array and Dictionary. Doing so allows us to add methods to AbstractSequence, and all the subclasses would automatically inherit those methods.

Yet in Swift, the code sharing in Sequence is implemented using protocols and protocol extensions. In this way, the Sequence protocol and its extensions also work with value types, such as structs and enums, which don't support subclassing.

Not relying on subclassing also makes types more flexible. In Swift, a class can only have a single superclass. When we create a class, we have to choose the superclass well, because we can only pick one; we can't subclass both AbstractSequence, and, say, Stream. This can sometimes be a problem. There are examples in Cocoa — e.g. with NSMutableAttributedString, where the designers had to choose between NSAttributedString and NSMutableString as a superclass.

Some languages have multiple inheritance, the most famous being C++. But this leads to something called the "diamond problem." For example, if multiple inheritance were possible, we could envision an NSMutableAttributedString that inherits from both NSMutableString and NSAttributedString. But what happens if both of those classes override a method of NSString? You could deal with it by just picking one of the methods. But what if that method is isEqual:? Providing good behavior for multiple inheritance is really hard.

Because multiple inheritance is so complicated, most languages don't support it. Yet many languages do support conforming to multiple protocols, which doesn't have the same problems. In Swift, we can conform to multiple protocols, and the compiler warns us when the use of a method is ambiguous.

Protocol extensions are a way of sharing code without sharing base classes. Protocols define a minimal viable set of methods for a type to implement. Extensions can then build on these minimal methods to implement more complex features.

For example, to implement a generic algorithm that sorts any sequence, you need two things. First, you need a way to iterate over the elements. Second, you need to be able to compare the elements. That's it. There are no demands as to how the elements are held. They could be in a linked list, an array, or any iterable container. What they are doesn't matter, either — they could be strings, integers, dates, or people. As long as you write down the two aforementioned constraints in the type system, you can implement sort:

```
extension Sequence where Iterator.Element: Comparable {
  func sorted() -> [Self.Iterator.Element]
}
```

To implement an in-place sort, you need more building blocks. More specifically, you need index-based access to the elements rather than just linear iteration. Collection captures this and MutableCollection adds mutation to it. Finally, you need to compare and offset indices in constant time. RandomAccessCollection allows for that. This may sound complex, but it captures the prerequisites needed to perform an in-place sort:

```
extension MutableCollection where
    Self: RandomAccessCollection,
    Self.Iterator.Element: Comparable {
    mutating func sort()
}
```

Minimal capabilities described by protocols compose well. You can add different capabilities of different protocols to a type, bit by bit. We saw this in the collection protocols chapter when we first built a List type by giving it a single method, cons. Without changing the original List struct, we made it conform to Sequence. In fact, we could've done this even if we weren't the original authors of this type, using a technique called *retroactive modeling*. By adding conformance to Sequence, we get all the extension methods of Sequence for free.

Adding new shared features via a common superclass isn't this flexible; you can't just decide later to add a new common base class to many different classes. When you do, you risk major refactoring. And if you aren't the owner of these subclasses, you can't do it at all!

Subclasses have to know which methods they can override without breaking the superclass. For example, when a method is overridden, a subclass might need to call the superclass method at the right moment: either at the beginning, somewhere in the middle, or at the end of the method. This moment is often unspecified. Also, by overriding the wrong method, a subclass might break the superclass without warning.

Protocol-Oriented Programming

In a graphical application, we might want different render targets: for example, we can render graphics in a Core Graphics CGContext and create an SVG. To start, we'll define a protocol that describes the minimum functionality of our drawing API:

```
protocol Drawing {
    mutating func addEllipse(rect: CGRect, fill: UIColor)
    mutating func addRectangle(rect: CGRect, fill: UIColor)
}
```

One of the most powerful features of protocols is that we can retroactively modify any type to add conformance to a protocol. For CGContext, we can add an extension that makes it conform to the Drawing protocol:

```swift
extension CGContext: Drawing {
  func addEllipse(rect: CGRect, fill: UIColor) {
    setFillColor(fill.cgColor)
    fillEllipse(in: rect)
  }

  func addRectangle(rect: CGRect, fill fillColor: UIColor) {
    setFillColor(fillColor.cgColor)
    fill(rect)
  }
}
```

To represent an SVG file, we create an SVG struct. It contains an XMLNode with children and has a single method, append, which appends a child node to the root node. (We've left out the definition of XMLNode here.)

```swift
struct SVG {
  var rootNode = XMLNode(tag: "svg")
  mutating func append(node: XMLNode) {
    rootNode.children.append(node)
  }
}
```

Rendering an SVG means we have to append a node for each element. We use a few simple extensions: the svgAttributes property on CGRect creates a dictionary that matches the SVG specification. String.init(hexColor:) takes a UIColor and turns it into a hexadecimal string (such as "#010100"). With these helpers, adding Drawing conformance is straightforward:

```swift
extension SVG: Drawing {
  mutating func addEllipse(rect: CGRect, fill: UIColor) {
    var attributes: [String:String] = rect.svgAttributes
    attributes["fill"] = String(hexColor: fill)
    append(node: XMLNode(tag: "ellipse", attributes: attributes))
  }

  mutating func addRectangle(rect: CGRect, fill: UIColor) {
    var attributes: [String:String] = rect.svgAttributes
    attributes["fill"] = String(hexColor: fill)
    append(node: XMLNode(tag: "rect", attributes: attributes))
```

```
     }
}
```

We can now write drawing code that's independent of the rendering target; it only assumes that context conforms to the Drawing protocol. If we initialized it with a CGContext instead, we wouldn't need to change any of the code:

```
var context: Drawing = SVG()
let rect1 = CGRect(x: 0, y: 0, width: 100, height: 100)
let rect2 = CGRect(x: 0, y: 0, width: 50, height: 50)
context.addRectangle(rect: rect1, fill: .yellow)
context.addEllipse(rect: rect2, fill: .blue)
context
/*
<svg>
<rect cy="0.0" fill="#010100" ry="100.0" rx="100.0" cx="0.0"/>
<ellipse cy="0.0" fill="#000001" ry="50.0" rx="50.0" cx="0.0"/>
</svg>
*/
```

Protocol Extensions

Another powerful feature of Swift protocols is the possibility to extend a protocol with full method implementations; you can do this to both your own protocols and existing protocols. For example, we could add a method to Drawing that, given a center point and a radius, renders a circle:

```
extension Drawing {
    mutating func addCircle(center: CGPoint, radius: CGFloat, fill: UIColor) {
        let diameter = radius/2
        let origin = CGPoint(x: center.x - diameter, y: center.y - diameter)
        let size = CGSize(width: radius, height: radius)
        let rect = CGRect(origin: origin, size: size)
        addEllipse(rect: rect, fill: fill)
    }
}
```

By adding addCircle in an extension, we can use it both with CGContext and our SVG type.

Note that code sharing using protocols has several advantages over code sharing using inheritance:

→ We're not forced to use a specific superclass.

→ We can conform existing types to a protocol (e.g. we made CGContext conform to Drawing). Subclassing isn't as flexible; we can't retroactively change the superclass of CGContext.

→ Protocols work with both structs and classes, but structs can't have superclasses.

→ Finally, when dealing with protocols, we don't have to worry about overriding methods or calling super at the right moment.

Overriding Methods in Protocol Extensions

As the author of a protocol, you have two options when you add a protocol method in an extension. First, you can choose to only add it in an extension, as we did above with addCircle. Or, you could also add the method declaration to the protocol definition itself, making the method a *protocol requirement*. Protocol requirements are dispatched dynamically, whereas methods that are only defined in an extension use static dispatch. The difference is subtle but important, both as a protocol author and as a user of conforming types.

Let's look at an example. In the previous section, we added addCircle as an extension of the Drawing protocol, but we didn't make it a requirement. If we want to provide a more specific version of addCircle for the SVG type, we can just "override" the method:

```
extension SVG {
    mutating func addCircle(center: CGPoint, radius: CGFloat, fill: UIColor) {
        var attributes: [String:String] = [
            "cx": "\(center.x)",
            "cy": "\(center.y)",
            "r": "\(radius)",
        ]
        attributes["fill"] = String(hexColor: fill)
        append(node: XMLNode(tag: "circle", attributes: attributes))
    }
}
```

If we now create an instance of SVG and call addCircle on it, it behaves as you'd expect: the compiler will pick the most specific version of addCircle, which is the version that's defined in the extension on SVG. We can see that it correctly uses the circle tag:

```
var sample = SVG()
sample.addCircle(center: .zero, radius: 20, fill: .red)
print(sample)
/*
<svg>
<circle cy="0.0" fill="#010000" r="20.0" cx="0.0"/>
</svg>
*/
```

Now, just like above, we create another SVG instance; the only difference is that we explicitly cast the variable to the Drawing type. What'll happen if we call addCircle on this Drawing-that's-really-an-SVG? Most people would probably expect that this call would be dispatched to the same implementation on SVG, but that's not the case:

```
var otherSample: Drawing = SVG()
otherSample.addCircle(center: .zero, radius: 20, fill: .red)
print(otherSample)
/*
<svg>
<ellipse cy="-10.0" fill="#010000" ry="20.0" rx="20.0" cx="-10.0"/>
</svg>
*/
```

It returned an ellipse element, and not the circle we were expecting. It turns out it used the addCircle method from the protocol extension and not the method from the SVG extension. When we defined otherSample as a variable of type Drawing, the compiler automatically boxed the SVG value in a type that represents the protocol. This box is called an *existential container*, the details of which we'll look into later in this chapter. For now, let's consider the behavior: when we call addCircle on our existential container, the method is statically dispatched, i.e. it always uses the extension on Drawing. If it were dynamically dispatched, it would've taken the type of the receiver (SVG) into account.

To make addCircle dynamically dispatched, we add it as a protocol requirement:

```
protocol Drawing {
    mutating func addEllipse(rect: CGRect, fill: UIColor)
    mutating func addRectangle(rect: CGRect, fill: UIColor)
    mutating func addCircle(center: CGPoint, radius: CGFloat, fill: UIColor)
}
```

We can still provide a default implementation, just like before:

And also like before, types are free to override addCircle. Because it's now part of the protocol definition, it'll be dynamically dispatched — at runtime, depending on the dynamic type of the receiver, the existential container will call the custom implementation if one exists. If it doesn't exist, it'll use the default implementation from the protocol extension. The addCircle method has become a *customization point* for the protocol.

The Swift standard library uses this technique a lot. A protocol like Sequence has dozens of requirements, yet almost all have default implementations. A conforming type can customize the default implementations because the methods are dynamically dispatched, but it doesn't have to.

Two Types of Protocols

As we stated in the introduction, protocols with associated types are different from regular protocols. The same is true for protocols with a Self requirement, i.e. those that refer to Self anywhere in their definition. In Swift 3, these protocols can't be used as standalone types. This restriction will probably be lifted in a future version once the full generics system is implemented, but until then, we have to deal with the limitations.

One of the simplest examples of a protocol with an associated type is IteratorProtocol. It has a single associated type, Element, and a single function, next(), which returns a value of that type:

```
public protocol IteratorProtocol {
    associatedtype Element
    public mutating func next() -> Self.Element?
}
```

In the chapter on collection protocols, we showed an example of a type that conforms to IteratorProtocol. This iterator simply returns 1 each time it's called:

```
struct ConstantIterator: IteratorProtocol {
    mutating func next() -> Int? {
        return 1
    }
}
```

As we've seen, IteratorProtocol forms the base for the collection protocols. Unlike IteratorProtocol, the Collection protocol doesn't have a simple definition:

```
protocol Collection: Indexable, Sequence {
    associatedtype IndexDistance: SignedInteger = Int
    associatedtype Iterator: IteratorProtocol = IndexingIterator<Self>
    // ... Method definitions and more associated types
}
```

Let's look at some of the important parts of the definition above. The collection protocol inherits from Indexable and Sequence. Because protocol inheritance doesn't have the same problems as inheritance through subclassing, we can compose multiple protocols:

```
protocol Collection: Indexable, Sequence {
```

Next up, we have two associated types: IndexDistance and Iterator. Both have a default value: IndexDistance is just an Int, and Iterator is an IndexingIterator. Note that we can use Self for the generic type parameter of IndexingIterator. Both types also have constraints: IndexDistance needs to conform to the SignedInteger protocol, and Iterator needs to conform to IteratorProtocol:

```
associatedtype IndexDistance: SignedInteger = Int
associatedtype Iterator: IteratorProtocol = IndexingIterator<Self>
```

There are two options when we make our own types conform to the Collection protocol. We can either use the default associated types, or we could define our own associated types (for example, in the collection protocols chapter, we made List have a custom associated type for SubSequence). If we decide to stick with the default associated types, we get a lot of functionality for free. For example, there's a conditional protocol extension that adds an implementation of makeIterator() when the iterator isn't overridden:

```
extension Collection where Iterator == IndexingIterator<Self> {
    func makeIterator() -> IndexingIterator<Self>
}
```

There are many more conditional extensions, and you can also add your own. As we mentioned earlier, it can be challenging to see which methods you should implement in order to conform to a protocol. Because many protocols in the standard library have default values for the associated types and conditional extensions that match those associated types, you often only have to implement a handful of methods, even for protocols that have dozens of requirements. To address this, the standard library has documented it in a section, "Conforming to the Sequence Protocol." If you write a custom protocol with more than a few methods, you should consider adding a similar section to your documentation.

Type Erasers

In the previous section, we were able to use the Drawing protocol as a type. However, with IteratorProtocol, this isn't (yet) possible, because it has an associated type. The compile error says: "Protocol 'IteratorProtocol' can only be used as a generic constraint because it has Self or associated type requirements."

```
let iterator: IteratorProtocol = ConstantIterator() // Error
```

In a way, IteratorProtocol used as a type is incomplete; we'd have to specify the associated type as well in order for this to be meaningful.

> The Swift Core Team has stated that they want to support *generalized existentials*. This feature would allow for using protocols with associated types as standalone values, and it would also eliminate the need to write type erasers. For more information about what to expect in the future, see the Swift Generics Manifesto[a].
>
> ───────────────
> a https://lists.swift.org/pipermail/swift-evolution/Week-of-Mon-20160229/011666.html

In a future version of Swift, we might be able to solve this by saying something like the following:

```
let iterator: Any<IteratorProtocol where .Element == Int> = ConstantIterator()
```

Currently, we can't yet express this. We can, however, use IteratorProtocol as a constraint for a generic parameter:

```
func nextInt<I: IteratorProtocol>(iterator: inout I) -> Int?
  where I.Element == Int {
    return iterator.next()
}
```

Similarly, we can store an iterator in a class or struct. The limitation is the same, in that we can only use it as a generic constraint, and not as a standalone type:

```
class IteratorStore<I: IteratorProtocol> where I.Element == Int {
  var iterator: I

  init(iterator: I) {
    self.iterator = iterator
  }
}
```

This works, but it has a drawback: the specific type of the stored iterator "leaks out" through the generic parameter. In the current type system, we can't express "any iterator, as long as the element type is Int." This is a problem if you want to, for example, put multiple IteratorStores into an array. All elements in an array must have the same type, and that includes any generic parameters; it's not possible to create an array that can store both IteratorStore<ConstantIterator> and IteratorStore<FibsIterator>.

Luckily, there are two ways around this — one is easy, the other one more efficient (but hacky). The process of removing a specific type (such as the iterator) is called *type erasure*.

In the easy solution, we implement a wrapper class. Instead of storing the iterator directly, the class stores the iterator's next function. To do this, we must first copy the iterator parameter to a var variable so that we're allowed to call its next method (which is mutating). We then wrap the call to next() in a closure expression and assign that closure to a property. We used a class to signal that IntIterator has reference semantics:

```
class IntIterator {
  var nextImpl: () -> Int?

  init<I: IteratorProtocol>(_ iterator: I) where I.Element == Int {
    var iteratorCopy = iterator
    self.nextImpl = { iteratorCopy.next() }
  }
}
```

Now, in our IntIterator, the specific type of the iterator (e.g. ConstantIterator) is only specified when creating a value. After that, the specific type is hidden, captured by the closure. We can create an IntIterator with any kind of iterator, as long as the elements are integers:

```
var iter = IntIterator(ConstantIterator())
iter = IntIterator([1,2,3].makeIterator())
```

The code above allows us to specify the associated type constraints (e.g. iter contains an iterator with Int elements) using Swift's current type system. Our IntIterator can also easily conform to the IteratorProtocol (and the inferred associated type is Int):

```
extension IntIterator: IteratorProtocol {
  func next() -> Int? {
    return nextImpl()
  }
}
```

In fact, by abstracting over Int and adding a generic parameter, we can change IntIterator to work just like AnyIterator does:

```
class AnyIterator<A>: IteratorProtocol {
  var nextImpl: () -> A?

  init<I: IteratorProtocol>(_ iterator: I) where I.Element == A {
    var iteratorCopy = iterator
    self.nextImpl = { iteratorCopy.next() }
  }

  func next() -> A? {
    return nextImpl()
  }
}
```

The specific iterator type (I) is only specified in the initializer, and after that, it's "erased."

From this refactoring, we can come up with a simple algorithm for creating a type eraser. First, we create a struct or class named AnyProtocolName. Then, for each associated type, we add a generic parameter. Finally, for each method, we store the implementation in a property on AnyProtocolName.

For a simple protocol like IteratorProtocol, this only takes a few lines of code, but for more complex protocols (such as Sequence), this is quite a lot of work.

Even worse, the size of the object or struct will increase linearly with each protocol method (because a new closure is added for each method).

The standard library takes a different approach to erasing types. We start by creating a simple class that conforms to IteratorProtocol. Its generic type is the Element of the iterator, and the implementation will simply crash:

```
class IteratorBox<A>: IteratorProtocol {
  func next() -> A? {
    fatalError("This method is abstract.")
  }
}
```

Then, we create another class, IteratorBoxHelper, which is also generic. Here, the generic parameter is the specific iterator type (for example, ConstantIterator). The next method simply forwards to the next method of the underlying iterator:

```
class IteratorBoxHelper<I: IteratorProtocol> {
  var iterator: I
  init(iterator: I) {
    self.iterator = iterator
  }

  func next() -> I.Element? {
    return iterator.next()
  }
}
```

Now for the hacky part. We change IteratorBoxHelper so that it's a subclass of IteratorBox, and the two generic parameters are constrained in such a way that IteratorBox gets I's element as the generic parameter:

```
class IteratorBoxHelper<I: IteratorProtocol>: IteratorBox<I.Element> {
  var iterator: I
  init(_ iterator: I) {
    self.iterator = iterator
  }

  override func next() -> I.Element? {
    return iterator.next()
  }
}
```

This allows us to create a value of IteratorBoxHelper and use it as an IteratorBox, effectively erasing the type of I:

```
let iter: IteratorBox<Int> = IteratorBoxHelper(ConstantIterator())
```

In the standard library, the IteratorBox and IteratorBoxHelper are then made private, and yet another wrapper (AnyIterator) makes sure that these implementation details are hidden from the public interface.

Protocols with Self Requirements

Protocols with Self requirements behave in a way similar to protocols with associated types. One of the simplest protocols with a Self requirement is Equatable. It has a single method (in the form of an operator) that compares two elements:

```
protocol Equatable {
    static func ==(lhs: Self, rhs: Self) -> Bool
}
```

Implementing Equatable for your own type isn't too hard. For example, if we have a simple MonetaryAmount struct, we can compare two values by comparing their properties:

```
struct MonetaryAmount: Equatable {
    var currency: String
    var amountInCents: Int

    static func ==(lhs: MonetaryAmount, rhs: MonetaryAmount) -> Bool {
        return lhs.currency == rhs.currency &&
            lhs.amountInCents == rhs.amountInCents
    }
}
```

We can't simply declare a variable with Equatable as its type:

```
// Error: 'Equatable' can only be used as a generic constraint
// because it has Self or associated type requirements
let x: Equatable = MonetaryAmount(currency: "EUR", amountInCents: 100)
```

This suffers from the same problems as associated types: from this (incorrect) definition, it's unclear what the Self type should be. For example, if it were possible to use Equatable as a standalone type, you could also write this:

```
let x: Equatable = MonetaryAmount(currency: "EUR", amountInCents: 100)
let y: Equatable = "hello"
x == y
```

There's no definition of == that takes a monetary amount and a string. How would you compare the two? However, we can use Equatable as a generic constraint. For example, we could write a free function, allEqual, that checks whether all elements in an array are equal:

```
func allEqual<E: Equatable>(x: [E]) -> Bool {
  guard let firstElement = x.first else { return true }
  for element in x {
    guard element == firstElement else { return false }
  }
  return true
}
```

Or we could use it as a constraint when writing an extension on Collection:

```
extension Collection where Iterator.Element: Equatable {
  func allEqual() -> Bool {
    guard let firstElement = first else { return true }
    for element in self {
      guard element == firstElement else { return false }
    }
    return true
  }
}
```

The == operator is defined as a static function of the type. In other words, it's not a member function, and it's statically dispatched. Unlike member functions, we can't override it. If you have a class that implements Equatable (for example, NSObject), you might get unexpected behavior when you create a subclass. For example, consider the following class:

```
class IntegerRef: NSObject {
  let int: Int
  init(_ int: Int) {
    self.int = int
  }
```

```
}
```

We can define a version of == that compares two IntegerRefs by comparing their int properties:

```
func ==(lhs: IntegerRef, rhs: IntegerRef) -> Bool {
    return lhs.int == rhs.int
}
```

If we create two IntegerRef objects, we can compare them, and everything works as expected:

```
let one = IntegerRef(1)
let otherOne = IntegerRef(1)
one == otherOne // true
```

However, if we use them as NSObjects, the == of NSObject is used (which uses === under the hood to check if the references point to the same object). Unless you're aware of the static dispatch behavior, the result might come as a surprise:

```
let two: NSObject = IntegerRef(2)
let otherTwo: NSObject = IntegerRef(2)
two == otherTwo // false
```

Protocol Internals

As we mentioned earlier, when we create a variable that has a protocol type, it's wrapped in a box called an existential container. Let's take a closer look at this.

Consider the following pair of functions. Both take a value that conforms to CustomStringConvertible and return the size of the value's type. The only difference is that one function uses the protocol as a generic constraint, whereas the other uses it as a type:

```
func f<C: CustomStringConvertible>(_ x: C) -> Int {
    return MemoryLayout.size(ofValue: x)
}
func g(_ x: CustomStringConvertible) -> Int {
    return MemoryLayout.size(ofValue: x)
}
```

```
f(5) // 8
g(5) // 40
```

Where does the size difference of 8 bytes versus 40 bytes come from? Because f takes a generic parameter, the integer 5 is passed straight to the function without any kind of boxing. This is reflected in its size of 8 bytes, which is the size of Int on a 64-bit system. For g, the integer is wrapped in an existential container. For regular protocols, an *opaque existential container* is used. Opaque existential containers contain a buffer (the size of three pointers, or 24 bytes) for the value; some metadata (one pointer, 8 bytes); and a number of *witness tables* (zero or more pointers, 8 bytes each). If the value doesn't fit into the buffer, it's stored on the heap, and the buffer contains a reference to the storage location. The metadata contains information about the type (for example, so that it can be used with a conditional cast). We'll discuss the witness table shortly.

For a class-only protocol, there's a special existential container called a *class existential container*, which only has the size of a single pointer because it doesn't need to store the value (only a reference) or the metadata (which is already in the class):

```
MemoryLayout<UITableViewDelegate>.size // 16
```

The witness table is what makes dynamic dispatch possible. It encodes the implementation of a protocol for a specific type: for each method in the protocol, there's an entry that points to the implementation for that specific type. Sometimes this is also called a *vtable*. In a way, when we created the first version of AnyIterator, we manually wrote a witness table.

Given the witness table, the surprising behavior of addCircle at the beginning of this chapter makes a lot more sense. Because addCircle wasn't part of the protocol definition, it wasn't in the witness table either. Therefore, the compiler had no choice but to statically call the protocol's default implementation. Once we made addCircle a protocol requirement, it was also added to the witness table, and therefore called using dynamic dispatch.

The size of the opaque existential container depends on the number of witness tables: it contains one witness table per protocol. For example, Any is a typealias for an empty protocol that has no witness tables at all:

```
typealias Any = protocol<>
```

```
MemoryLayout<Any>.size // 32
```

If we combine multiple protocols, one 8-byte chunk gets added per protocol. So combining four protocols adds 32 bytes:

```
protocol Prot { }
protocol Prot2 { }
protocol Prot3 { }
protocol Prot4 { }
typealias P = Prot & Prot2 & Prot3 & Prot4

MemoryLayout<P>.size // 64
```

Performance Implications

Existential containers add a level of indirection and therefore generally cause a performance decrease over generic parameters. In addition to the possibly slower method dispatch, the existential container also acts as a barrier that prevents many compiler optimizations. For the most part, worrying about this overhead is premature optimization. However, if you need maximum performance in a tight loop, it'll be more efficient to use a generic parameter rather than a parameter that has a protocol type. This way, you can avoid the implicit protocol box.

If you try to pass [String] (or any other type) into a function that takes [Any] (or any other array of a protocol rather than a specific type), the compiler will emit code that maps over the entire array and boxes every value, effectively making the function call itself — not the function body — an $O(n)$ operation (where n is the number of elements in the array). Again, this won't be an issue in most cases, but if you need to write highly performant code, you might choose to write your function with a generic parameter rather than a protocol type:

```
// Implicit boxing
func printProtocol(array: [CustomStringConvertible]) {
    print(array)
}
```

```
// No boxing
func printGeneric<A: CustomStringConvertible>(array: [A]) {
    print(array)
}
```

Conclusion

Protocols in Swift are important building blocks. They allow us to write flexible code that decouples the interface and implementation. We looked at the two different kinds of protocols and how they're implemented. We used type erasers and looked at the performance differences between protocol types and generic types with a protocol constraint. We also looked at unexpected behavior due to the differences between static and dynamic dispatch.

Protocols had a big impact on the Swift community. Yet we also want to warn against overusing them. Sometimes, using a simple concrete type like a struct or a class is much easier to understand than a protocol, and this increases the readability of your code. However, there are also times when using a protocol can increase readability of your code — for example, when you deal with legacy APIs retrofitted to a protocol.

One of the big upsides of using protocols is that they provide a *minimal viable interface*, which means they specify exactly what the interface looks like. This lets us create multiple types that conform to the interface. Also, it makes it easier to write test code. Rather than having to set up a complicated tree of dependencies, we can just create a simple test type that conforms to the protocol.

Interoperability

One of Swift's greatest strengths is the low friction when interoperating with C and Objective-C. Swift can automatically bridge Objective-C types to native Swift types, and it can even bridge with many C types. This allows us to use existing libraries and provide a nice interface on top.

In this chapter, we'll create a wrapper around the CommonMark[1] library. CommonMark is a formal specification for Markdown, a popular syntax for formatting plain text. If you've ever written a post on GitHub or Stack Overflow, you've probably used Markdown. After this practical example, we'll take a look at the tools the standard library provides for working with memory, and we'll see how they can be used to interact with C code.

Hands-On: Wrapping CommonMark

Swift's ability to call into C code allows us to take advantage of the abundance of existing C libraries. Writing a wrapper around an existing library's interface in Swift is often much easier and involves less work than building something from scratch; meanwhile, users of our wrapper will see no difference in terms of type safety or ease of use compared to a fully native solution. All we need to start is the dynamic library and its header files.

Our example, the CommonMark C library, is a reference implementation of the CommonMark spec that's both fast and well tested. We'll take a layered approach in order to make CommonMark accessible from Swift. First, we'll create a very thin Swift class around the opaque types the library exposes. Then, we'll wrap this class with Swift enums in order to provide a more idiomatic API.

Wrapping the C Library

Let's begin by wrapping a single function with a nicer interface. The cmark_markdown_to_html function takes in Markdown-formatted text and returns the resulting HTML code in a string. The C interface looks like this:

```
// Convert 'text' (assumed to be a UTF-8 encoded string with length
// 'len') from CommonMark Markdown to HTML, returning a null-terminated,
// UTF-8-encoded string.
```

---

1 http://commonmark.org

```
char *cmark_markdown_to_html(const char *text, size_t len, int options);
```

When Swift imports this declaration, it presents the C string in the first
parameter as an UnsafePointer to a number of Int8 values. From the
documentation, we know that these are expected to be UTF-8 code units. The
len parameter takes the length of the string:

```
func cmark_markdown_to_html
    (_ text: UnsafePointer<Int8>!, _ len: Int, _ options: Int32)
    -> UnsafeMutablePointer<Int8>!
```

We want our wrapper function to work with Swift strings, of course, so you
might think that we need to convert the Swift string into an Int8 pointer.
However, bridging between native and C strings is such a common operation
that Swift will do this automatically for us. We do have to be careful with the
len parameter, as the function expects the length of the UTF-8-encoded string
in bytes, and not the number of characters. We get the correct value from the
string's utf8 view, and we can just pass in zero for the options:

```
func markdownToHtml(input: String) -> String {
    let outString = cmark_markdown_to_html(input, input.utf8.count, 0)!
    return String(cString: outString)
}
```

Notice that we force-unwrap the string pointer the function returns. We can
safely do this because we know that cmark_markdown_to_html always returns
a valid string. By force-unwrapping inside the method, the library user can
call the markdownToHTML method without having to worry about optionals —
the result would never be nil anyway.

> The automatic bridging of native Swift strings to C strings assumes
> that the C function you want to call expects the string to be UTF-8
> encoded. This is the correct choice in most cases, but if the C API
> assumes a different encoding, you can't use the automatic bridging.
> However, it's often still easy. For example, if you need an array of
> UTF-16 code points, you can use Array(string.utf16).

Wrapping the cmark_node Type

In addition to the straight HTML output, the cmark library also provides a way
to parse a Markdown text into a structured tree of elements. For example, a

simple text could be transformed into a list of block-level nodes such as paragraphs, quotes, lists, code blocks, headers, and so on. Some block-level elements contain other block-level elements (for example, quotes can contain multiple paragraphs), whereas others contain only inline elements (for example, a header can contain a part that's emphasized). No element can contain both (for example, the inline elements of a list item are always wrapped in a paragraph element).

The C library uses a single data type, cmark_node, to represent the nodes. It's opaque, meaning the authors of the library chose to hide its definition. All we see in the headers are functions that operate on or return pointers to cmark_node. Swift imports these pointers as OpaquePointers. (We'll take a closer look at the differences between the many pointer types in the standard library, such as OpaquePointer and UnsafeMutablePointer, later in this chapter.)

> In the future, we might be able to use the "import as member" feature of Swift to import these functions as methods on cmark_node. Apple has used this to provide more "object-oriented" APIs for Core Graphics and Grand Central Dispatch in Swift. It works by annotating the C source code with the swift_name attribute. Alas, this feature doesn't really work for the cmark library yet. It might work for your own C library. There are some bugs around import as member, for example, it doesn't always work with opaque pointers (which is exactly what's used in cmark).

Let's wrap a node in a native Swift type to make it easier to work with. As we saw in the chapter on structs and classes, we need to think about value semantics whenever we create a custom type: is the type a value, or does it make sense for instances to have identity? In the former case, we should favor a struct or enum, whereas the latter requires a class. Our case is interesting: on one hand, the node of a Markdown document is a value — two nodes that have the same element type and contents should be indistinguishable, hence they shouldn't have identity. On the other hand, since we don't know the internals of cmark_node, there's no straightforward way to make a copy of a node, so we can't guarantee value semantics. For this reason, we start with a class. Later on, we'll write another layer on top of this class to provide an interface with value semantics.

Our class simply stores the opaque pointer and frees the memory cmark_node uses on deinit when there are no references left to an instance of this class. We only free memory at the document level, because otherwise we might free nodes that are still in use. Freeing the document will also automatically free all the children recursively. Wrapping the opaque pointer in this way will give us automatic reference counting for free:

```
public class Node {
  let node: OpaquePointer

  init(node: OpaquePointer) {
    self.node = node
  }

  deinit {
    guard type == CMARK_NODE_DOCUMENT else { return }
    cmark_node_free(node)
  }
}
```

The next step is to wrap the cmark_parse_document function, which parses a Markdown text and returns the document's root node. It takes the same arguments as cmark_markdown_to_html: the string, its length, and an integer describing parse options. The return type of the cmark_parse_document function in Swift is OpaquePointer, which represents the node:

```
func cmark_parse_document
  (_ buffer: UnsafePointer<Int8>!, _ len: Int, _ options: Int32)
  -> OpaquePointer!
```

We turn the function into a convenience initializer for our class. Note that the function can return nil if parsing fails. Therefore, our initializer should be failable and return nil (the optional value, not the null pointer) if this occurs:

```
public init?(markdown: String) {
  let parsed = cmark_parse_document(markdown, markdown.utf8.count, 0)
  guard let node = parsed else { return nil }
  self.node = node
}
```

As mentioned above, there are a couple of interesting functions that operate on nodes. For example, there's one that returns the type of a node, such as paragraph or header:

```
cmark_node_type cmark_node_get_type(cmark_node *node);
```

In Swift, it looks like this:

```
func cmark_node_get_type(_ node: OpaquePointer!) -> cmark_node_type
```

cmark_node_type is a C enum that has cases for the various block-level and inline elements that are defined in Markdown, as well as one case to signify errors:

```
typedef enum {
  // Error status
  CMARK_NODE_NONE,

  // Block
  CMARK_NODE_DOCUMENT,
  CMARK_NODE_BLOCK_QUOTE,
  ...

  // Inline
  CMARK_NODE_TEXT,
  CMARK_NODE_EMPH,
  ...
} cmark_node_type;
```

Swift imports plain C enums as structs containing only an Int32. Additionally, for every case in an enum, a top-level variable is generated. Enums marked with the NS_ENUM macro, used by Apple in its Objective-C frameworks, are imported as native Swift enumerations. Additionally, you can annotate your enum cases with swift_name to make them member variables:

```
struct cmark_node_type : RawRepresentable, Equatable {
  public init(_ rawValue: UInt32)
  public init(rawValue: UInt32)
  public var rawValue: UInt32
}

var CMARK_NODE_NONE: cmark_node_type { get }
var CMARK_NODE_DOCUMENT: cmark_node_type { get }
```

In Swift, the type of a node should be a property of the Node data type, so we turn the cmark_node_get_type function into a computed property of our class:

```
var type: cmark_node_type {
  return cmark_node_get_type(node)
}
```

Now we can just write node.type to get an element's type.

There are a couple more node properties we can access. For example, if a node is a list, it can have one of two list types: bulleted or ordered. All other nodes have the list type "no list." Again, Swift represents the corresponding C enum as a struct, with a top-level variable for each case, and we can write a similar wrapper property. In this case, we also provide a setter, which will come in handy later in this chapter:

```
var listType: cmark_list_type {
  get { return cmark_node_get_list_type(node) }
  set { cmark_node_set_list_type(node, newValue) }
}
```

There are similar functions for all the other node properties (such as header level, fenced code block info, and link URLs and titles). These properties often only make sense for specific types of nodes, and we can choose to provide an interface either with an optional (e.g. for the link URL) or with a default value (e.g. the default header level is zero). This illustrates a major weakness of the library's C API that we can model much better in Swift. We'll talk more about this below.

Some nodes can also have children. For iterating over them, the CommonMark library provides the functions cmark_node_first_child and cmark_node_next. We want our Node class to provide an array of its children. To generate this array, we start with the first child and keep adding children until either cmark_node_first_child or cmark_node_next returns nil, signaling the end of the list. Note that this C null pointer automatically gets converted to an optional:

```
var children: [Node] {
  var result: [Node] = []
  var child = cmark_node_first_child(node)
  while let unwrapped = child {
    result.append(Node(node: unwrapped))
    child = cmark_node_next(child)
  }
  return result
}
```

We could also have chosen to return a lazy sequence rather than an array (for example, by using sequence or AnySequence). However, there's a problem with this: the node structure might change between creation and consumption of the sequence. In that case, the code below will return wrong values, or even worse, crash. Depending on your use case, returning a lazily constructed sequence might be exactly what you want, but if your data structure can change, returning an array is a much safer choice.

With this simple wrapper class for nodes, accessing the abstract syntax tree produced by the CommonMark library from Swift becomes a lot easier. Instead of having to call functions like cmark_node_get_list_type, we can just write node.listType and get autocompletion and type safety. However, we aren't done yet. Even though the Node class feels much more native than the C functions, Swift allows us to express a node in an even more natural and safer way, using enums with associated values.

A Safer Interface

As we mentioned above, there are many node properties that only apply in certain contexts. For example, it doesn't make any sense to access the headerLevel of a list or the listType of a code block. Enumerations with associated values allow us to specify only the metadata that makes sense for each specific case. We'll create one enum for all possible inline elements, and another one for block-level items. That way, we can enforce the structure of a CommonMark document. For example, a plain text element just stores a String, whereas emphasis nodes contain an array of other inline elements. These enumerations will be the public interface to our library, turning the Node class into an internal implementation detail:

```
public enum Inline {
    case text(text: String)
    case softBreak
    case lineBreak
    case code(text: String)
    case html(text: String)
    case emphasis(children: [Inline])
    case strong(children: [Inline])
    case custom(literal: String)
    case link(children: [Inline], title: String?, url: String?)
    case image(children: [Inline], title: String?, url: String?)
}
```

Similarly, paragraphs and headers can only contain inline elements, whereas block quotations always contain other block-level elements. A list is defined as an array of Block elements that represent the list items:

```
public enum Block {
  case list(items: [[Block]], type: ListType)
  case blockQuote(items: [Block])
  case codeBlock(text: String, language: String?)
  case html(text: String)
  case paragraph(text: [Inline])
  case heading(text: [Inline], level: Int)
  case custom(literal: String)
  case thematicBreak
}
```

The ListType is just a simple enum that states whether a list is ordered or unordered:

```
public enum ListType {
  case Unordered
  case Ordered
}
```

Since enums are value types, this also lets us treat nodes as values by converting them to their enum representations. We follow the API Design Guidelines[2] by using initializers for type conversions. We write two pairs of initializers: one pair creates Block and InlineElement values from the Node type, and another pair reconstructs a Node from these enums. This allows us to write functions that transform either InlineElement or Block values and reconstruct a CommonMark document, which can then be rendered into HTML, into man pages, or back into Markdown text.

Let's start by writing an initializer that converts a Node into an InlineElement. We switch on the node's type and construct the corresponding Inline value. For example, for a text node, we take the node's string contents, which we access through the literal property in the cmark library. We can safely force-unwrap literal because we know that text nodes always have this value, whereas other node types might have nil values for literal. For example, emphasis and strong nodes only have child nodes, and no literal value. To parse the latter, we map over the node's children and call our initializer recursively. Instead of duplicating that code, we create an inline function, inlineChildren, that only gets called when needed. The default case should never get reached, so we choose to trap the program if it does. This follows the convention that returning an optional or using throws should generally only be used for expected errors, and not to signify programmer errors:

```
extension Inline {
  init(_ node: Node) {
    let inlineChildren = { node.children.map(Inline.init) }
    switch node.type {
    case CMARK_NODE_TEXT:
      self = .text(text: node.literal!)
    case CMARK_NODE_SOFTBREAK:
      self = .softBreak
    case CMARK_NODE_LINEBREAK:
      self = .lineBreak
    case CMARK_NODE_CODE:
      self = .code(text: node.literal!)
    case CMARK_NODE_HTML_INLINE:
      self = .html(text: node.literal!)
    case CMARK_NODE_CUSTOM_INLINE:
      self = .custom(literal: node.literal!)
    case CMARK_NODE_EMPH:
      self = .emphasis(children: inlineChildren())
    case CMARK_NODE_STRONG:
      self = .strong(children: inlineChildren())
    case CMARK_NODE_LINK:
      self = .link(children: inlineChildren(), title: node.title, url: node.urlString)
    case CMARK_NODE_IMAGE:
      self = .image(children: inlineChildren(), title: node.title, url: node.urlString)
    default:
      fatalError("Unrecognized node: \(node.typeString)")
    }
  }
}
```

Converting block-level elements follows the same pattern. Note that block-level elements can have either inline elements, list items, or other block-level elements as children, depending on the node type. In the cmark_node syntax tree, list items get wrapped with an extra node. In the listItem property on Node, we remove that layer and directly return an array of block-level elements:

```
extension Block {
  init(_ node: Node) {
    let parseInlineChildren = { node.children.map(Inline.init) }
    let parseBlockChildren = { node.children.map(Block.init) }
    switch node.type {
```

```
case CMARK_NODE_PARAGRAPH:
  self = .paragraph(text: parseInlineChildren())
case CMARK_NODE_BLOCK_QUOTE:
  self = .blockQuote(items: parseBlockChildren())
case CMARK_NODE_LIST:
  let type = node.listType == CMARK_BULLET_LIST ?
    ListType.Unordered : ListType.Ordered
  self = .list(items: node.children.map { $0.listItem }, type: type)
case CMARK_NODE_CODE_BLOCK:
  self = .codeBlock(text: node.literal!, language: node.fenceInfo)
case CMARK_NODE_HTML_BLOCK:
  self = .html(text: node.literal!)
case CMARK_NODE_CUSTOM_BLOCK:
  self = .custom(literal: node.literal!)
case CMARK_NODE_HEADING:
  self = .heading(text: parseInlineChildren(), level: node.headerLevel)
case CMARK_NODE_THEMATIC_BREAK:
  self = .thematicBreak
default:
  fatalError("Unrecognized node: \(node.typeString)")
  }
 }
}
```

Now, given a document-level Node, we can easily convert it into an array of
Block elements. The Block elements are values: we can freely copy or change
them without having to worry about references. This is very powerful for
manipulating nodes. Since values, by definition, don't care how they were
created, we can also create a Markdown syntax tree in code, from scratch,
without using the CommonMark library at all. The types are much clearer too;
you can't accidentally do things that wouldn't make sense — such as accessing
the title of a list — as the compiler won't allow it. Aside from making your code
safer, this is a very robust form of documentation — by just looking at the
types, it's obvious how a CommonMark document is structured. And unlike
comments, the compiler will make sure that this form of documentation is
never outdated.

It's now very easy to write simple functions that operate on our new data types.
For example, if we want to build a list of all the level one and two headers from
a Markdown document for a table of contents, we can just loop over all
children and check whether they are headers and have the correct level:

```
func tableOfContents(document: String) -> [Block] {
  let blocks = Node(markdown: document)?.children.map(Block.init) ?? []
```

```
  return blocks.filter {
    switch $0 {
    case .heading(_, let level) where level < 3: return true
    default: return false
    }
  }
}
```

Before we build more operations like this, let's tackle the inverse transformation: converting a Block back into a Node. We need this because we ultimately want to use the CommonMark library to generate HTML or other text formats from the Markdown syntax tree we've built or manipulated, and the library can only deal with cmark_node_type.

Our plan is to add two initializers on Node: one that converts an Inline value to a node, and another that handles Block elements. We start by extending Node with a new initializer that creates a new cmark_node from scratch with the specified type and children. Recall that we wrote a deinit, which frees the root node of the tree (and recursively, all its children). This deinit will make sure that the node we allocate here gets freed eventually:

```
extension Node {
  convenience init(type: cmark_node_type, children: [Node] = []) {
    self.init(node: cmark_node_new(type))
    for child in children {
      cmark_node_append_child(node, child.node)
    }
  }
}
```

We'll frequently need to create text-only nodes, or nodes with a number of children, so let's add three convenience initializers to make that easier:

```
extension Node {
  convenience init(type: cmark_node_type, literal: String) {
    self.init(type: type)
    self.literal = literal
  }
  convenience init(type: cmark_node_type, blocks: [Block]) {
    self.init(type: type, children: blocks.map(Node.init))
  }
  convenience init(type: cmark_node_type, elements: [Inline]) {
    self.init(type: type, children: elements.map(Node.init))
  }
```

```
}
```

Now we're ready to write the two conversion initializers. Using the initializers we just defined, it becomes very straightforward: we switch on the element and create a node with the correct type. Here's the version for inline elements:

```
extension Node {
  convenience init(element: Inline) {
    switch element {
    case .text(let text):
      self.init(type: CMARK_NODE_TEXT, literal: text)
    case .emphasis(let children):
      self.init(type: CMARK_NODE_EMPH, elements: children)
    case .code(let text):
      self.init(type: CMARK_NODE_CODE, literal: text)
    case .strong(let children):
      self.init(type: CMARK_NODE_STRONG, elements: children)
    case .html(let text):
      self.init(type: CMARK_NODE_HTML_INLINE, literal: text)
    case .custom(let literal):
      self.init(type: CMARK_NODE_CUSTOM_INLINE, literal: literal)
    case let .link(children, title, url):
      self.init(type: CMARK_NODE_LINK, elements: children)
      self.title = title
      self.urlString = url
    case let .image(children, title, url):
      self.init(type: CMARK_NODE_IMAGE, elements: children)
      self.title = title
      urlString = url
    case .softBreak:
      self.init(type: CMARK_NODE_SOFTBREAK)
    case .lineBreak:
      self.init(type: CMARK_NODE_LINEBREAK)
    }
  }
}
```

Creating a node from a block-level element is very similar. The only slightly more complicated case is lists. Recall that in the above conversion from Node to Block, we removed the extra node the CommonMark library uses to represent lists, so we need to add that back in here:

```
extension Node {
  convenience init(block: Block) {
    switch block {
```

```
      case .paragraph(let children):
        self.init(type: CMARK_NODE_PARAGRAPH, elements: children)
      case let .list(items, type):
        let listItems = items.map { Node(type: CMARK_NODE_ITEM, blocks: $0) }
        self.init(type: CMARK_NODE_LIST, children: listItems)
        listType = type == .Unordered
          ? CMARK_BULLET_LIST
          : CMARK_ORDERED_LIST
      case .blockQuote(let items):
        self.init(type: CMARK_NODE_BLOCK_QUOTE, blocks: items)
      case let .codeBlock(text, language):
        self.init(type: CMARK_NODE_CODE_BLOCK, literal: text)
        fenceInfo = language
      case .html(let text):
        self.init(type: CMARK_NODE_HTML_BLOCK, literal: text)
      case .custom(let literal):
        self.init(type: CMARK_NODE_CUSTOM_BLOCK, literal: literal)
      case let .heading(text, level):
        self.init(type: CMARK_NODE_HEADING, elements: text)
        headerLevel = level
      case .thematicBreak:
        self.init(type: CMARK_NODE_THEMATIC_BREAK)
    }
  }
}
```

Finally, to provide a nice interface for the user, we define a public initializer
that takes an array of block-level elements and produces a document node,
which we can then render into one of the different output formats:

```
extension Node {
  public convenience init(blocks: [Block]) {
    self.init(type: CMARK_NODE_DOCUMENT, blocks: blocks)
  }
}
```

Now we can go in both directions: we can load a document, convert it into
[Block] elements, modify those elements, and turn them back into a Node.
This allows us to write programs that extract information from Markdown or
even change the Markdown dynamically. By first creating a thin wrapper
around the C library (the Node class), we abstracted the conversion from the

underlying C API. This allowed us to focus on providing an interface that feels like idiomatic Swift. The entire project is available on GitHub[3].

An Overview of Low-Level Types

There are many types in the standard library that provide low-level access to memory. Their sheer number can be overwhelming, but they're named consistently. Here are the most important naming parts:

→ A **managed** type has automatic memory management. The compiler will allocate, initialize, and free the memory for you.

→ An **unsafe** type doesn't provide automated memory management (as opposed to *managed*). You have to allocate, initialize, deallocate, and deinitialize the memory explicitly.

→ A **buffer** type works on multiple (contiguously stored) elements, rather than a single element.

→ A **pointer** type has pointer semantics (just like a C pointer).

→ A **raw** type contains untyped data. It's the equivalent of a void* in C. Types that don't contain *raw* in their name have typed data.

→ A **mutable** type allows the mutation of the memory it points to.

If you want raw storage but don't need to interact with C, you can use the ManagedBuffer class to allocate the memory. This is what Swift's collections use under the hood to manage their memory. It consists of a single header value (for storing data such as the number of elements) and contiguous memory for the elements. It also has a capacity property, which isn't the same as the number of actual elements: for example, an Array with a count of 17 might own a buffer with a capacity of 32, meaning that 15 elements can be added before the Array allocates more memory. There's also a variant called ManagedBufferPointer, which we won't discuss here.

Sometimes you need to do manual memory management. For example, in a C API, you might pass in an object as context for a function. However, C doesn't know about Swift's memory management. If the API is synchronous, you can just pass in a Swift object, convert it back, and all will be fine (we'll look at this in detail in the next section). However, if the API is asynchronous, you have to

3 https://github.com/objcio/commonmark-swift

manually retain and release that object, because otherwise it might get deinitialized once it goes out of scope. In order to do that, there's the Unmanaged type. It has methods for retain and release, as well as initializers that either modify or keep the current retain count.

An UnsafePointer is the simplest of the pointer types and similar to a const pointer in C. It's generic over the data type of the memory it points to. You can create an unsafe pointer from one of the other pointer types using an initializer. Swift also supports a special syntax for calling functions that take unsafe pointers. You can pass any *mutable* variable of the correct type to such a function by prefixing it with an ampersand, thereby making it an *in-out expression*:

```
var x = 5
func fetch(p: UnsafePointer<Int>) -> Int {
   return p.pointee
}
fetch(p: &x) // 5
```

This looks exactly like the inout parameters we covered in the functions chapter, and it works in a similar manner — although in this case, nothing is passed back to the caller via this value because the pointer isn't mutable. The pointer that Swift creates behind the scenes and passes to the function is guaranteed to be valid only for the duration of the function call. Don't try to return the pointer from the function and access it after the function has returned — the result is undefined. As we stated before, an Unsafe type doesn't provide any memory management, so we're relying on the fact that x is still in scope when we call fetch:

There's also a mutable variant, named UnsafeMutablePointer. This struct works just like a regular C pointer; you can dereference the pointer and change the value of the memory, which then gets passed back to the caller via the in-out expression:

```
func increment(p: UnsafeMutablePointer<Int>) {
   p.pointee += 1
}
var y = 0
increment(p: &y)
y // 1
```

Rather than using an in-out expression, you can also allocate memory directly using UnsafeMutablePointer. The rules for allocating memory in Swift are similar to the rules in C: after allocating the memory, you first need to initialize it before you can use it. Once you're done with the pointer, you need to deallocate the memory:

```
// Allocate and initialize memory for two Ints
let z = UnsafeMutablePointer<Int>.allocate(capacity: 2)
z.initialize(to: 42, count: 2)
z.pointee // 42
// Pointer arithmetic:
(z+1).pointee = 43
// Subscripts:
z[1] // 43
z.deallocate(capacity: 2)
// Garbage memory
z.pointee // 42
```

In C APIs, it's also very common to have a pointer to a sequence of bytes with no specific element type (void* or const void*). The equivalent counterparts in Swift are the UnsafeMutableRawPointer and UnsafeRawPointer types. C APIs that use void* or const void* get imported as these types. Usually, you'd directly convert these types into Unsafe[Mutable]Pointer or other typed variants by using one of their instance methods (such as assumingMemoryBound(to:), bindMemory(to:), or load(fromByteOffset:as:)).

Sometimes a C API has an opaque pointer type. For example, in the cmark library, we saw that the type cmark_node* gets imported as an OpaquePointer. The definition of cmark_node isn't exposed in the header, and therefore, we can't access the pointee's memory. You can convert opaque pointers to other pointers using an initializer.

In Swift, we usually use the Array type to store a sequence of values contiguously. In C, a sequence is often returned as a pointer to the first element and a number of elements. If we want to use such a sequence as a collection, we could turn the sequence into an Array, but that makes a copy of the elements. This is often a good thing (because once they're in an array, the elements are memory managed by the Swift runtime). However, sometimes you don't want to make copies of each element. For those cases, there are the Unsafe[Mutable]BufferPointer types. You initialize them with a pointer to the start element and a count. From then on, you have a (mutable) random-access collection. The buffer pointers make it a lot easier to work with C collections.

Finally, in a future version of Swift, the Unsafe[Mutable]RawBufferPointer types will be added. These make it easier to work with raw memory as collections (they provide the low-level equivalent to Data and NSData).

Function Pointers

Let's have a look at wrapping the standard C qsort sorting function. The type as it's imported in Swift's Darwin module (or if you're on Linux, Glibc) is given below:

```
public func qsort(
    _ __base: UnsafeMutableRawPointer!,
    _ __nel: Int,
    _ __width: Int,
    _ __compar: @escaping @convention(c) (UnsafeRawPointer?,
    UnsafeRawPointer?)
    -> Int32)
```

The man page (man qsort) describes how to use the qsort function:

> The qsort() and heapsort() functions sort an array of nel objects, the initial member of which is pointed to by base. The size of each object is specified by width.
>
> The contents of the array base are sorted in ascending order according to a comparison function pointed to by compar, which requires two arguments pointing to the objects being compared.

And here's a wrapper function that uses qsort to sort an array of Swift strings:

```
func qsortStrings(array: inout [String]) {
  qsort(&array, array.count, MemoryLayout<String>.stride) { a, b in
    let l = a!.assumingMemoryBound(to: String.self).pointee
    let r = b!.assumingMemoryBound(to: String.self).pointee
    if r > l { return -1 }
    else if r == l { return 0 }
    else { return 1 }
  }
}
```

Let's look at each of the arguments being passed to qsort:

→ The first argument is a pointer to the base of the array. Swift arrays automatically convert to C-style base pointers when you pass them into a function that takes an UnsafePointer. We have to use the & prefix because it's an UnsafeMutableRawPointer (a void *base in the C declaration). If the function didn't need to mutate its input and were declared in C as const void *base, the ampersand wouldn't be needed. This matches the difference with inout arguments in Swift functions.

→ Second, we have to provide the number of elements. This one is easy; we can use the count property of the array.

→ Third, to get the width of each element, we use MemoryLayout.stride, *not* MemoryLayout.size. In Swift, MemoryLayout.size returns the true size of a type, but when locating elements in memory, platform alignment rules may lead to gaps between adjacent elements. The stride is the size of the type, plus some padding (which may be zero) to account for this gap. For strings, size and stride are currently the same on Apple's platforms, but this won't be the case for all types — for example, MemoryLayout<Character>.size is 9 and MemoryLayout<Character>.stride is 16. When translating code from C to Swift, you probably want to write MemoryLayout.stride in cases where you would have written sizeof in C.

→ The last parameter is a pointer to a C function that's used to compare two elements from the array. Swift automatically bridges a Swift function type to a C function pointer, so we can pass any function that has a matching signature. However, there's one big caveat: C function pointers are just pointers; they can't capture any values. For that reason, the compiler will only allow you to provide functions that don't capture any external state (for example, no local variables and no generics). It signifies this with the @convention(c) attribute.

The compar function accepts two raw pointers. Such an UnsafeRawPointer can be a pointer to anything. The reason we have to deal with UnsafeRawPointer (and not UnsafePointer<String>) is because C doesn't have generics. However, we know that we get passed in a String, so we can interpret it as a pointer to a String. We also know the pointers are never nil here, so we can safely force-unwrap them. Finally, the function needs to return an Int32: a positive number if the first element is greater than the second, zero if they're equal, and a negative number if the first is less than the second.

It's easy enough to create another wrapper that works for a different type of elements; we can copy and paste the code and change String to a different type and we're done. But we should really make the code generic. This is where we hit the limit of C function pointers. At the time of writing this book, the Swift compiler segfaulted on the code below. And even if it hadn't, the code is still impossible: it captures things from outside the closure. More specifically, it captures the comparison and equality operators, which are different for each generic parameter. There's nothing we can do about this — we simply encountered a limitation of the way C works:

```swift
// Valid syntax, but invalid code
extension Array where Element: Comparable {
  mutating func quicksort() {
    qsort(&self, self.count, MemoryLayout<Element>.stride) { a, b in
      let l = a!.assumingMemoryBound(to: Element.self).pointee
      let r = b!.assumingMemoryBound(to: Element.self).pointee
      if r > l { return -1 }
      else if r == l { return 0 }
      else { return 1 }
    }
  }
}
```

One way to think about this limitation is by thinking like the compiler. A C function pointer is just an address in memory that points to a block of code. In the case of functions that don't have any context, this address will be static and known at compile time. However, in case of a generic function, an extra parameter (the generic type) is passed in. Therefore, there are no addresses for specialized generic functions. This is the same for closures. Even if the compiler could rewrite a closure in such a way that it'd be possible to pass it as a function pointer, the memory management couldn't be done automatically — there's no way to know when to release the closure.

In practice, this is a problem for many C programmers as well. On OS X, there's a variant of qsort called qsort_b, which takes a block — instead of a function pointer — as the last parameter. If we replace qsort with qsort_b in the code above, it'll compile and run fine.

However, qsort_b isn't available on most platforms. And other functions aside from qsort might not have a block-based variant, either. Most C APIs that work with callbacks offer a different solution. They take an extra UnsafeRawPointer as a parameter and pass that pointer on to the callback function. The user of the API can then use this to pass an arbitrary piece of data to each invocation of the callback function. qsort also has a variant, qsort_r, which does exactly this. Its type signature includes an extra parameter, thunk, which is an UnsafeRawPointer. Note that this parameter has also been added to the type of the comparison function pointer because qsort_r passes the value to that function on every invocation:

```
public func qsort_r(
    _ __base: UnsafeMutableRawPointer!,
    _ __nel: Int,
    _ __width: Int,
    _: UnsafeMutableRawPointer!,
    _ __compar: @escaping @convention(c)
  (UnsafeMutableRawPointer?, UnsafeRawPointer?, UnsafeRawPointer?)
    -> Int32
)
```

If qsort_b isn't available on our platform, we can reconstruct it in Swift using qsort_r. We can pass anything we want as the thunk parameter, as long as we cast it to an UnsafeRawPointer. In our case, we want to pass the comparison closure. We can automatically create an UnsafeRawPointer out of a variable defined with var by using an in-out expression. So all we need to do is store the comparison closure that's passed as an argument to our qsort_b variant in a variable named thunk. Then we can pass the reference to the thunk variable into qsort_r. Inside the callback, we cast the void pointer back to its real type, Block, and then simply call the closure:

```
typealias Block = (UnsafeRawPointer?, UnsafeRawPointer?) -> Int32
func qsort_block(_ array: UnsafeMutableRawPointer, _ count: Int,
          _ width: Int, f: @escaping Block)
{
  var thunk = f
  qsort_r(array, count, width, &thunk) { (ctx, p1, p2) -> Int32 in
    let comp = ctx!.assumingMemoryBound(to: Block.self).pointee
    return comp(p1, p2)
  }
}
```

Using qsort_block, we can redefine our qsortWrapper function and provide a nice generic interface to the qsort algorithm that's in the C standard library:

```
extension Array where Element: Comparable {
  mutating func quicksort() {
    qsort_block(&self, self.count, MemoryLayout<Element>.stride) { a, b in
      let l = a!.assumingMemoryBound(to: Element.self).pointee
```

```
        let r = b!.assumingMemoryBound(to: Element.self).pointee
        if r > l { return -1 }
        else if r == l { return 0 }
        else { return 1 }
      }
   }
}

var x = [3,1,2]
x.quicksort()
x // [1, 2, 3]
```

It might seem like a lot of work to use a sorting algorithm from the C standard library. After all, Swift's built-in sort function is much easier to use, and it's faster in most cases. However, there are many other interesting C APIs out there that we can wrap with a type-safe and generic interface using the same technique.